THE GENRE OF COMMUNAL LAMENT
IN THE BIBLE
AND THE ANCIENT NEAR EAST

SOCIETY
OF BIBLICAL
LITERATURE

DISSERTATION SERIES
J. J. M. Roberts, Old Testament Editor
Pheme Perkins, New Testament Editor

Number 127

THE GENRE OF COMMUNAL LAMENT
IN THE BIBLE
AND THE ANCIENT NEAR EAST
by
Paul Wayne Ferris, Jr.

Paul Wayne Ferris, Jr.

THE GENRE
OF COMMUNAL LAMENT
IN THE BIBLE
AND THE ANCIENT NEAR EAST

Scholars Press
Atlanta, Georgia

THE GENRE OF COMMUNAL LAMENT
IN THE BIBLE
AND THE ANCIENT NEAR EAST

Paul Wayne Ferris, Jr.

Ph.D., 1984
Dropsie College
for Hebrew and Cognate Learning

Advisor:
Stephen Geller

© 1992
The Society of Biblical Literature

Library of Congress Cataloging in Publication Data

Ferris, Paul W.
    The genre of communal lament in the Bible and the ancient Near
East / Paul Wayne Ferris, Jr.
    p. cm. — (Dissertation series ; no. 127)
    Includes bibliographical references.
    ISBN 1-55540-542-8 (alk. paper). — ISBN 1-55540-543-6 (pbk. :
alk. paper)
    1. Laments in the Bible. 2. Bible. O.T. Lamentations—
Criticism, interpretation, etc. 3. Laments—Iraq—History and
criticism. 4. Assyro-Babylonian literature—Relation to the Old
Testament. I. Title. II. Series: Dissertation series (Society of
Biblical Literature) ; no. 127.
BS1199.L27F47 1990
224'.3'06—dc20   91-39722
                         CIP

Printed in the United States of America
on acid-free paper

To
Lois Anne Ferris
Paul Wayne Ferris III
Heide Lynne Ferris
Jeremy Tyler Fransen Ferris

and To
Mr. and Mrs. Paul Ferris Sr.

Contents

CHAPTER THREE

The Lament Phenomenon in the Ancient Near East
as it Relates to the Hebrew Communal Laments

CHAPTER FIVE

Comparisons and Contrasts Between the Sumero-Akkadian and the Hebrew Communal Laments

Acknowledgements

This study has had a long and rather convoluted history. I was encouraged to study the biblical laments by my mentor, Professor Walter Kaiser, at a time when they were just beginning to receive scholarly attention.

This project was carried out under the guidance of Dr. Stephen Geller who has distinguished himself as a scholar of Hebrew poetry. His careful critique and advice have in no small way contributed to whatever achievements have been made in this study. To the other members of my committee, Professors Stephen Lieberman and Sol Cohen, I am also greatly indebted for their diligent efforts to help me improve this study.

My gratitude must also be expressed to the Columbia Biblical Seminary, its President and Dean as well as to my colleagues for their unflagging support.

To my wife, Lois, and children, Paul III, Heide and Jeremy, and to my parents, Mr. & Mrs Paul Ferris Sr., I dedicate this work as a token of my love and deep appreciation for their support over the years.

Finally, I am deeply grateful to Dr. J.J.M. Roberts and especially to Dr. David Petersen and his staff as well as the staff at Scholars Press for their invaluable assistance in preparing the manuscript for publication.

Abbreviations

AASOR	*Annual of the American Schools of Oriental Research*
AbrN	*Abr-Nahrain*
AJSL	*American Journal of Semitic Languages and Literatures*
ANET	J. Pritchard, *Ancient Near Eastern Texts*
AnOr	*Analecta Orientalia*
AS	*Assyriological Studies*
BASOR	*Bulletin of the American Schools of Oriental Research*
BDB	F. Brown, S. Driver, C. Briggs, *Hebrew and English Lexicon of the Old Testament*
BHS	*Biblia Hebraica Stuttgartensia*
Bib	*Biblica*
BKAT	*Biblischer Kommentar: Altes Testament*
BL	S. Langdon, *Babylonian Liturgies*
BSac	*Bibliotheca Sacra*
BZAW	*Beihefte zur ZAW*
CAD	*The Assyrian Dictionary of the University of Chicago*
CAH	*Cambridge Ancient History*
CBC	M. Cohen, *Balag-compositions*
CRAIBL	*Compte Rendus de l'Académie des Inscriptiones et Belles-Lettres*
CBQ	*Catholic Biblical Quarterly*
CSH	M. Cohen, *Sumerian Hymnology*
GN	*Gottesname*, divine name
HAT	*Handbuch zum Alten Testament*

HRTN	S. Langdon, *Historical & Religious Texts from Nippur*
HSM	Harvard Semitic Monographs
HTR	*Harvard Theological Review*
HUCA	*Hebrew Union College Annual*
IB	*Interpreter's Bible*
ICC	*International Critical Commentary*
Int	*Interpretation*
JAOS	*Journal of the American Oriental Society*
JBL	*Journal of Biblical Literature*
JCS	*Journal of Cuneiform Studies*
JQR	*Jewish Quarterly Review*
JR	*Journal of Religion*
JSS	*Journal of Semitic Studies*
LEr	M. Green, "Lamentation over the Destruction of Eridu"
LIIBE	R. Castellino, *Lamentazioni Individuali e gli Inni in Babylonia e in Israel*
LK	S. Kramer, "Kesh and Its Fate"
LU	S. Kramer, *Lamentation over the Destruction of Ur*
LSU	S. Kramer, "Lamentation over the Destruction of Sumer and Ur"
OAS	R. Kutscher, "*a-ab-ba hu-luh-ha,*" *O Angry Sea*
OECT	*Oxford Editions of Cuneiform Texts*
Or	*Orientalia*
PASOR	*Proceedings of the American Schools of Oriental Research*
RA	*Revue d'assyriologie et d'archeologie orientale*
RAI	*Actes de la Rencontre assyriologique internationale*
RGG	*Religion in Geschichte und Gegenwart*
RS	*Ras Shamra*
SAHG	A. Falkenstein, W. von Soden, *Sumerische und Akkadische Hymnen und Gebete*
SBLDS	Society of Biblical Literature Dissertation Series
SBP	S. Langdon, *Sumerian and Babylonian Psalms*
SK	H. Zimmern, *Sumerische Kultlieder aus altbabylonischer Zeit* I-II, VS II, X
SKly	J. Krecher, *Sumerische Kultlyrik*
SNVAO	Skrifter utgitt av det norske videnskaps–akademi i Oslo
SLT	S. Langdon, *Sumerian Liturgical Texts*
StOr	*Studia Orientalia*
TynBul	*Tyndale Bulletin*
UET	*Ur Excavations, Texts*
UT	C. Gordon, *Ugaritic Textbook*

VAB	*Vorderasiatische Bibliothek*
VS	*Vorderasiatische Schriftdenkmaler der Königlichen Museen zu Berlin*
VT	*Vetus Testamentum*
YNER	Yale Near Eastern Researches
ZA	*Zeitschrift für Assyriologie*
ZAW	*Zeitschrift für die alttestamentliche Wissenschaft*
ZZB	D. Edzard, *Die "zweite Zwischenzeit" Babyloniens*

1

Introduction

1.1 *Current State of Lament Study*

This study has grown out of a developing interest in the biblical book of Lamentations. The phenomenon of public lament is unfortunately quite foreign to current Western culture. This was not so in the ancient Near East. It is fair to say, however, that the typical Westerner's awareness of most aspects of ancient Near Eastern culture is almost entirely limited to the Hebrew Bible. Yet even from this limited vantage point, a perusal of the literature, both popular and scholarly, over the past century and a half indicates that the biblical lamentations have not received much attention.

1.1.1 Recent Developments

However, there has been some change recently. Within the last quarter century or so the biblical book of Lamentations has indeed begun to draw a significantly greater degree of attention.[1] However, when the various other biblical laments are dealt with, the treatment is usually brief: often only a few lines. Generally, perhaps due to the format of the commentaries, the laments are treated on an individual basis. A unified study of the communal lament and the genre out of which it grew is lacking.

---

[1] E.g., the contributions of Albrektson, Gordis, Gottwald, Kraus, Rudolph and Weiser.

1.1.2 Gunkel and Form-critical Studies

Over a half-century ago the study of the various genres of Hebrew literature received its greatest impetus from the work of Hermann Gunkel (1862-1932). Gunkel approached biblical studies out of historical criticism. It was his abiding interest in historical backgrounds that caused him to develop a history of selected portions of Hebrew literature. In a way not yet done in literary or historical criticism, he urged the use of extra-biblical literature in an attempt to explicate the origins, forms and functions of a given piece of literature. He was concerned how a piece of literature was related to others of like origin, form and function. He encouraged the study of how a literary genre functioned in the life of a community or individual, its purpose and how and when it was used.[2] From the quite apparent conservatism of Semitic poetry Gunkel postulated that customs and convention exerted a strong and pervasive influence over verbal expression, especially in cultic or other religious literature not only in Israel, but throughout the ancient Near East. He also observed that, for example, "in the Psalms . . . we find an extraordinary sameness of content—in different Psalms we find the same thoughts, moods, forms of expression, metaphors, rhetorical figures, phrases."[3] Gunkel began to apply this method to both Old and New Testament literature. For instance, in his first major work he analyzes Gen. 1:1 - 2:4a and Revelation 12.[4] But it was his approach as applied to the Psalter that has so affected the analysis of the laments.[5]

1.1.3 Genre Categorization

Largely on the basis of postulated categories of similar literary expressions, Gunkel suggested in somewhat broad strokes what might indeed serve as the main literary *Gattungen*, classes or types.

---

[2] Note "Fundamental Problems of Hebrew Literary History," in *What Remains of the Old Testament*, trans. A. K. Dallas (N. Y.: Macmillan, 1928), pp. 57-68; cf. "Die israelitische Literatur," *Die Kultur der Gegenwart*, ed. Hinneburg, Div. I/vol. 7 (Berlin: B. G. Teubner, 1906), pp. 51-102.

[3] "Fundamental Problems," pp. 58-59.

[4] *Schöpfung und Chaos in Urzeit und Endzeit* (Göttingen: Vandenhoeck & Ruprecht, 1895).

[5] *Ausgewählte Psalmen* (Göttingen: Vandenhoeck & Ruprecht, 1904; 4th rev. ed., 1917); *Die Psalmen übersetzt und erklärt*, 4th ed. (Göttingen: Vandenhoeck & Ruprecht, 1926); "The Poetry of the Psalms: Its Literary History and Its Application to the Dating of the Psalms," in *Old Testament Essays*, ed. D. C. Simpson (London: Griffin, 1927), pp. 118-142; *Einleitung in die Psalmen: Die Gattungen der religiösen Lyrik Israels* (completed by J. Begrich), (Göttingen: Vandenhoeck and Ruprecht, 1933). See also John Hayes' summary of Gunkel's position in "Old Testament Form Criticism," *An Introduction to Old Testament Study*, (Nashville: Abingdon, 1979), pp. 121-154.

1.1.3.1 *Sitz im Leben*

Gunkel believed that an analysis of the history of a literary type should include not only the identification of the main literary forms but also "the history through which these types have passed (including the sociological setting), [and the identification] of the process of collecting and stylizing according to artistic conventions and the survey of cognate literary types and affinities."[6]

This sociological setting from which a literary type was seen to have developed and against which it must be understood was called the *Sitz im Leben* by Gunkel.

> Every ancient literary type originally belonged to a quite definite side of the national life of Israel. Just as among ourselves the "sermon" belongs to the pulpit, while the "fairy-tale" has its home in the nursery, so in ancient Israel the Song of Victory was sung by maidens to greet the returning war-host; the Lament was chanted by hired female mourners by the bier of the dead; the Thora was announced by the priest in the sanctuary; the Judgment (*mishpaṭ* was given by the judge in his seat; the prophet uttered his Oracle in the outer court of the temple; the elders at the gate gave forth the Oracle of Wisdom. To understand the literary type we must in each case have the whole situation clearly before us and ask ourselves, Who is speaking? Who are the listeners? What is the *mise en scène* at the time? What effect is aimed at? In many cases a type is employed by a special class of speaker, and its use reveals of what class he is. Just as today a "sermon" implies a professional "preacher," so in ancient time the Thora and the hymn of worship were given through the priest, the oracular saying was uttered by the "wise men," and the lay was the utterance of a "singer." There may even have been a professional class of popular "story-tellers."[7]

This new attention to what Gunkel termed the *Sitz im Leben* is one of the major features of what came to be known as the form-critical method. It focuses on the social usage of a genre. He attempted to reconstruct as closely as possible the "pure" original—presumably oral—situation from which the more complex written form developed. It was with this contrast between the real-life oral situation and the contrived written form in mind that he argued: "The oldest genre, that which has its *Sitz im Leben*, envisages specific listeners and strives for certain effects are for that very reason almost always entirely pure."[8] This "*Sitz*" became a key factor in genre identification as it sought to identify a given literary piece with both an originating situation and the recurring situation which perpetu-

---

6 "Fundamental Problems," pp. 60-61.
7 Ibid. pp. 61-62.
8 "Die israelitische Literatur," pp. 55-56.

ated the piece. In the first edition of *Die Religion in Geschichte und Gegenwart* Gunkel stated categorically that the identification of the types of Cult Songs was to be done "always according to their setting in life, that is, according to the various situations in which the songs were sung."[9]

1.1.3.2 Thought and Mood Content

The attention given to the *Sitz im Leben*, however, was to be only one factor in genre studies. Gunkel argued that the thought and the mood of the literature and the specific linguistic forms as well as the *Sitz im Leben* were constituent parts of what he came to call "genre." In the second edition of *Die Religion in Geschichte und Gegenwart* he added:

> The principal literary types are represented by those songs which were sung on the most frequently recurring occasions. A common setting in life is thus *one* of the distinguishing characteristics of songs belonging to the same literary type. *Another* distinguishing characteristic is the great number of thoughts and moods which these songs share, while *yet another*—a very distinctive characteristic—is the literary forms (*Formensprache*) which are prevalent in them.[10]

It is significant to note that Gunkel seemed rather consistently to regard matters of mood and thought content as prior, logically, procedurally and most likely developmentally, to matters of linguistic or literary form.[11] In practice, however, the emphasis in genre identification is often placed on fixed literary forms and even a fixed *Sitz im Leben*.

1.1.4 Influence of Form-Critical Studies

1.1.4.1 Sigmund Mowinckel

Though at first Gunkel's approach was regarded with skepticism, the value of his work obviously did not go unnoticed. Among those of the next generation of scholars who would be influenced by Gunkel was Sigmund Mowinckel (1884-1965).

Coming from what is often referred to as the Scandinavian school, Mowinckel seemed almost predisposed to adapt significantly rather than adopt outright the method as he built on Gunkel's foundations. While adopting Gunkel's generic categories and form-critical analysis largely

---

9 *The Psalms*, trans. T. M. Horner (Philadelphia: Fortress, 1967), p. 10, from RGG, I (Tübingen: Mohr, 1930).

10 Ibid. Italics mine. Cf. H. Gunkel and J. Begrich, *Einleitung in die Psalmen*, p. 22.

11 *Reden und Aufsätze* (Göttingen: Vandenhoeck and Ruprecht, 1913), p. 32; *Die Propheten* (Göttingen: Vandenhoeck and Ruprecht, 1917), p. 109; "Jesaia: eine prophetische Liturgie," ZAW 42 (1924): 177-208; *What Remains*, p. 115.

intact, Mowinckel, under the influence of the Assyriologist Heinrich Zimmern,[12] endeavored to establish a religio-cultural framework for understanding many or most of the Psalms. He postulated the cultic activities surrounding the feast days of ancient Israel, especially the New Year's festival, "the real 'festival of Yahweh,' or 'day of Yahweh.'" The laments, on the other hand, belonged "to the days of humiliation and prayer which were 'proclaimed' on special occasions of crisis, and might be called the 'casual' or *ad hoc* festivals."[13] Thus, beyond the correlation of the form of the Psalms with the cultus in general which Gunkel had endeavored to demonstrate, Mowinckel tried to show a correlation of the Psalter with particular cultic situations and factors of national life. Mowinckel focused more on the mood and the content of the Psalms than Gunkel did. Indeed, Mowinckel warned that "the form may be overrated so as to . . . make one overlook important inner correspondences between the psalms which outwardly [by means of the formal literary criteria] appear to belong to different groups, but which are governed by the same ideas, and thus prove to belong together, perhaps as psalms for some specific festival."[14]

Mowinckel's approach has been variously labelled "cult-functional" or "cult-historical" as over against Gunkel's approach. But the two can properly be subsumed under the rubric of form criticism.

1.1.4.2 Claus Westermann

The hiatus in research and writing caused by the Second World War occasioned a notable contrast between pre-war and post-war biblical studies, especially in Germany. This applied to form-critical analyses as well. Post-war German biblical scholarship was influenced in no small way by Barthian theology and the biblical theology movement and form criticism came to be pressed to more theological ends.[15]

Prominent among the practitioners of the form-critical method in the post-war era is Claus Westermann. In his *Praise of God in the Psalms* he

---

[12] S. Mowinckel, Psalmenstudien, vol. II: Das Thronbesteigungsfest Jahwäs und der Ursprung der Eschatologie. SNVAO. (Kristiana: J. Dybwad, 1922), p. xi.

[13] *The Psalms in Israel's Worship*, trans. D. R. Ap-Thomas, vol. I (Oxford: Oxford Univ. Press, 1962), p. 193.

[14] Ibid., p. 31.

[15] For example, G. von Rad applies form criticism as an instrument to aid in adducing a biblical theology in his *Old Testament Theology*, trans. D. M. G. Stalker, 2 vols. (New York: Harper, 1962). For a discussion of these developments see J. Barr's 1970 Croall Lectures at Edinburgh, *The Bible in the Modern World* (New York: Harper and Row, 1973), especially chapter 1. See also B. Childs, *Biblical Theology in Crisis* (Philadelphia: Westminster, 1970) for a discussion of specifically American developments in post-war biblical studies. See also H. H. Rowley, *Rediscovery of the Old Testament* (Philadelphia: Westminster, 1946).

argues that neither Gunkel's literary nor Mowinckel's cultic categories offers the best working system. Rather, he postulates two foundational categories: plea and praise. From these all other "branches" can be traced. The definition of the function of the *Sitz im Leben* is significantly modified as well. It now refers to that "basic occurrence which transpires in 'cult' when men speak to God: the polarity of speaking to God as plea and as praise."[16]

Thus form criticism came to be directed more or less toward the *mysterium* of the relationship and "dialog" between God and man.[17] Westermann presses the form-critic beyond the forms of the surface structures to ask: What happens in a lament and what are the components of what happens?[18]

1.2 *Problem of Generic Classification*

1.2.1 Question of Priority

This brief survey, while indicating some of the significant features and contributions of the form-critical method to date, also points up a recurring problem. The problem centers on the question: Should the issues of literary forms, linguistic style and structure take precedence over the issues of content and purpose in identifying a genre? Gunkel seems to have recognized the *logical* priority of the matters of content and purpose over the matters of form in genre analysis.[19] This is quite significant. Gerstenberger has pointed out that "because of our remoteness from the ancient scene, grammatical and syntactical analysis had to take precedence."[20] The main significance of this for the study of the lament literature is, of course, the bearing which this tension between form and content has upon the development of working criteria—how does one identify a communal lament? It must be agreed with Gerstenberger that the tendency has been to focus almost exclusively on matters of form, linguistic style and surface structure, etc. But while it may well be that a specific formal structure might be a definitive characteristic for some

---

16 Trans. K. R. Crim (Richmond, Va.: John Knox, 1965), pp. 153-154.

17 Ibid., pp. 65-70. See also his "Struktur und Geschichte der Klage im Alten Testament," ZAW 66 (1954): 44-80; "The Role of the Lament in the Theology of the Old Testament," Int 28 (1974): 20-38. These two articles are reprinted in the new edition of *Praise* entitled *Praise and Lament in the Psalms* (Atlanta: John Knox, 1981).

18 "Struktur," p. 46.

19 See above, p. 4.

20 E. Gerstenberger, "Psalms," in *Old Testament Form Criticism*, ed. J. H. Hayes (San Antonio, Tex.: Trinity Univ. Press, 1974), p. 182, to which might be added lexicography.

genres, it seems problematic to start there and there alone when dealing with the communal laments.

R. Knierim outlines the difficulties in fixing criteria for determining a specific genre.[21] He points out that "form criticism has employed a monolithic conception of genre and assumed the homogeneity of the typical factors in it. This may—paradoxically—have been counterproductive to its own original intentions."[22]

An indication of the problem may be seen in the absence of a real consensus when it comes to identifying communal laments as in indicated the chart below (fig. 1).

Gunkel seems to have been closer to the mark in placing emphasis— if only theoretically—upon the "thoughts and moods," the *Sitz im Leben* and the *raison d'être* which interrelates them. The difficulty has been in working out the proper balance. Both the characteristic forms/structures on the one hand, and the content and purpose/function on the other hand must be utilized in determining generic classification. That is, a whole complex of factors must be studied in order to determine the shared generic conception which constitutes both the meaning and understanding which is the "intrinsic genre" of a given text.[23]

1.2.2 Question of Methodology

But another point must be made at this juncture. Such a working system of generic classification ought not to be reduced to the lowest common denominator and then canonized. Rather, it functions best as a heuristic device, open to modification and theoretically even elimination. The study of ancient Near Eastern literature in general and Hebrew Bible in particular would seem to benefit significantly if it were to be based on a flexible or adaptable notion of "genre." It will not do to foist either 19th or 20th century notions and categories upon a phenomenon so historically and culturally distant.

---

[21] "Old Testament Form Criticism Reconsidered," Int 27 (1973): 435-468.

[22] Ibid., p. 467.

[23] E. D. Hirsch, *Validity in Interpretation* (New Haven, Conn.: Yale Univ. Press, 1967), pp. 80-81. Both Hirsch and H. G. Gadamer, P. Ricoeur and T. Todorov press beyond an idealist notion of genre as merely a device of classification and develop aspects of a notion of genre as a generative principle on the analogy of N. Chomsky's generative function of grammar. H. G. Gadamer, *Truth and Method* (New York: Seabury, 1975); E. D. Hirsch, *Validity*; idem, *The Aims of Interpretation* (Chicago: Univ. of Chicago Press, 1976); P. Ricoeur, "The Hermeneutical Function of Distanciation," *Philosophy Today* 17 (Summer 1973): 129-141.; T. Todorov, *The Fantastic: A Structural Approach to the Literary Genre* (Cleveland: Case Western Reserve Univ. Press, 1973).

It may prove more fruitful to analyze forms and structure and test to see how they function as indicators of one specific genre or another. But as Blenkinsopp has observed regarding the gap between the phenomenon and its modern analysts: "It does not seem that Mesopotamian scribes were much exercised with distinctions of genre."[24] And it appears, as I shall endeavor to demonstrate below, that much the same could be said for the Hebrews. While it is true that the Mesopotamian utilized various rubrics which seem to be identified with one genre or sub-genre or another,[25] these speakers/writers simply do not appear to be bound by a fixed set of precisely defined rules. In other words, one finds in fact that content does not always correspond to imposed limitations of form. For example, the *eršemma*, as we shall see below: while most often is a form to be identified as a sub-genre of the communal lament, occasionally may be otherwise associated. An example of such is Cohen's no. 29. "Not only does this text which is appended to a *balag*-lamentation not possess the heart-pacification unit [typical of the *eršemma*], but its very content and structure is identical to that of the *eršahunga*, another hymnal classification in the liturgy of the *gala*-priest."[26] The occurrence of formulaic language which has come to be identified characteristically with a specific genre does not necessarily require one to subsume the text in which it occurs under that particular generic category. In other words, it is true that both the Sumero-Akkadian and the Hebrew laments bear rubrics which seem to classify the compositions thus marked as one type or another. But even though there appear to be distinctive rubrics, Kutscher has pointed out, e.g., that the *balag* rubric is inconsistently applied because "to the scribes who designated the 'genre' of compositions the term was not generic at all, but functional, implying that such a composition was to be recited or chanted, accompanied by the *balag*-instrument."[27]

1.3 Purpose

This study is an attempt to offer a unified comparative description of the Hebrew genre of communal lament: its form and function. This description is based on a thematic analysis of the Hebrew communal

---

[24] "The Search for the Prickly Plant: Structure and Function Found in the Gilgamesh Epic," in *Structuralism*, ed. S. Wittig (Pittsburgh: Pickwick, 1975), p. 57.

[25] See C. Wilcke, "Formale Gesichtspunkte in der sumerischen Literatur," AS 20 (1976): 205-316, see esp. sec. 11, "Unterschriften und Rubriken."

[26] M. Cohen, *Sumerian Hymnology: The Eršemma* (Cincinnati: Hebrew Union College, 1981), p. 29.

[27] R. Kutscher, *Oh Angry Sea*, YNER 9 (New Haven: Yale, 1975), p. 3.

lament in light of the phenomenon of public lamentation in neighboring cultures as preserved in their literature. To this end it will address questions such as: What is a communal lament? What is the connection between the individual or personal laments and the communal or congregational laments? What are the characteristic forms of the communal lament? Of the elements of the characteristic forms, which are essential? What is the relationship of the literary forms to the ritual and/or other situations in the culture? What is the origin of the apparent guild of the מקוננות and did they have a standardized repertoire? If so, how was their repertoire developed? Who composed the laments and how did they develop from one function or form to another? That is, what is the relationship between the liturgical and literary forms? What was the role of the prophet and/or priest in this regard?

I will attempt to show how the liturgical dirge was developed into a literary sub-genre beginning, as it appears was often the case, as a private expression of grief and evolving to the point where there appears to emerge a professional guild whose job it was to compose—or at least adapt—and perform the dirge.

1.4 *Working Definitions*

1.4.1 Genre

The notion of genre has a breadth of meaning in biblical studies. On the one hand its terminology, e.g., *Gattung*, is applied to the larger categories of the literature. On the other hand, it may refer to more narrowly defined groups of compositions, e.g., *Formen*. "Form" may be applied to individual compositions and focus on its structure or scheme. In this study, the term "genre" is used in a way consistent with its use in literary analysis in general.[28] It is used to designate a selection of literary compositions which share a common theme and mood, and similar intent and function.[29] The term is not being used in its narrower sense to specify a "structural scheme."

1.4.2 Communal Lament

The primary issue, of course, is: What is a communal lament? By what criteria is the corpus of communal lament to be identified? Westermann's treatment of the Psalms of praise seems instructive at this

---

[28] See A. Marino, "Toward a Definition of Literary Genres," in *Yearbook of Comparative Criticism*, vol. 8, *Theories of Literary Genre*, ed. J. P. Strelka (University Park, Pa.: Pennsylvania State University Press, 1978), pp. 51, 54.

[29] See Knierim, "Form Criticism."

point. He argues that the formal verbal data, while significant, is insufficient alone to define or identify the category. He notes that the Psalms demonstrate a very "real way of praising, in words or sentences that do not even contain the word 'praise'."[30] The functional ambiguity in form-critical procedure mentioned above is at issue here. And Westermann makes the important point that categories are often to be distinguished, not by "different *forms* of speech . . . but the difference lies in *that which is spoken of*."[31]

In this study I will use the following as a working definition: A communal lament is a composition whose verbal content indicates that it was composed to be used by and/or on behalf of a community to express both complaint, and sorrow and grief over some perceived calamity, physical or cultural, which had befallen or was about to befall them and to appeal to God for deliverance.[32] How they were composed; how they were publicly expressed; whether or not a given lament may have been used on the occasion of more than one calamity or in memory of such a calamity are secondary questions the answers to which may vary. This definition is intended to cover matters of thought and mood, *Sitz im Leben* and linguistic and poetic structures.

1.4.3 Individual Lament

In corresponding fashion, an individual lament is a composition whose verbal content indicates that it was composed to be used by and/or on behalf of an individual to express sorrow and grief over some perceived calamity which had befallen or was about to befall him and to appeal to God for deliverance. Most often the "calamity" of the individual lament was related to some form of harassment of the subject by an enemy. Examples of the individual lament would be Pss. 6, 13, 22, 27, etc.

---

30 *Praise*, p. 15.

31 Italics mine. *Praise*, p. 19, n. 5, where, e.g., he points out that "at the beginning [of his *Einleitung*] Gunkel said that the category [hymn vs. song of thanks] could be recognized most clearly by the introduction (p. 25), but according to p. 83 the hymn and the song of thanks generally agree in the introduction and in the conclusion. (This is said more sharply on p. 267). This confusion could have been avoided if Gunkel had maintained the distinction, according to which the two types can be clearly distinguished in the main part of the song. The 'Song of Thanks' reports one specific action of God, and the 'Hymn' praises God's activity and his being for us in their fulness."

32 Those compositions which express penitence over guilt, whether an individual or communal expression, are classified as penitential psalms rather than laments, e.g., Ps. 52. Some may make a correlation between said guilt and some calamity which had befallen or was about to befall and individual or community, but still focus on the matter of penitence.

1.4.4 Funeral Dirge

A funeral dirge is a composition whose verbal content indicates that it was composed in honor of a deceased person sometimes eulogizing the individual, sometimes merely bewailing the loss. It was apparently used by either individuals or by groups at funeral observances.

1.4.5 Descriptive Terms

A certain amount of repetition of themes, forms and terms is to be expected in poetic compositions as a poetic device. Such is certainly the case with the material treated in this study. In order to distinguish between two different kinds of repetition found particularly in the Sumero-Akkadian laments, I will use the term "refrain" to mean those passages which recur at intervals in a composition and which often serve to set off sections of the composition. Shorter phrases and terms repeated frequently within a unit or among several units of a composition will be termed "repetends."

1.5 *Delimitations*

1.5.1 Literary Data

One of the significant distinctives of Gunkel's approach to the question of the *Sitz* of a genre was the assumption of an original, i.e., *ante scriptum*, oral setting. In order to understand a piece of literature, Gunkel argued "we have to keep in mind the [original] situation [in which it was told]. . . . The ordinary situation we have to think of is this: During an idle winter evening the family is sitting by the hearth [recounting stories from the olden days].[33] "Every old literary genre originally had .its appointed place in the *Sitz im Volksleben* of Israel.[34]

> The oldest genre did not originally exist on paper in life where the original unit was brief, complying with the low capacity of the listeners for absorption, especially those ancient listeners. From the indicated *Sitz im Leben* it is furthermore explained that these old genres have a *pure style*. They are calculated for a certain situation and are thoroughly appropriate.[35]

To assume that there may in all probability have been an oral period in the history of a literary piece and/or genre is most reasonable. However, to posit just what that original setting "must" have been is quite another question. To attempt to reconstruct the growth of a genre

---

33 *Die Sagen der Genesis* (Göttingen: Vandenhoeck and Ruprecht, 1901), p. xviii.
34 *Reden und Aufsätze* (Göttingen: Vandenhoeck and Ruprecht, 1913), p. 33, cf. p. 35.
35 Italics mine. *Die Religion in Geschichte und Gegenwart* (Tübingen: Mohr, 1909), I:1193.

in an assumed oral period is to attempt the almost impossible by virtue of the absence or at least the paucity of primary data with which to work. To argue gratuitously that these pure originals were necessarily short due to some conceived mental deficiency on the part of the "ancient listeners" is to demonstrate a blatant cultural chauvinism. M. Buss has raised a number of significant questions in regard to this aspect of the form-critical method:

> Can a contrast between writing and 'life' be effectively maintained? Is it true that simple literature is as a rule prior to sophisticated (oral or written) production? Do the "oldest," practical genres have an "altogether pure style?" Are situations in primitive life clearly demarcated, so that there is only one basic circumstance for each genre? These questions probably need to be answered in the negative; H. Gunkel allowed himself to go beyond available evidence.[36]

It must be the written form which serves as the basis for study. Indeed, particularly in recent Old Testament studies, form criticism has been increasingly addressing the written forms.[37] This is due, at least in part, to the growing number of extant extra-biblical literary parallels, many of which are at least as old if not older than the biblical texts in question. With such a volume of written data with which to work, the need to attempt to reconstruct and analyze a hypothetical oral composition behind the written text becomes greatly diminished. Therefore this study will focus itself upon the written forms of the "communal lament" which has been preserved in extant standard texts.

1.5.2 Format

The approach taken, then, is to analyze the basic elements of communal lament in extant Mesopotamian literature looking for any variety in types and structure of the laments. The thematic elements of the Sumero-Akkadian communal lament forms are then isolated. Then the issue of the *Sitz im Leben* is addressed. The circumstances which mark the occasion of continued usage and/or adaptation, if any, are described.

In performing the social analysis of the laments, I have endeavored not to prejudge the question of corporate origin vs. individual origin but rather pursue the historical question: "Where did the lament come from?" To this question the practitioners of the form-critical method have consistently answered in terms of a corporate origin. I remain to be con-

---

36 "The Idea of *Sitz im Leben*—History and Critique," ZAW 90 (1978): 159.

37 For example, K. Baltzer, *The Covenant Formulary* (Philadelphia: Fortress, 1971); M. Kline, *The Treaty of the Great King* (Grand Rapids, Mich.: Eerdmans, 1963); K. Kitchen, *Ancient Orient and the Old Testament* (Chicago: Inter-Varsity, 1966), pp. 90-102, 130-135.

vinced that this is always the case. Rather, it seems that the evidence supports the conclusion that the origin of a given lament could quite feasibly be either, or possibly even both, corporate and/or individual.

Attention is then turned to related aspects of the phenomenon of lament in the ancient Near East as they bear upon the Hebrew communal lament. A summary of the content, form and function of the individual laments is given. Then a summary of the phenomenon of the funeral dirges: their occasion, content and performers are presented. Following this, the occurrence and adaptation of the lament to other aspects of society are treated. Lastly, the matter of musical accompaniment is taken up.

In chapter four the basic form of the communal lament in the Bible is analyzed following the same basic approach as was applied to the Sumero-Akkadian laments.

I then deal with the question of influence between the Mesopotamian and Hebrew laments: What relationship, if any, existed? Were there common roots in the ancient Near Eastern experience and culture? To what degree are the types identical or at least similar? How do the respective structures compare? How do the functions of the laments in the respective societies compare? What evidence is there of "borrowing" or influence between the examples of lament?

Apart from certain technical terms, I have endeavored to present all of this discussion in English so that rather than, e.g., quoting an authority in German or French, I have translated the given passage into English. Likewise, I have translated the Hebrew to facilitate the illustrative purpose of the citations.

1.5.3 Purpose

As stated above,[38] this study is an attempt to develop a unified comparative description of the Hebrew communal lament in light of the phenomenon of public lament in neighboring cultures as preserved in their literature. It will not pursue the various characteristics which lament may for one reason or another share with other forms of poetry beyond the lament literature.[39] Our study will be directed toward the

---

[38] See p. 8.

[39] For example, the overlap with other genres of apparent key terms, technical terms, and idioms or formulae commonly associated with lamentation. It is somewhat tenuous to assume that the mere occurrence of איכה or אוי e.g., in another genre is a necessary sign of recipient influence. Also, the issue of metrics has been discussed at length by Cross, Eissfeldt, Freedman, Gray, Sievers, Stuart et al., and will not be pursued in this study.

question of the influence the various communal laments may have had upon one another.

1.5.4 Laments to be Studied

As indicated above,[40] thought and mood as indicated by content takes priority over but does not exclude matters of form in identifying laments. Though there is a general lack of agreement as to just which of the biblical Psalms are indeed communal laments,[41] in light of the above-mentioned criteria, the following passages will be analyzed: Psalms 31, 35, 42, 43, 44, 56, 59, 60, 69, 74, 77, 79, 80, 83, 85, 89, 94, 102, 109, 137, 142, Lamentations.

In chapter four I attempt to show how each of these compositions manifests the themes and the expressions which indicate that they were composed to be used by or on behalf of the community to express grief and appeal for deliverance. Psalms 31, 35, 42/43, 56, 59, 69, 109 and 142 are identified as communal laments by Mowinckel. These are among those he describes as "quite personal, but in reality . . . national (congregational) psalms."[42] In these cases, Mowinckel argues that "in the I-form . . . the king represents the people, even in public distress."[43] I concur. For example, Psalm 31 demonstrates all the component thematic elements we have identified as belonging to a communal lament,[44] and although it is couched in the first person, the community is the focus of the expression as indicated in the hymn of praise in verses 24-25:

> Love the LORD, all you His loyal ones!
> The LORD guards the faithful,
> And rewards in full the proud doer.
> Be strong and He will encourage your heart,
> All you who wait expectantly on the LORD.

In a similar vein, Psalm 35 is identified in the title as a Psalm of David, yet in the body of the song, the community is enjoined to praise the LORD in verse 27. The composition of Psalms 42 and 43 also indicates a communal context, viz., the crowd which went in procession to the festival at the house of God. Both Psalms 42/43 and 44 contain notations indicating they are *maskils* as are 74, 89 and 142. Psalms 31, 42/43, 44, 56, 59, 60, 69, 77, 80, 85 and 109 are designated to the "choir director." From

---

[40] See above, p. 4.
[41] See fig. 1.
[42] Mowinckel, *Psalms*, vol. I, p. 219.
[43] Ibid., p. 194.
[44] See below, ch. 4. Note especially fig. 3.

another perspective, in Psalm 56 and 59 it is the nations, the heathen who attack and oppress, thus indicating not the enemy of an individual but of the community. Psalms 44, 60, 74, 79 and 80 all deal with some aspect of military defeat which better fits a communal setting than an individual one.[45] Psalm 77 seems also to be set against the backdrop of the national experience and the one reciting the lament speaks for the community in corporate solidarity. Psalms 42/3, 69, 79, 89, 102 and 137 are some of the more obvious communal laments, dealing as they do with the destruction of the city of Jerusalem.

The extra-biblical laments treated will be those communal laments of the extant corpus of Sumero-Akkadian lament literature which are available in translation. Many of the texts were treated around the turn of the century and, in some cases, neither the transliteration nor the translation is up to date. A significant sampling of these is included in the laments translated and published almost a quarter century ago. I have endeavored to use the best available translations, but at times the only material available material is three-quarters of a century old. Happily, new and better editions are forthcoming.

Indeed, the corpus has been growing thanks to the contributions of E. Ebeling, S. N. Kramer, A. Falkenstein and W. von Soden and more recently by J. Krecher. Within the last decade, significant contributions have been made by W. Hallo, R. Kutscher, M. Cohen and M. Green. Together, these include the vast majority, if not the totality of the extra-biblical ancient Near Eastern communal laments pursued in this study.

---

[45] See below, fig. 4.

FIGURE 1

Identification of Communal Laments

Psa.	SD 1891	HG(A) 1904	HG(B) 1931	SM 1924	OE 1934	CW 1961	AW 1962	OK 1969	AA 1972	LS 1974
9/10				Y						
12				X						?
13				Y						
14	X			X						
21							z			
31				Y						
33							z			
35				Y						
42/3				Y						
44	X	X	X	X	X	X	X			X
46						X				
55				Y						
56				Y						
58				X						?
59				Y						
60	X	X	X	X	X	X	z	X	X	X
68							z			
69				Y						
74	X	X	X	X	X	X	X	X	X	X
77										?
79	X	X	X	X	X	X	X	X	X	X
80	X	X	X	X	X	X	X	X	X	X
82	X									?
83	X	X		X	X		X	X	X	?
85	X					X	z	X	X	X
89			X	X	X		z	X	X	X
90						X	z	X	X	X
94	X		X	X						?
102	X			Y						
106						X				?
108	X									?
109				Y						
115						X				
123	X						z			X
124									X	
126							z		X	?
129							z			
137	X						X	X	X	X
142				Y						
144				X					X	

LEGEND

x = Identify as Communal Lament   y = Very Personal Communal Lament
z = Psalm with Communal Lament Theme   ? = Possibly a Communal Lament

SD = S. R. Driver   OE = O. Eissfeldt   OK = O. Kaiser
HG = H. Gunkel   CW = C. Westermann   AA = A. Anderson
SM = S. Mowinckel   AW = A. Weiser   LS = L. Sabourin

—— ❦ **2** ❧ ——

Basic Forms of Communal Lament
in Mesopotamia

2.1 *Introduction*

A survey of the Sumero-Akkadian literature which expresses communal lamentation reveals a range of terms which are used to designate a variety of sub-classes.[46]

2.1.1 Terms for Lament

If there was a technical term for the genre of lament in Sumerian, it is as yet unknown. The classic city laments do not bear any generic designation and, as far as is known, none is assigned elsewhere.

2.1.1.1 *Balag*

Though *balag* is the term which came to designate the class of literature which expresses lamentation over some public disaster, it does not seem to be used of the classic city laments such as the "Lamentation over the Destruction of Ur."[47] The term *balag* apparently originally denoted a musical instrument and then by extension "a kind of song, probably a

---

[46] T. Jacobsen, "Review of S. N. Kramer, *Lamentation over the Destruction of Ur*," AJSL 58 (1941): 222.
[47] Ibid.

dirge, accompanied by the *b[alag]*-instrument" as well as the one who performs on such instrument.[48] Kutscher concludes that the reason so few *balag*-type compositions of the Old Babylonian period are labelled as such is that, at that time, the term was not yet a genre title as it later turned out to be.[49] Jacobsen pointed out the two-fold aspect of the later *balag*: the "*ér* and *ershemma*."[50] Thus, the first part of the *balag* composition is designated in the later texts: *balag*-GN "*balag* for 'divine name'." "In the rituals it is called *taqribtu* (?), always written *ÉR*." The second part is designated in the songs themselves as well as in the ritual *er-šem/šem-[4]-ma*.[51] Jacobsen saw a comparison with the complaint and the pacification elements of the "Lament over Ur" and felt comfortable in applying the term to it as a genre designation.[52] The problem, of course, is that there are indeed Old Babylonian *balag*s which, while demonstrating certain affinities with the classic city laments, are nevertheless quite distinct.

The Akkadian term *girranu* "ritual wailing" occurs in some Sumerian texts. It is somehow identified with *balag* and *ér*.[53]

2.1.1.2 Ér

The canonical *ka-gal* = *abullu* from the texts of Tiglath-pileser I contains an acrographic listing with 22 entries under *ér*.[54] The following is a partial list with definitions:[55]

irgididakku: lament to the accompaniment of the flute
irgigidakku: "
irkatardudu: lament with doxology
irkitusakku: lament of the dwelling place
irnamtaggadu: lament to obtain absolution for sins
irsaharhubbakku: lament (to be recited while) covered with dust
irsipittu: lament. Cf. Akk. *sipittu*
irsizkurakku: lament with prayer (or sacrifices)
irsabadari: lament
irsannisakku: prayer in the form of a lamentation

---

48 CAD, s.v. "balaggu." See below, chapter 3, p. 85.
49 *OAS*, p. 3.
50 "Review of LU," citing IV R 53, p. 222.
51 J. Krecher, *Sumerische Kultlyrik* (Wiesbaden: Otto Harrassowitz, 1966), p. 21.
52 "Review of LU," pp. 222-223.
53 CAD, s.v.
54 B. Landsberger, *Materials for the Sumerian Lexicon*, vol. 13, ed. M. Civil (Rome: Pontifical Biblical Institute, 1971), p. 232.
55 CAD, s.v.

In view of the range of the use of the *ír/ér* term, Green suggests that this might be the term to designate the genre to which the classic city laments belong, but she concludes it is unlikely.[56]

2.1.2 Brief Description of Lamentations Available in Translation

Shortly after the turn of the century several collections of translations of Sumerian and Babylonian religious literature were published by S. Langdon, H. Zimmern, A. Ungnad and H. Gressmann.[57]

2.1.2.1 Stephen Langdon

Langdon's work is of the greatest interest here because of his treatment of *eršemma* and *balag* psalms. He first published treatment of the "Lamentation to the Goddess of Sirpurla.[58] A year later he published his *Sumerian and Babylonian Psalms*. In this book, he collected and translated from previously published texts, such as the *Cuneiform Texts from Babylonian Tablets in the British Museum*, vol. 15, by Pinches, King and Thompson; *Cuneiform Inscriptions of Western Asia*, vol. 4, by H. C. Rawlinson, G. Smith, and T. Pinches; *Sumerisch-Babylonische Hymnen* by G. Reisner; *Akkadische und Sumerische Keilschrifttexte* by P. Haupt; and *Beitrage zur Assyriologie* by F. Delitzsch and P. Haupt.

In his *Babylonian Liturgies* published four years later Langdon also treated a series of *balag* and *eršemma* liturgies.[59]

2.1.2.2 Samuel N. Kramer

Sumerian literature received a fair amount of attention from the next generation of scholars. Throughout the forties, fifties and sixties men like A. Falkenstein, T. Jacobsen, S. Kramer, and M. Witzel devoted much energy to the relatively new field of Sumerian literature.

---

[56] M. W. Green, "Eridu in Sumerian Literature," (Ph.D. dissertation, University of Chicago, 1975), pp. 282-283.

[57] H. Zimmern, *Babylonische Hymnen und Gebete in Auswahl*, (Leipzig: J. C. Hinrichs, 1905); S. Langdon, *Sumerian and Babylonian Psalms*, (Paris: Librairie Paul Geuthner, 1909); A. Ungnad and H. Gressmann, *Altorientalische Texte und Bilder zum alten Testament* (Tubingen: J. C. B. Mohr, 1909); H. Zimmern, *Babylonische Hymnen und Gebete, Zweite Auswähle* (Leipzig: J. C. Hinrichs, 1911); S. Langdon, *Babylonian Liturgies* (Paris: Librairie Paul Geuthner, 1913), and *Historical and Religious Texts from the Temple Library of Nippur*, Babylonian Expedition of the University of Pennsylvania, vol. 31, ed. H. Hilprecht,(Munich: Rudolph Merkel, 1914).

[58] AJSL 24 (1907-1908): 282-285.

[59] The consensus is that Langdon's treatments need to be updated in light of currently available data. In some few cases this has been addressed (eg. Cohen, Falkenstein, Krecher), but the sheer volume of extant literature that has yet to be transcribed and translated, much less receive critical attention, has mitigated against this updating process. Thus, for a majority of the smaller or otherwise apparently less significant lament texts, Langdon still offers the "latest" treatment.

In 1940 Kramer published his critical treatment of the *Lamentation Over the Destruction of Ur*.[60] In 1969, he published a translation of the "Lamentation Over the Destruction of Sumer and Ur."[61] In the same year, he published a preliminary report on the "Lamentation over the Destruction of Nippur."[62] And in 1971, Kramer published a translation of the "Lament to Aruru over Keš."[63]

2.1.2.3 Joachim Krecher

In 1966, J. Krecher published an extensive study of an Old Babylonian *balag* lament over Isin in which he treats both *balag* and *eršemma* as well as the *šu-illa* and *ersahunga* songs and offers an analysis of the genre designation and the utilization of *emesal* cult lyrics from Seleucid times back to Old Sumerian times. Krecher builds on the foundation laid by Langdon by utilizing additional material which had since become available. Thus, in several aspects, Krecher offers an update of Langdon's work.[64]

2.1.2.4 Raphael Kutscher

In 1975, R. Kutscher published *Oh Angry Sea (a-ab-ba hu-luh-ha): The History of a Sumerian Congregational Lament*, which grew out of his doctoral dissertation at Yale.[65] The *a-ab-ba hu-luh-ha* is a lament series over Nippur and Babylon dedicated to their respective patron deities, Enlil and Marduk.

2.1.2.5 Mark Cohen

In 1972, M. Cohen submitted his Ph.D. dissertation entitled, "An Analysis of the *balag*-Compositions to the God Enlil Copied in Babylon During the Seleucid Period," a critical treatment of thirty-five recon-

---

[60] *Lamentation Over the Destruction of Ur*, AS 12 (Chicago: Univ. of Chicago, 1940) (LU). This was followed quickly by T. Jacobsen's review and historical analysis in AJSL 58 (1941): 219-224. Eight years later A. Falkenstein published a "Review of *Lamentation over the Destruction of Ur* by Samuel Noah Kramer," ZA 49 (1949): 320-324. A translation of the 436 line lament by Kramer also appears in J. B. Pritchard's ANET (Princeton, NJ: Princeton University, 1955). See also M. Witzel's treatment, "Die Klage über Ur," Or NS 14 (1945): 185-234 and 15 (1946): 46-63.

[61] ANET, pp. 611-619. (LSU)

[62] *Eretz Israel* 9 (1969): 89-93.

[63] "Keš and Its Fate: Laments, Blessings, Omens," in *Gratz College Anniversary Volume*, eds. I. Passow, S. Lachs (Phila.: Gratz College, 1971), pp. 165-175. (LK)

[64] *Sumerische Kultlyrik* (Wiesbaden: Otto Harrassowitz, 1966). (SKly)

[65] *Oh Angry Sea (a-ab-bahu-luh-ha): The History of a Sumerian Congregational Lament]*, YNER, 6 (New Haven, CT: Yale Univ. Press, 1975). (OAS)

structed *balags*.[66] In 1975, he published *balag-Compositions: Sumerian Lamentation Liturgies of the Second and First Millennium* B.C., a treatment of *balag*s in general with a translation of five laments.[67]

Six years later, he published a work on the *eršemma*[68] in which he treats seventeen *eršemma*s preserved only in Old Babylonian copies, ten *eršemma*s preserved in both Old Babylonian and first millennium B.C. copies, and four which have been preserved only in first millennium copies.

2.1.2.6 Margaret Green

The most recent addition to the growing collection of laments occurred in 1978 when M. Green published a critical edition of the 65 line Eridu Lament (LEr).[69]

2.1.3 Early Sumerian Laments

No examples of the genre under consideration have yet been discovered from the neo-Sumerian or Ur III period. The neo-Sumerian laments which we do have come from the Old Babylonian period. They fall into two basic categories: the city-lament and the Dumuzi dirge.

There are only six distinctive Sumerian city-laments extant. Three of these Kutscher calls "major":[70] the "Lamentation over the Destruction of Ur," the "Lamentation over the Destruction of Sumer and Ur" and the "Lamentation over the Destruction of Nippur." The other three are the "Lamentation over the Destruction of Sumer and Uruk," the "Lamentation over the Destruction of Eridu," and the "Lamentation over the *ekimar*."

Some discussions of the Sumerian lament have included the "Curse of Agade." Scholarly consensus is that the "Curse," while including lament themes, is of a more historiographic genre, or, as Falkenstein would have it, political propaganda.[71]

---

[66] University of Pennsylvania.

[67] *Sources from the Ancient Near East*, vol. 1, (Malibu, CA: Undena, 1975). (CBC)

[68] *Sumerian Hymnology: The Ersemma*, HUCA Supplements, no. 2 (Cincinnati: Hebrew Union Col., 1981). (CSH)

[69] JCS 30 (1978):127-167. *Kirugus* 6-8 had already been published by C. Wilcke, "Der aktuelle Bezug der Sammlung der sumerischen Tempelhymnen und eines Fragment Klagelieder," ZA 62 (1972): 49-61. The JCS article is based on her dissertation, "Eridu in Sumerian Literature," (University of Chicago, 1975.) "The Uruk Lament" has just been published by M. Green but unfortunately too late to be included in this study, appearing this summer in JAOS 104 (1984):253-279.

[70] OAS, p. 1.

[71] M. Lambert, "La litterature sumerienne," RA 56 (1962):81-82. See also S. Kramer, *The Sumerians*, (Chicago: Univ. of Chicago, 1963) p. 62-66, and "The Curse of Agade," ANET, p.

The current status of the treatment of the classical Sumerian city-laments is as follows:

2.1.3.1 "The Lamentation over the Destruction of Ur"

Thus far, the 436 line "Lament over Ur" and the 165 line "Lament over Eridu" are the only texts to have been published in a critical edition. The edition of the Ur lament was done almost half a century ago. An alternate translation based on Kramer's collation is offered by M. Witzel.[72] A new edition is being prepared for publication by H. Vanstiphout.

The "Lament over Ur" as well as the "Lament over Sumer and Ur" are demonstrably magnificent literary works. Characteristic of the neo-Sumerian city-laments, the "Lament over Ur" is primarily written in the main Sumerian dialect, *emegir*. The first two of its eleven *kirugus*, however, are in the *emesal* dialect[73] which seems to have been reserved for female subjects in the Sumerian literary texts.[74]

There seems to be general agreement with T. Jacobsen[75] in assigning the *terminus ad quem* of the Ur Lament to the reign of Lipit-Ishtar of Isin (c. 1934 B.C.) some three quarters of a century after the destruction of the city at the hand of the Elamites and Sua in ca. 2006 B.C.[76] D. Edzard would date its composition closer to the time of the destruction—"barely later than one generation after the event," that is, closer to the time of the beginning of the restoration project than to the time of its conclusion.[77] The *terminus a quo* is obviously the 2006 B.C. destruction.

2.1.3.2 "The Lamentation over the Destruction of Sumer and Ur"

The "Lamentation over the Destruction of Sumer and Ur" has also been translated by Kramer.[78] The reference in the text of this lament to the capture of Ibbi-Sin (lines 35-37) suggests a *terminus a quo* of the fall of Ur III placing this lament roughly contemporary with the "Lament over

---

646; A. Falkenstein, "Fluch über Agade," ZA 57 (1965):43 ff.; J. Cooper, *The Curse of Agade,* Johns Hopkins Near Eastern Studies (Baltimore: Johns Hopkins University, 1983).

[72] Or NS, 14 (1945): 185-234 and 15 (1946): 46-63.

[73] LU, pp. 1-2; OAS, p. 3. Cf. contra re. Ur and Nippur laments: CBC, pp. 11, 32; LN.

[74] See below fn. 90.

[75] "Review of LU," pp. 219-221.

[76] "According to the system calculated by M.B. Rowton for the revision of *CAH*, I and II." C. Gadd, "Second Lamentation for Ur," in *Hebrew and Semitic Studies Presented to Godfrey Rolles Driver,* ed. D. W. Thomas and W. D. Hardy (Oxford: Clarendon, 1963), p. 59 n. 41.

[77] Edzard, ZZB, (Wiesbaden: Harrassowitz, 1975), pp. 57-58. Falkenstein disagrees with Jacobsen and links the composition to the occasion of the invasion of Ilu-Suma of Assyria in the early 1800's B.C., "Review of LU," AJSL, p. 321.

[78] ANET, pp. 611-619.

Ur." Approximately 80% of what Kramer concludes was originally a 500+ line text of five *kirugu*s has been "fairly well preserved" in more than thirty tablets and fragments.[79] This lament was once treated as two separate laments: the "Second Lamentation for Ur,"[80] and the "Ibbi-Sin Lament."[81] "With the publication of eleven new tablets and fragments in UET 6/2, . . . the text of the composition could be reconstructed, and . . . it became clear that it was actually a single composition."[82] As it turned out, Gadd's "Second Lamentation" was a treatment of the third *kirugu*, and Falkenstein's "Ibbisin-Klage" was a treatment of the first *kirugu* of the same lament.

2.1.3.3 "Lamentation over the Destruction of Eridu"

In her critical edition of the "Lament over Eridu," Green has used eight sources to reconstruct some 163 lines which are divided into eight *kirugu*s. It is not clear just how many lines the original had. Its identification in the Sumerian literary catalogs is uncertain due to the loss of the text's incipit.

Typical of the Neo-Sumerian city-laments, the "Lament over Eridu" is written predominantly in *emegir*. *Kirugu*s 5:7 through 7:2 contain a lament spoken by one of Eridu's patron gods, Damgalnunna, in the *emesal* dialect.

Internal data is even less specific for dating the composition of the Lament. The data seems to point to its composition during the reign of either Išme-Dagan (1953-34 B.C.) or Nur-Adad (1865-49 B.C.). Green points out that Išme-Dagan is known to have produced a number of hymns, and this lament might well fit that situation. Also, there exists an Išme-Dagan hymn which portrays a banquet-offering scene similar to that associated with the lament observance. However, from the available documentation we learn that Nur-Adad of Larsa rebuilt Enki's ziggurat at Eridu, and as far as is known from documentary evidence, he is the only Isin-Larsa ruler to have engaged in construction or restoration at Eridu. "But since no other Sumerian literary composition is known which can be assigned to Nur-Adad, it is somewhat less likely, although not impossible, that the Eridu Lament, which has close affinities to the other members of the text genre, was composed under his sponsor-

---

79 ANET, p. 612, n. 49.

80 C. J. Gadd, "Second Lamentation for Ur," *Hebrew and Semitic Studies Presented to G. R. Driver*], eds. D. W. Thomas and W. D. McHardy (Oxford: Clarendon, 1963), pp. 59-71.

81 A. Falkenstein, "Die Ibbisin-Klage," *Die Welt des Orients* I (1950), pp. 377-384. Cf. SAHG (Stuttgart: Artemis, 1953), pp. 189-192.

82 Kramer, ANET, p. 612, n. 49.

ship."[83] By all accounts the evidence is fragmentary and ambiguous. However, by virtue of the relative evidence identifying Nur-Adad with the rebuilding of the shrine at Eridu, I would tentatively date the composition of the Lament to the reign of Nur-Adad.

2.1.3.4 Other Classic City Laments

Several other major laments are not yet available in translation and thus will not be treated in this study. Work is reportedly being done to prepare the 276 line "Lament over the Destruction of Nippur" for publication and translation.[84] Like the Nippur Lament, the "Lament over Uruk" awaits publication.[85]

M. Lambert lists along with the Laments over Ur, Sumer and Ur, and Nippur, the "Lamentation over Ekimar" which is identified as a text describing the destruction of the E-ki-mar by the Martu and Su-bir$_{(4)}$ peoples.[86]

2.1.3.5 Summary

Of these six neo-Sumerian city-laments known, only two have been published in critical editions (the Ur and Eridu laments), one has been published from an extensive collection of various texts (Sumer and Ur lament), and the other three have been published as transcribed or transliterated text having received some comment in the literature (Uruk, Nippur and *ekimar* laments). The use of the Sumerian dialects in the

---

[83] Green conjectures a date ca. the time of Išme-Dagan, LEr, pp. 128-130.

[84] M. Green reported in 1975 that A. Sjöberg was working on a new edition of the Nippur Lament. In his 1983 publication of *The Curse of Agade*, Cooper notes that H. Vanstiphout is preparing to publish the Nippur Lament from a Pennsylvania Sumerian Dictionary ms. It has been discussed by D. Edzard and S. Kramer et al. who indicate that the Lament mentions the Amorites' (*ti-da-nu-um*) destruction of Nippur as well as Išme-Dagan's hand in restoring it. Thus the content does give some clue to possible origin. The *terminus a quo* obviously must be the reign of Išme-Dagan and the attention given him in the text might favor dating it to his reign. See ZZB, p. 86ff.; C. Gadd & S. Kramer, UET VI/2, *Literary & Religious Texts*, 1966, p. 2.; Kramer, "Lament over Nippur." M. Green suggests there are better grounds for dating its origin to the reign of Nur-Adad of Larsa (c. 1865 B.C.) (LEr, p. 319). While documentation is significant if not essential in determining absolute dates, the fragmentary nature of the extant corpus of Ancient Near Eastern literature makes an argument from silence most tenuous.

[85] Now in preparation by M. Civil and M. Green. It also names Išme-Dagan as restorer. Green questions whether the destruction mentioned refers to the fall of Ur III or of the incursion of Ilu-šuma of Assur (c. 1940 B.C.). Again, from external documentation, Green posits Nur-Adad as sponsor of its composition.

[86] The extant text consists of 30 fragmentary lines. "La littérature sumerienne à propos d'ouvrages récents," RA, 55 (1961): 191, no. 41. Brief notes on this lament have been published by Kramer, *Sumerian Literary Texts from Nippur in the Museum of the Ancient Orient at Istanbul*, AASOR, 23 (1944):103.

laments is a debated point. *Emegir*, the main Sumerian dialect is used in varying degrees in these city-laments. In some, it seems to be predominant, while in others, its use seems to be more restricted. Scholarly consensus places the origin of five of the six in the neo-Sumerian period (2200-1900 B.C.) and most of these within 75 years of the fall of Ur III. Išme-Dagan (1953-1934 B.C.) seems the most likely sponsor of the composition of most of the laments. The sixth, the "Lament over Eridu" was quite possibly composed some three-quarters of a century later.

2.1.4 Later Sumerian Laments

During the Old Babylonian period two new lament sub-genres appear virtually simultaneously.[87] These came to be known as *balag*s and *eršemma*s. The *balag* apparently took its name from the fact that it was chanted to the accompaniment of an instrument called *balag*.[88] Similarly, the *eršemma*, which is supposed to mean "wail of the *šem*-drum," apparently receives its name from the practice of reciting this type of composition to the accompaniment of that instrument.[89]

It is interesting to note that whereas the classical city laments were written predominantly in the main Sumerian dialect, *emegir*, the extant *balag*s and *eršemma*s are composed in the *emesal* dialect. Both the use of the *emesal* dialect for these laments and their preservation can be explained by the apparent fact that it was the dialect used by a religious institution—the *gala*-priesthood—and religious institutions tend to be conservative by nature. Krecher and Cohen both argue that it was the *gala*-priests who "owned, copied and recited" the *emesal* texts.[90]

---

[87] M. Cohen states: "subjectively we believe the *eršemma* to be the older genre," supporting that assumption by comparing the literary characteristics of both. "The *eršemma* is a compact, well-structured composition, centering upon one theme. The *balag*-lamentation, on the other hand, is a very lengthy, rambling work, sometimes having no basic story line." He argues that the press of priestly demands forced the *gala*-priests to create patchwork laments from already existing sources. CSH, pp. 37-38.

[88] See H. Hartmann, "Die Musik der sumerischen Kultur" (Ph.D. dissertation, Johann Wolfgang Goethe Universität, 1960), pp. 52-67, 210-211.

[89] Ibid. pp. 216-219.

[90] CSH, p. 4. Cf. SKly, p. 34. I. Diakonoff outlines the shift of opinion re the nature of *emesal*. Originally regarded as a "women's language," the current opinion has "nearly universally" been reversed. Diakonoff takes issue, however, and argues that there is ample evidence to support the conclusion that the *emesal* "was actually a women's language." In summary, he posits that the dialect "was used 1.) for the speech of women and goddesses in epics, proverbs, and similar texts, 2.) for the speech of the messengers and servants of the goddesses, 3.) for the speech of incantation singers (*gala*) in proverbs, and 4.) in some hymns and prayers." (pp. 113-116). "Ancient Writing and Ancient Written Language," AS 20 (Chicago: Univ. of Chicago, 1976), pp. 99-121.

We may speculate that the status enjoyed by the classical city-laments as well as their basic religious character was sufficient impetus for them to be emulated for liturgical use. Whereas the city-laments were apparently written for a single use, the *balags* were composed for recurrent use as is indicated by their subject matter and their being listed in ritual calendars.[91]

Various clues point to the Old Babylonian period as the period of the origin of at least some of the *balag* lamentations which have survived only in much later editions. For example, some four or five extant Old Babylonian compositions contain the *balag* rubric.[92] Also, Krecher has noted that the composition of *emesal* cult lyrics in the form of *balags* and *eršemmas* was discontinued at the close of the Old Babylonian period, though the lyrics continued to be copied. He concludes that "the emesal songs which are known from more recent times really belong to the forms (*Gattungen*) of *balag* and *eršemma* which have already been attested in Old Babylonian times and have not been composed in the more recent period.[93] With this Kutscher concurs, though not with as much certitude. His view is merely that "there are some hints which point to a possible Old Babylonian origin of the late congregational city laments.[94]

2.1.5 Akkadian Laments

Although there is one extant, rather brief Akkadian lament which is mentioned below, there are apparently no parallels of the classic city-laments in extant Akkadian literature; Akkadian does play a role in the later laments. Akkadian is used in interlinear translations, apparently beginning in the Middle Babylonian period.[95] These interlinear translations seem to be common in the *ersahunga* compositions, and most of the *šu-illa* laments are in Akkadian rather than Sumerian.[96]

But there is evidence that Akkadian was also used exclusively in lament compositions. R. Borger lists three Akkadian lamentations.[97] The first one, in which Ishtar laments over Erech and Agade, is included in

---

[91] Though all extant ritual texts which include the entry of *balags* are from the first millennium. See T. Jacobsen, "Kramer Review," p. 223; W. Hallo, "The Cultic Setting of Sumerian Poetry," RAI-17 (Ham-sur-Heuere: Univ. Lib. de Bruxelles, 1970): 116-134; CBC, p. 11.

[92] See SKly, p. 30, cf. C. Wilcke, "Formale Gesichtspunkte in der sumerischen Literatur," AS 20 (Chicago: Univ. of Chicago, 1976), p. 285.

[93] SKly, p. 18.

[94] OAS, p. 5.

[95] CBC, p. 6, CSH, p. 2.

[96] See below Ch. 3. See also J. Cooper, "Sumerian and Akkadian in Sumer and Akkad," Or NS 42 (1973):239-246.

[97] *Handbuch der Keilinschriftliteratur* vol. 3, p. 83.

the material covered in this study.[98] Langdon suggested that calamity in the lament "probably refers to the Aramean invasion of Babylon in the time of Erba-Marduk [770 circa] mentioned in the Chronicle BM 27859 rev. 10-12 and in Nabuna'id's *Stele* cols. III and IV."[99]

2.1.6 Language of the Laments

As has already been mentioned, the two languages which are used in the laments are Sumerian and Akkadian. And the Sumerian texts occur in either *emegir*, the main dialect, or *emesal*, the dialect which has come to be identified with the *gala*-priesthood.

The Sumerian *emegir* texts are represented by the oldest, classic city-laments. In post-Sumerian times, they serve as exemplars of formal Sumerian for the "Academy." But, as we have seen, even these texts contain sections composed in *emesal*.

There are two potentially conflicting theories about the identification of the speakers of the *emesal* dialect. One is that *emesal* is the dialect reserved for use by females in Sumerian literary texts. This seems to be based upon the use of *emesal* in some Inanna and Dumuzi texts.[100] There is ample evidence to support the conclusion that females did play a major role in the cultural phenomenon of communal lament—both as the speaker in certain literary texts (primary speaker) and as performers of the lament rituals (secondary speakers or "readers"). The apparent conflict arises from the existence and role of the gala priesthood. It has been pointed out that *emesal* seems to have been virtually the exclusive property of the *gala*-priesthood which, while perhaps not exclusively male, was not exclusively female. As we shall discuss later, both male and female subjects are cited in the lament literature. In addition to the female roles we find, for example, the *mu-lu-ir-ri*, "him of tears" or the "lamenting man" in the "Lament over the Destruction of Ur," lines 46-47, 63-64, 71-72[101], or the *mu-lu akkil-a*, "lord of lament" or "wailing man."[102]

As already indicated, some of the classic laments, e.g. the "Lamentation over Ur," use both dialects. Rather than indicating a necessary change in the sex of the speaker, Cohen argues that the gender

---

[98] The second and third entries Borger indicates are questionable or subject to further study. The third one is CT 15: 45-48 which has been translated by P. Jensen in *Keilinschriftliche Bibliothek*, ed. E. Schrader, vol. 6, p. 80 ff.; A. Heidel, *Gilgamesh Epic and Old Testament Parallels*, 2d ed., (Chicago: University of Chicago, 1949), p. 121 ff., et al. It appears not to be a lament.

[99] SBP, p. 351.

[100] See SKly, pp. 11-14.

[101] Kramer, AJSL, p. 22, nn.40,41.

[102] BL, p. 63, CXXXXIII, line 10. See above n. 90.

change (implied by the dialect change), where it occurs, may be better explained as a literary device used to indicate a role change on the part of a single speaker.[103]

2.2 *Structure of the Sumero-akkadian Lament*

One thing becomes apparent when one scans the extant laments: there is no uniform structure. However, when the constituent elements are analyzed, a theoretical structure can be derived from the dynamics of the relationships of the various thematic elements. Of course, the shape of the structure of the large classical city-laments is not the same as that of the *eršemma*s. There are several factors which cause this, but perhaps the most salient are the factors of form and function. For example, the specific function of the *eršemma* poems as a sequel to the *balag* laments results in a variation of form.[104]

But there is no uniformity of structure even among the extant classical city laments. However, there is a marked similarity of structure and content among them.

2.2.1 Classical City Laments

2.2.1.1 Structure of the Ur Lament

The "Lament over Ur" is the largest classical city lament to have been published in a critical edition and so will be used as the primary example. The detailed outline of the "Lament over Ur" might be represented as follows:

I. COMPLAINT OF ABANDONMENT: *kirugu* 1
    A. Deity has abandoned its stable/house/city/sheepfold,   a.)
    B. It has been delivered to the wind,   b.)
    ─────
    C. *Kirugu* rubric
    D. Antiphon with rubric

II. CALL TO LAMENTATION: *kirugu* 2
    A. Summons to city to set up bitter lament, 40-45
        1. Call for lament, 40-41, 44
        2. Cause for lament: Righteous city destroyed, 42-43, 45
        3. Repetend: "Thy lament which is bitter," "bitter is its lament"
    B. Refrain:"Thy lament which is bitter—how long will it
       grieve the weeping PN?" 46-47
    C. Specific summons to lament, 48-62

─────
[103] CBC, p. 32.
[104] SKly, pp. 29, 34. Cf. CBC, p. 9.

1. Call to PN (to lament) a.)
2. Repetend: "a bitter lament set up as thy lament" b.)
D. Refrain:"Thy lament which is bitter—how long will it grieve the weeping PN?" 63-64
E. Lament to Ur, 65-70
    1. Direct address: Destruction lamented, 65-66
    2. Direct address: Innocent offspring perished, 67-68
    3. Direct address: "marza" and "me" transformed, 69-70
F. Refrain:"Thy lament which is bitter—how long will it grieve the weeping PN?" 71-72

G. *Kirugu* rubric
H. Antiphon with rubric

III. NINGAL'S SUPPLICATION TO NANNA: *kirugu* 3-4
A. City joins deity in lamenting, 77-79
B. Wife of deity importunes husband, 80-85
    1. For the sake of his city/house a.)
    2. Repetend: "bitterly she weeps" b.)
C. Ningal's Lament, 86-169
    1. Introduction, 86-87
    2. Raging Storm—"its wail has filled me full," 88-91
    3. Bitter terror, 92-109
        a. Terrified by day, I fled not, 92-95
        b. No peace by night, I fled not, 96-101
        c. Like animals, I pursued my own, 102-107
        d. City destroyed, perishes, 108-109
    4. Appeal, 110-111
        a. Scream for storm to "return to the plain," 110
        b. Storm rose not to depart, 111
    5. Destroyed house, 112-133
        a. Shortened reign brings weeping and lament 112-113
        b. Wrath and distress displace soothing feasts, 114-117
        c. Attacked house received bitter laments, 118-121
        d. Righteous, royal house in ruins, 122-132
            i. like garden hut, its sides caved in
            ii. like tent exposed to wind and rain
            iii. like sheepfold torn down
        e. Possessions have been "dissipated, 133"

D. *Kirugu* rubric
E. Antiphon with rubric

F. Declaration of faithfulness, 137-144
    1. After destruction decreed and accomplished, 137-142
    2. Queen did not abandon city or forsake land, 143-144

G. Supplication to Premier Deities, 145-161
    1. Addressees: Enlil and Anu, 145-146
    2. Substance:
        a. "Let not city be destroyed," 147-148
        b. "Let not its people perish," 149
    3. Response:
        a. "Anu changed not his word," 150
        b. "Enlil with its 'It is good; so be it' soothed not my heart," 151
H. Supplication to Divine Council, 152-161
    1. Addressees: the Anunnaki and Anu and Enlil, 152-156
    2. Substance:
        a. "Let not city be destroyed," 157-158
        b. "Let not its people perish," 159
    3. Response:
        a. "Anu changed not his word," 160
        b. "Enlil with its 'It is good; so be it' soothed not my heart," 161
I. Accusation against Divine Council, 162-169
    1. Deific actions:
        a. They directed the destruction of my city, 162-163
        b. They decreed the massacre of my people, 164
        c. They deprived me of my city, 165-167
    2. Deific obstinacy, 168-169
        a. "Anu changes not his command," 168
        b. "Enlil alters not the command which he had
           issued," 169

J. *Kirugu* rubric
K. Antiphon with rubric

IV. DESCRIPTION OF DEVASTATION OF THE STORM: *kirugu* 5
    A. Enlil Directs the "storms" in hate, 173-204   a.)
        1. Removes the good storm of overflow, 174-175
        2. Summons and directs the evil storm "Kingaluda,"
           and the evil winds "Gibil," 176-181
        3. The storm:
           a. howls and roars unrestrained, 182-184
           b. attacks the boats of the city, 185-186
           c. burns with scorching heat, 187-189
           d. darkens the land with dust, 190-194
           e. attacks the land as *gisburru*, 195-196
           f. "by tears is not adjured," 197
           g. brings trembling and destruction to city, 198-202
           h. is pervasive, 203-204
    B. Repetend: "the people groan"   b.)

    C. *Kirugu* rubric

D. Antiphon with rubric

V. DESCRIPTION OF THE DEVASTATION OF BATTLE: *kirugu* 6
    A. Storm lamented to Nanna, 208-210
        1. Addressee: Father Nanna
        2. Substance:
            a. Good storm taken from city
            b. City made into ruins
        3. Repetend: "the people groan"
    B. Carnage described, 211-246
        1. Dead bodies heaped in streets, 211-218
        2. Injured ones neglected, 219-224
        3. None escape, 225-226
        4. Domestic life ravaged, 227-236
            a. Famine, 227
            b. Fire, 228
            c. Flood, 229
            d. Judgment and counsel destroyed, 231-232
            e. Familial ties broken, 233-235
            f. People deported, 236
        5. Patron goddess finally abandons city, 237-238
        6. Possessions defiled, 239
        7. City and storehouses burned, 240-241
        8. Ekishnugal destroyed by Subarians and Elamites, 242-246
        —Repetend: "the people groan"
    C. Aggrieved Queen Laments, 247-250
        1. Repetend: "Alas for my city," "Alas for my house"
        2. Complaint:
            a. My city and house destroyed, 249
            b. Ur destroyed and its people dispersed, 250

D. *Kirugu* rubric
E. Antiphon with rubric

VI. NINGAL'S LAMENT SOLILOQUY: *kirugu* 7
    A. Introduction, 254-256
        1. Mother Ningal stands aside like enemy, 254
        2. Woman/princess loudly and bitterly wails, 255-256
    B. Attribution of responsibility, 257-260
        1. Anu cursed city: city destroyed, 257
        2. Enlil became inimical, hurled flame: house destroyed, 258-260
    C. Locus of lamentation, 261-264
        1. Outside the city, 261, 263
        2. Inside the city, 262, 264
        3. Repetend lament: "Alas for my city," "Alas for my house"
    D. Description of calamity, 265-283

     1. Innocent city lost leadership, 265-268

     2. Waterworks dried up, 269-270

     3. Fields and grove abandoned, destroyed, and overgrown, 271-274

     4. Treasures plundered, 275-281

       —Repetend: "'O my possessions' I will say"

     5. Living creatures depart, 282-283

       a. Birds have flown away, 282

       b. Daughters and sons carried off, 283

       c. Repetend: "Alas for my city/men"

E. Lament refrain, 284-287

     1. "Woe is me"

       a. Daughters carry strange banner in strange city

       b. Youth bound

       c. City no longer exists

       d. I am not its queen

     2. "O Nanna, Ur which no longer exists—I am not its mistress."

F. Complaint of foreign occupation, 288-291

     1. House and city demolished, 288, 290

     2. Claim of righteousness, 289a

     3. Strange city and house built, 289b, 291

G. Lament, 292-327

     1. "Woe is me" 292-293

       a. City destroyed

       b. Shrine destroyed

       c. People dead

     2. "Woe is me," where shall I sit/stand? 294

     3. "Woe is me,"

       a. My city replaced by strange city, 295

       b. My house replaced by strange house, 296

       c. For my city, "Alas my city" I will say, 297

       d. For my house, "Alas my house" I will say, 298

     4. Demonstration of grief, 299-301

       a. Tore hair

       b. Struck chest: "Alas for my city" she cries

       c. Eyes flooded with tears

     5. "Woe is me,"

       a. My city replaced by strange city, 302

       b. My house replaced by strange house, 303

     6. "Woe is me,"

       a. My house is a stable torn down, 304a

       b. My "cows have been dispersed," 304b

       c. My ewes have been killed, 305

     7. "Woe is me,"

       a. I have been exiled, 306a, 307a

    b. I have found to place to rest, 306b, 307b
    c. I am a stranger in a strange city, 308
        i. I am cursed and abused, 309
        ii. I dare not respond, 310
 8. Supplication, 311-314
    a. Addressee: Lord of the city
    b. Purpose: For the sake of his house and city
    c. Repetend: "bitterly I weep"
 9. "Woe is me,"
    a. O my city-fate, 315
    b. O my house, 316
    c. O my brickwork of Ur, 317
    d. O my righteous house, 318
        i. I lay down in debris, 319
        ii. I do not rise up, 320
 10. "Woe is me,"
    a. Untrustworthy was thy building;
       bitter thy destruction, 321
    b. O Ur, O Enunkug;
       attacked and destroyed without cause, 322-325
    c. Storm ordered in hate, not abated, 326
    d. O my house of Sin 327

H. *Kirugu* rubric
I. Antiphon with rubric

VII. LAMENT TO AND SUPPLICATION FOR NINGAL: *kirugu* 8
 A. Commiseration, 331-380
    1. Appeal, 331-332
    2. Calamity recounted, 333-370
       a. City destroyed
       b. House demolished
       c. Shrine laid waste
       d. Worship defiled and discontinued
       e. Resources ruined
    3. Appeal, 371-380
       a. House lifts hands: "Where pray?"
       b. Accusation: You departed
       c. "How long?"
           i. Stand aside like enemy?
           ii. Hurl challenges like enemy?
       d. Accusation: You abandoned
       e. Return:
           i. Like ox to stable
           ii. Like sheep to fold
           iii. Like child to chamber

iv. Like maid to house
B. Supplication, 381-384
   1. Objects: Anu and Enlil
   2. Subjects:
      a. Decree "tis enough," favorable fate
      b. Restore city
      c. Restore queenship

C. *Kirugu* rubric
D. Antiphon with rubric

VIII. SUPPLICATION TO NANNA ABOUT THE STORM: *kirugu* 9-10
  A. Complaint, 388-406
    1. Storm destroyed material culture, 388-392
    2. Storm destroyed religious culture, 393
    3. Storm destroyed civil culture, 394-396

  B. *Kirugu* rubric
  C. Antiphon with rubric

  D. Complaint continued
    1. Storm indiscriminate, 400-403
    2. Storm destroyed domestic culture, 404
    3. Storm destroyed agriculture, 405
  E. Appeal, 406-435
    1. Entirely destroy the storm, 406-414
    2. Be gracious to the black-headed people! 408

  F. *Kirugu* rubric
  G. Antiphon with rubric

IX. SUPPLICATION TO NANNA FOR RESTORATION: *kirugu* 11
  A. Appellants: the humble and faithful, 418-422
  B. Appeal:
    1. May restored city be glorious, 423
    2. May it not be destroyed, 424a
    3. May it proceed before thee, 424b
  C. Prayer forthcoming, 425-427
  D. Request:
    1. Undo sins, 429
    2. Soothe heart, 430
    3. Receive offerings, 431
    4. Purify every evil heart, 432-434
  E. Praise, 435

  F. *Kirugu* rubric

2.2.1.2 Structural Model of the City-Lament

An analysis of these classic city laments reveals certain elements which the three seem to share in common and points out certain other elements which are not universally shared. (See fig. 2: Structural Comparison of Major City-Laments.)

A model of the city-lament based on the "Lament over Ur" would take the following shape:

> I. Detailed Complaint
> II. Lament Proper
> III. Intercession of a Patron
> IV. Appeal for Restoration

2.2.1.3 Detailed Complaint

These three city-laments set out in great detail the cause of their lament. As was shown in the section on thematic elements, the calamity in question is described. The condition of the city walls and the shrine and its contents and personnel are spelled out to the deity being addressed. The situation of the society, its material, religious, social, civil, and domestic aspects, is recited. This detailing may not be confined to one *kirugu*, but rather treated in various parts of the composition. It ought to be noted that even in the lament proper there is a detailing of the complaint, as might well be expected.

Invariably, the ultimate responsibility is assigned to the highest level of the pantheon: An and Enlil, and their decree. Secondarily, in all three of the city-laments there is an accusation directed to the gods for having abandoned their cities and their shrines and for having caused the disorder. However, in the "Lament over Eridu," there seems to be some frustration over the disagreements among the gods in this matter of loyalty/abandonment. In the first and fifth *kirugu*s, Enki remains outside his city as if it were an alien city as does Damgalnunna, the "Mother of the Lofty Temple." The city is addressed as the one "whose woman does not dwell there." This is set in contrast in the sixth *kirugu* with several gods, including Mullil (Enlil) who destroyed their cities "but did not abandon [them]."

As already noted, the laments also assign a mediate responsibility to political enemies such as the Elamites.

FIGURE 2

Structural Comparison of Major City-Laments

Lament over Ur (KLU)		Lament over Sumer & Ur (KLSU)		Lament over Eridu (GEL)	
I.	Complaint of abandonment: kirugu 1, lines 1-39	I.	Detailed complaint re Storm and its effects: kirugu 1, lines 1-118	I.	Detailed complaint re Storm and its effects: kirugu 1
II.	Call to lamentation: kirugu 2, lines 40-76	II.	Complaint and lament of Sumerian cities: kirugu 2, lines 119-282	II.	Description of phases of the Storm's attack: kirugu 2-4
III.	Ningal's supplication to Nanna re storm and its effects: kirugu 3-4, lines 77-172	III.	Complaint of Ur: kirugu 3, lines 283-339	III.	Lament of Damgalnunna and her supplication to Enki: kirugu 5-7:7
IV.	Description of devastation of the Storm: kirugu 5-6, lines 173-253	IV.	Complaint and supplication of Sin to Enlil: kirugu 4, lines 340-489	IV.	Appeal for restoration: kirugu 7:8-8:3
V.	Ningal's lament soliloquy: kirugu 7, lines 254-330	V.	Appeal for restoration and imprecation: kirugu 5, lines 490-500+x+1		
VI.	Lament for Ningal: kirugu 8, lines 331-387				
VII.	Supplication to Nanna re Storm: kirugu 9-10, lines 388-417				
VIII.	Appeal to Nanna for restoration: kirugu 11, lines 418-436				

2.2.1.4 Lament Proper

A summons is sometimes issued to engage in lamentation. It is usually directed to the city or cities in question and occasionally to specific buildings identified respectively with those cities. The summons may include specific verbal formulae to be recited. It rarely, if ever, includes specific directions for non-verbal expressions. However, it is clear from other parts of the laments that non-verbal expressions such as the tearing of hair, the beating of the breast, and the profusion of tears were an integral part of lamenting.[105]

There are basically two classes of plaintiffs represented in the texts. One is that of the patron deity. More than one may be involved, espe-

---

[105] See LEr 5:4-6; CSH 79:33-35.

cially if the lament is concerned with more than one city or shrine. The other class is usually characterized as the "city" itself.

The lament proper uses several stock terms and phrases such as "Oh...," "Woe...," "Alas for...," as well as the nondescript groanings of the people, the sighings and mournful wailing of people and gods alike. These stock phrases often occur as a repetend which punctuates a narrative of complaint or of lamentation or as part of a refrain which marks a literary unit.

2.2.1.5 Intercession of a Patron Deity

In the "Lament over Ur," it is Ningal, wife of Ur's patron deity Nanna, who intercedes with him on behalf of the beleaguered city. In the "Lament over Sumer and Ur," it is Nanna-Sin himself who intercedes with his father Enlil on behalf of the city and temple. In the "Lament over Eridu," the intercession is not so clear. The grief of the patron deities over the destruction and chaos in Eridu is narrated in the fifth *kirugu* to be followed by the lament of Damgalnunna which continues through the sixth and into the seventh *kirugu*. Beginning with the third line of the seventh *kirugu*, an appeal is made to Enki to be pacified and to return his attention to his city and temple. It is most probable that the speaker of this prayer is his wife, the goddess Damgalnunna, though the prayer is immediately followed by a reference to a humble man who sings a lament and recites a prayer.

2.2.1.6 Appeal

Each of the city laments contains an appeal at or near the end of the composition. Appeals in the city laments are addressed primarily to An or Enlil or both. Even in the Lament over Sumer and Ur where Enki and Ninhursag are cited along with An and Enlil as having decreed the fate being lamented, it is Enlil who is singled out as the object of appeal.

Supplication is made either by an unnamed party, presumably the populace, or by a lower level deity such as the wife of the patron, or by the patron himself to his superior. Examples of each can be found in the city-laments.

In one sense, the data of the city-laments conflict on the matter of confession as part of the appeal. As noted in the section on thematic elements, in some places innocence is claimed, though this claim may be made relative to the Elamites, etc., who are described as rebellious. On the other hand, The Ur Lament contains a brief petition to "undo the sins of its..." and "May every evil heart of its people be pure before thee! May the heart of those who dwell in the land be good before thee!" However, neither the "Lament over Sumer and Ur" nor the "Lament over Eridu" appear to be concerned with confession.

2.2.2 *Balags*

The *balags* tend toward one or the other of two basic forms. One consists basically of complaint and appeal, whereas the other contains extended adulation in addition to the complaint and appeal elements. The *balag* with the incipit "The steer in his fold"[106] is one of the longer published *balags* and will be used as the primary example of the former. The *balag* with the beginning "Elevated warrior of the land"[107] is of almost equal length and will serve as an example of the latter form. In either case, it must be noted that the fragmentary nature of many of the extant texts makes it necessary to draw only tentative conclusions about formal structures.

2.2.2.1 Structure of *balag* – "The Steer in His Fold"

The detailed outline of the first *balag* might be represented thus:

I. COMPLAINT AND APPEAL: *kirugu* 1
  A. Introduction: Local deity mourns, 1-2
  B. Titulary, 3-6
    1. Honored lord, 3
    2. Inscrutable lord, 4
    3. Immutable word, 5-6
  C. Complaint against Mullil, 7-23
    1. Initiation, 7-8
    2. Entrapment, 9-12
    3. Invasion, 13-14
    4. Displacement, 15-16
    5. Inaccessibility, 17-18
    6. Destruction of city and shrine, 19-20
    7. Assault on clerics and supplicants, 21-23
  D. Quasi-Appeal, 24-29
    1. Address, 24a
    2. "How long?" 24b-29
  E. Complaint continued, 30-42
    1. Land smitten, 30-34
    2. Heavens disestablished, 35-38
    3. Humanity massacred, 39-42
  F. Appeal, 43-95

---

106 CBC, pp. 16-20.
107 Ibid., pp. 22-26.

  1. May Mullil be soothed, 43-44
  2. May Mullil receive prayer of divine supplicants, 45-95
      a. Receptivity enjoined, 45-83
          —Repetend: "may...utter a prayer to you!"
          "may...stand before you in prayer!"
      b. Substance of prayer:
          —Repetend: "may he utter to you! May he utter
          a prayer to you!"
          i. "You should not abandon..." 84-92
          ii. "Indeed you are its lord/shepherd," 93-94
          iii. "You are a storm locked up in a house," 95

  G. *Kirugu* rubric

II. COMPLAINT AND APPEAL: *kirugu* 2
    A. Appeal, 96
(indeterminate number of lines missing)
    B. Complaint of social disorder, 97-102

  C. *Kirugu* rubric
III. APPEAL TO MULLIL: *kirugu* 3
    A. May [Mullil] be soothed, 103-104
    B. May Mullil receive prayer of divine supplicants, 105-117
    C. "How long will you remain seated?" 118-130
(indeterminate number of lines missing)
    D. "Gaze about!" at destroyed city and shrine, 131-138
    E. Complaint of social disorder, 139-144
    F. May An stand before you and soothe you, 145-146

  G. *Kirugu* rubric

IV. COMPLAINT: *kirugu* 4
    A. Epithets, 147-160
    B. Quasi-Appeal: "When will your heart tire?" 161-163
    C. Complaint of betrayal and destruction, 164-168

  D. *Kirugu* rubric

2.2.2.2 Introduction

The *balag* opens with the declaration that the steer (Iskur) mourns
grievously in his fold and is followed by Enlil's titulary attributes. The
attributes are expressed in terms common to other portions of a *balag* as
well as other forms of lamentation. For example: lord of the lands, honored one, unfathomable one, he whose word is true, etc.

Characteristic of Sumerian poetry, the entire lament is marked by extended use of repetends and refrains such as "utter a prayer to you," which recurs at the end of lines 49-83 and then is modified to "may he utter to you! May he utter a prayer to you," which continues twelve more lines. Lines 46-50 are repeated as lines 105-109. Lines 97-102 recur as 139-144, and lines 103-104 as 145-146.

2.2.2.3 Complaint

Such is also the case with complaint in this example. The first phrase, and occasionally a second, of each line in this unit is either a title or epithet of the deity and is followed by a declaration of some aspect of the god's action in bringing about the calamity in question. Included in this section is a quasi-lament in the form of a series of six "how long?" questions. I have called this a quasi-lament because although the questions imply a desire for resolution of the situation, they are couched in negative terms as matters of complaint. They are also sandwiched between two extended sections of complaint.

2.2.2.4 Appeal

The complaint is followed by an extended appeal marked by the monotonous repetend: "May [PN] utter a prayer to you!" This is varied by the insertion of the names of many of the different gods of the pantheon. The two major elements of the appeal were the "be soothed" motif and the receptivity-to-prayer motif.

One observation illustrated by this *balag* is that the structure marked by the *kirugu* rubric may not always coincide with the structure of the content as represented in the outline above.[108] In the case before us, the appeal appears to continue into at least the first line of the second *kirugu*. This cannot be absolutely established for this example because after the first line an indeterminate number of lines have been broken away from the second *kirugu* so that in all only seven lines remain. This makes it difficult to ascertain the exact relationship between the first line and the remainder of the second *kirugu*.

One feature that would tend to support this observation is that an eight or nine line refrain is mechanically divided, six and two (three), by

---

[108] See C. Wilcke, "Formale Gesichtspunkte in der sumerischen Literatur," AS 20 (Chicago: Univ. of Chicago, 1976), pp. 254-255, where he indicates that although normally the kirugu rubric seems to agree with the strophic structure of a composition, there are examples where the contrary is true. See also A. Falkenstein's suggestion that the term means to "bow to the ground," "Sumerische religiose Texte," ZA 49 (1949): 104 ff. Cf. W. von Soden, *Akkadisches Handwörterbuch* s.v. "kirugu."

the rubric marking the end of the second *kirugu*. The identical refrain recurs undivided at the end of the third *kirugu*. This second occurrence follows contiguous text whereas the first immediately follows a break in the text. The division in the first instance coincides with a change in subject matter. The first six lines of the refrain deal with complaint, narrating the aspects of the calamity. The last three (the third line does not appear in the second instance) express an appeal to the god to be soothed.

2.2.2.5 Complaint

The complaint section begins with an extended passage composed entirely of epithets each followed by a repetend. Then brief accusatory complaints are lodged.

2.2.2.6 Structure of *balag* – "Elevated Warrior of the Land"

The structure of the second form-type can be represented thus:

I. PRAISE AND ACCUSATORY COMPLAINT: *kirugu* 1
    A. Introduction
        1. Epithet, 1a, 2a
        2. Expression of inscrutability, 1b, 2b
    B. Laud Offered, 3-35
        1. Alternating laudatory repetend,   a.) a'.)
        2. Titulary,   b.)
           a. Titulary of position, 4-22
           b. Titulary of attribute, 23-32
        3. Expression of inscrutability, 33-35
    C. Glory Described, 36-43
        1. vis-a-vis creation, 36-38
        2. vis-a-vis pantheon, 39-43
    D. Accusatory complaint, 44-60
        1. Assignment of responsibility, 44-51
        2. Description of scope of calamity, 52-59

    ———
    E. *Kirugu* rubric
    F. Antiphon with rubric

II. COMPLAINT AND APPEAL: *kirugu* 2
    A. Declaration of means of calamity, 61-69
    B. Charge to lesser deities, 70-81
    C. Imprecation, 82-83
    D. Complaint, 84-98

    ———
    E. *Kirugu* rubric

    ———

IV. LAMENT: *kirugu* 3
   A. Wail of the populace, 99-115
   B. Wail of the goddess, 116-120
   C. Appeal to the lamenting goddess to "turn back," 121-143
   D. Complaint of the goddess, 144-167
   ———
   E. *Kirugu* rubric
(Remainder of text missing)

2.2.2.7 Structural Model of *balag* Type-B

A structural model of this form of *balag* would take the following shape:

        I. Praise
        II. Accusatory Complaint
        III. Appeal
        IV. Lament Proper

2.2.2.8 Praise

The tendency toward repetition in the *balag*s applies to the element of praise. The passages can be extensive. In some instances, the a-colon will contain a fixed cycle of appellatives followed in the b-colon by a series of attributive statements. In other instances, the opposite takes place. The attributes are relatively constant and the appellatives are a long series of names of the pantheon. In either case, the overwhelming tone of this structural element is highly laudatory.

2.2.2.9 Accusatory Complaint

This unit contains details of the complaint which is the focus of the lament. I have not designated the unit simply a "complaint" because the thrust of it seems to focus attention on the deity in question as the prime cause of the calamity.

2.2.2.10 Appeal

The appeal may be addressed in two somewhat different directions. In some laments, the appeal is made directly to An or Enlil. In others, it is directed to another deity, pleading with him to intercede on behalf of the land, city and/or shrine and to return to his city.

2.2.2.11 Lament Proper

Elements of both complaint and appeal are commonly included in the lament proper. The main distinguishing features of the lament proper, however, are the use of direct discourse and the use of stock lament expressions such as "woe is...," and "Oh...!" The lament proper is attributed either to the populace or to a deity or to both.

2.2.2.12 Summary

As a comparison of the structures of the two types shows, most of the elements of the lament are common. The primary difference between the two types is one of emphasis: type B places a marked emphasis on praise of the deity.

2.2.3 Eršemmas

At least by the first millennium, the *eršemma* was structurally related to the *balag* laments. A number of sources external to the *eršemma*s themselves indicate the practice of the gala-priests of reciting the two subgenre together, the *eršemma* serving as a sort of conclusion to the lament rite.[109]

Though the data is fragmentary, from the extant *eršemma*s Cohen has observed that all the *eršemma*s which are preserved only in Old Babylonian copies consist of a single structural unit whereas those preserved in First Millennium copies may, and often do, contain two or three structural units. What Cohen is referring to, however, falls within the category of structure rather than content. In the First Millennium *eršemma*s, rather than the *kirugu* rubric as found in the *balag*s, there is instead a heavy line incised across the tablet dividing one section from another.[110]

2.2.3.1 Structure of an Old Babylonian *eršemma*

I. PRAISE OF ISKUR, 1-14
   A. Epithets
   B. Repetend: "Your name is to the limits of heaven."
II. COMMISSION OF ISKUR, 15-26
   A. Commission to assail rebellious land
   B. Repetend: "Harness the storms for yourself."
III. RESPONSE OF ISKUR, 26-30
   A. Iskur gave heed
   B. Results: Iskur is a howling storm.

IV. *Eršemma* rubric[111]

------

[109] See G. Dossin, "Un rituel du Culte d'Istar," *RA* 35 (1938): 1-13. See also Krecher's discussion of the Mari ritual, *SKly*, p. 34; CSH, pp. 40-42.
[110] CSH, p. 21.
[111] CT 15:15-16. CSH, pp. 52-54.

2.2.3.2 Structural Model of Old Babylonian *eršemma*

I. Praise of deity
II. Commission of deity
III. Response of deity

2.2.3.3 Structure of a First Millennium *eršemma*

UNIT A:
I. THE ANGRY WITNESS, 1-19
    A. Anger unassuaged, 1-12
        1. Addressees: Baba and entourage and the shrine
        2. Repetend: "When I am angry, who can calm me?"
    B. Anger caused, 13-19
        1. Her pillaged house/city
        2. Her mournful cry:
           a. "Oh my city! Oh my house!"
           b. "Oh my spouse! Oh my child!"
II. THE SPARED MOURNER, 20-23
    A. Enlil's kind treatment, 20-22
    B. Lament for deportees: "Woe!" 23
III. THE LAMENTED DESTRUCTION, 24-28
    A. Destruction described   a.)
    B. Destruction lamented   b.)
   —Repetend: "Tears on her behalf, heartfelt sighs on her behalf!"

UNIT B:
IV. THE APPEALED PACIFICATION, 29-38
    A. Subjects: lesser deities
    B. Object: Baba/Ninisina/Nintinugga/Inanna
   —Repetend: "may he pacify your heart!"

V. *Eršemma* rubric: "An *eršemma* of Nintinugga. The *eršemma*
   (for the lamentation) *mu-tin-nu-nuz dim-ma.*"[112]

2.2.3.4 Model of First Millennium *eršemma*s

Physically, as noted above, this *eršemma* has a two part structure separated by a scribal incision across the tablet indicated above by the dotted line. The structure of the narrative content, however, may be represented thus:

I. Complaint
II. Lament
III. Appeal (Pacification unit)

---

[112] *SBH* 49, 49a, III, IVR 52:1. Ibid., pp. 139-143.

In some of the *eršemmas*, there is no formal lament offered or even mentioned. Rather, praise is offered to "the lord of the lands." Thus an alternate structure might be:

I. Praise

II. Appeal (Pacification unit)

2.2.3.5 Complaint

The speaker of this section of this example is not identified. The language would make it appear to be a god but not An or Enlil. Possibly it is Ninurta as intermediary between An and Enlil on the one hand and Baba/Nintinugga on the other.

The details of the cause for a complaint seem to vary widely among the *eršemmas*. In this case, it is only two lines long. Most of the space is taken by a series of appellatives followed by the repetend expressing the unassuaged anger of the speaker.

2.2.3.6 Lament

The lament unit apparently comes from the mouth of the goddess Baba. It is typically some deity who utters the lament in the *eršemmas*. Many of the same lamenting expressions in the *balag*s are used in the *eršemma*. The same is true of the non-verbal expressions of lament, such as weeping and prostration, etc.[113]

2.2.3.7 Praise

In some of the *eršemmas*, there is neither complaint nor lament in the composition, though either may be referred to obliquely. This may be the result of the connection of an *eršemma* with a *balag* which invariably contains both. Rather, certain *eršemmas* contain a sizeable unit composed almost entirely of appellatives and epithets referring to a cross section of the pantheon or else a list of cities thus broadening the range of propriety. Whereas the classic city laments cite only a limited number of cities and their gods, these later laments list many more cities and gods in keeping with their apparent multipurpose nature.

2.2.3.8 Appeal

Particularly in the First Millennium *eršemmas*, the "appeal" is invariably a heart-pacification composition identified as an *eršabhuma*, which is usually transliterated *er-ša-hun-ga*. This unit consists of three elements: 1.)

---

[113] See above, n. .

initial repetend, "May he pacify your heart! "May he calm your liver!" 2.) brief listing of deity, each followed by 3.) either a repetend "May he be pacified" or the like, or a repetend "May a prayer be uttered to you" or the like.[114]

2.2.4 Summary

Structurally, the city-lament and the *balag* are similar—so much so that the classic city-laments have been classified as *balag*s.[115] The *kirugu* and *gišgigal* rubrics marking multiple stanzas are features these two have in common as over against the *eršemma*s. Because the *balag*s are more general in content, they tend to be more simple and marked by much redundancy.

Regarding content structure, though there are specific elements common to the laments, only a hypothetical structure can be offered. There is no uniformity of content, structure either among the city-laments or the later *balag*s.

The *eršemma*, formally related to the *balag* as it is, has a different mechanical structure. The exemplars of the older *eršemma*s uniformly consist of one structural unit whereas those of the First Millennium may only have one but often have two or three structural units so indicated by a scribal incision across the breadth of the tablet.[116]

The structure of the content of the *eršemma* is more varied. Even the Old Babylonian texts may have more than one unit. One structural feature the *eršemma* shares with the *balag* is redundancy, a feature shared with nearly all Sumerian literature.

In the broadest terms, the basic structure of the genre as a whole might be reduced to three elements. The first is the invocation and adulation, which in some cases is quite lengthy. The second element is a complaint or lament which varies in detail between the various sub-genre, but, taken as a whole covers the gamut of issues. And the last element is an appeal for deliverance and restoration which is generally brief, not confined to any one position in the structure and not always in detailed correspondence with the specific items of the complaint.

Though formulaic expressions recur frequently and appear widely among the laments, there is no uniform pattern. Also, there appears to be no definitive uniform structure to which all of the communal laments can

---

[114] CSH, pp. 21-22.

[115] As suggested by Kutscher, OAS, pp. 2-3. He argues that *balag* is a functional label rather than a generic one, and since the classic city laments were ostensibly composed for single use, the label was not necessary.

[116] CSH, p. 21.

be expected to conform. Since the main communal laments tended to be preserved by scribal schools and adapted by the *gala* priests in subsequent generations and cultures, there does appear to be a marked similarity between the various groups of Sumero-Akkadian laments. It is clear, however, that literary devolution rather than evolution occurred. The later laments were indeed lesser in stature: less creative, more repetitive, less substantive in content, more mechanical and stereotyped.[117]

2.3 *Sitz im Leben*

2.3.1 Introduction

For the sake of clarity, I am dividing the treatment of the *Sitz im Leben* into three categories. Some of the lament compositions, like the classic city laments, were occasioned by a specific, historically documented catastrophe and the contents of the composition make frequent reference to various historical foci.

Other compositions are relatively general in their content and give no indication of being occasioned by an historically specific event. Rather, from external documentation it seems that they were probably composed for liturgical purposes.[118] In some instances, they are used in connection with the remodeling or rebuilding of a temple,[119] or the covering of a Temple drum.[120] In other instances, they have been associated with the *namburbi* rites[121] and other ritual observances. In either case, their purpose seems to be directed more toward the appeasement of deity and the averting of potential catastrophe.

The last category might be termed mytho-cultic as exemplified by the Tammuz laments. This group of laments shares many motifs and terms with the other categories but refers not to historical events past or present but to mythical subjects.[122] The *balag*s and *eršemma*s fall into these last two categories.

2.3.2 Related Literature

The themes of lament occur in other forms of Sumero-Akkadian literature as well. Kramer feels that the "incipient germ" of the Sumerian

---

[117] OAS, p. 4.
[118] Dossin, "Un rituel du Culte d'Istar"; S. Langdon, "Calendars of Liturgies and Prayers," AJSL 42 (1926): 110-127, etc.
[119] See A. Sachs, ANET, pp. 339-342.
[120] Ibid., pp. 334-338.
[121] R. Caplice, "Namburbi Texts in the British Museum," Or NS 39 (1970): 118-120.
[122] SKly, pp. 11, 49 ff.

lament can be "traced as far back as the days of Urukagina, in the 24th century," and the listing of shrines destroyed by Lugalzaggesi. What Kramer points to is rather intangible, however. In the midst of "the stark itemizing of the shrines destroyed," he sees the "implication of bitterness" and a "tone of resignation to the divine will."[123] A clearer example of the theme may be seen in the "Curse of Agade," dated ca. 2100-2000 B.C., not a lamentation per se, but a historiographic document[124] containing, as it does, complaints of the crushing Flood, abandonment of the shrine by the holy Inanna, a prostrated kingship, a plundered city, the appeals and imprecations and the benediction of praise to Inanna. There are also the elegies, funereal dirges, such as the Ludingirra dirges.[125] Other examples include "The Death of Gilgamesh," the Tammuz-laments, "Man and His God"—the Sumerian Job.

2.3.3 Classic City Laments

The classic city laments identify a specific city or series of cities that have been destroyed. Further, three of the city-laments mention a specific king. The "Lament over Sumer and Ur" refers to the Elamite captivity of Ibbi-Sin of the Ur III dynasty. The Uruk and Nippur laments both mention Išme-Dagan of Isin. He is named in these compositions as the one responsible for the restoration of the city in question and who is imploring the god to return with prayers and offerings. In the Nippur Lament Enlil commissions Išme-Dagan "to rebuild the mighty Ekur and to restore everything that befits it; to restore its *giguna* and make it as bright as the sun; to reinstate its rites and rituals that the enemy has suppressed and its *me* that have been dispersed."[126] In the eighth *kirugu* Išme-Dagan is credited with restoring not just Nippur but virtually all of Sumer and Akkad. Edzard posits a date during "the reign of Ismedagan, or certainly his forerunners" for the destruction of Nippur and Babylon referred to in the Nippur Lament.[127] Indeed, a liver omen from Mari speaks of a clash between Kish and Isin in which Išme-Dagan suffers defeat.[128] This,

---

123 Kramer, Lament over Nippur, p. 89.
124 See above, p. 21.
125 S. N. Kramer, Two Elegies on a Pushkin Museum Tablet: A New Sumerian Literary Genre (Moscow: Oriental Literature Publ., 1960).
126 Kramer, "Lament over Nippur," p. 92.
127 ZZB, p. 90.
128 RA 35 (1938): pl. 6, no. 11.

coupled with the effect the Amorite raids were having on the settled areas, likely describes at least part of the setting of the Nippur Lament.[129] The Ur and Eridu laments do not name either the king whose city or kingdom was demolished or the king responsible for its rebuilding. There is little room for doubt, however, that the events spoken of the in the Ur Lament are those which marked the fall of the Ur III dynasty. Jacobsen criticized Kramer's vagueness in stating that the "Ur Lament" was "both composed and inscribed some time during the Isin-Larsa-Babylon I period (as yet we lack criteria for more exact dating)."[130] Jacobsen argues that the clarity and detail of the description contained in the composition argue for a date relatively close to the events described: "it must have been written no more than seventy or eighty years after the destruction."[131] Edzard agrees, positing a date for the Ur Lament "barely later than one generation after the event."[132] The one bit of internal data which would narrow this time-frame further is contained in the last *kirugu*:

423 O Nanna, may thy city which has been returned to its place, step forth gloriously before thee!

424 Like a bright star let it not be destroyed; may it proceed before thee!

This plea seems to fit the setting of a restoration ceremony rather than that of a more recent demolition. By Jacobsen's account of the restoration process, the composition should probably be dated toward the end of the period from the reign of Shu-Ilishu (c. 1984-1974) to that of Lipit-Ishtar (c. 1934-1923) who claimed: "On the command of Enlil and Nanna he restored Ur to its place."[133] One other observation is that the apparent time-frame as indicated by the general tense of the composition might best fit the final aspects of the restoration process, viz., some sort of installation service for the patron deity.

The "Lament over Eridu" is somewhat more difficult to date, at least from internal data. No kings are named in the lament.

---

129 D. O. Edzard, "The Third Dynasty of Ur—Its Empire and Its Successor States," in *Delacorte World History*, eds. J. Bottero, E. Cassin, J. Vercoutter, vol. 2: *The Near East: The Early Civilizations* (New York: Delacorte, 1967), pp. 166-167.

130 LU, p. vii.

131 "Review," p. 221. Kramer, unconvinced by Jacobsen's argument, stated: "unless I am very much mistaken, he has considerably oversimplified the problems involved." ANET p. 455, n. 5.

132 ZZB, pp. 57-58.

133 RA 33 (1936): 24-25, no. 6 cited by Jacobsen, "Review," p. 221.

Green adduces external data to suggest two possible dates: either the reign of I me-Dagan of Isin (c. 1953-1934) or of Nur-Adad of Larsa (c. 1865-1849). Evidence for the former is merely stylistic as there does not seem to be any indication that Išme-Dagan sponsored any restoration projects at Eridu. On the other hand, there is both archaeological and documentary evidence for Nur-Adad's (1865-1849 B.C.) involvement at Eridu roughly a century and a half after the fall of Ur. A brick-inscription from the Nur-Adad's ziggurat at Eridu reads:

> I, Nur-Adad, the mighty man, the faithful farmer of Ur, king of Larsa, who purified the rites of the shrine Ebabbar: Eridu, which long ago had been damaged—I wanted to (re)build it so that I might make its reign prosperous. For Enki I built his beloved holy dwelling. I restored its primeval design for him.

Thus the weight of the evidence, incomplete as it may be, seems to favor the later date for the Eridu Lament.[134] If this date is correct, there seems to be a formal development. The Eridu lament, though it shares some formal characteristics with the other two examples studied, is substantially shorter. Three exemplars, however, seem insufficient to establish any firm conclusion. It is interesting to note that the other classical city laments are considerably longer.[135]

The classical city laments are set apart not only by the specificity of their content, but also by the fact that to date there are no known examples in Akkadian literature which parallel them in style and content. Whereas it is not uncommon to find a Sumerian *balag* and *eršemma* preserved with an Akkadian translation, to date no Akkadian translations of the classical city laments have been published.

2.3.4 *Balags*

This second category is related to the first but clearly distinct. It has been observed that the classical city laments share many of the characteristics of the later *balags*.[136] These too are concerned with large scale disaster, either real or impending.[137] But the *balags* which were concerned

---

134 Nevertheless, Green prefers the earlier date. LEr, pp. 128-130.

135 See p. 21.

136 OAS, p. 2.

137 Kutscher argues for no connection between the neo-Sumerian laments which exist in Old Babylonian copies and later laments which exist in neo-Assyrian and Seleucid copies, OAS, p. 1. To the contrary, Cohen argues that the *balags* were a literary outgrowth of the earlier classical city laments. He bases his argument on the similarities in structure and content, ritual use, and adequate time for such an evolution to occur. CBC, pp. 9-11. A problem seems to exist for either position. On the one hand, there does seem to be a significant similarity between the Old Babylonian *balags* and the later *balag* compositions which seem to imply a

with cities are very general in their content as compared with the classical city laments. Though much of the terminology is similar, the descriptions of the calamity presented in the balags are much less vivid and detailed. Rather than commemorating a specific historical calamity, these laments seem to have been composed for ritual use to assuage the anger of the gods and to moderate their capriciousness.

In some cases this might have been related to the process of remodeling a temple during which the ire of its god might be aroused. Cohen notes the frequent theme of the kišubim: "This supplication...return the 'x-temple' to place."[138]

It has been suggested that other balags seem to have been related to a periodic rite intended to placate the gods concerning unwitting transgression. Such a use, for example, is illustrated in the namburbi rituals which employ both balags and eršemmas.[139]

It has also been observed that the city lists preserved in the extant balags tend to indicate a northern shift in demographics which would correspond with what we know of the course of events from the 18th century B.C. on.[140]

2.3.5 Eršemmas

There is scant data regarding the eršemma of the Old Babylonian period, viz., a single text dealing with a ritual observance at Mari.[141] There does seem to be a clear indication in that text that the balag and eršemma were somehow related in the same ritual. First millennium sources on the other hand are replete with examples of balags which concluded with an appended eršemma.

Not all eršemmas were thus used, however. A number appear to have been composed for use independent of a balag and are listed under the heading kidudu.[142]

The actual origin of the eršemma is difficult to ascertain. This is in part because the eršemmas share with the balags not only a stock of characteristic terms but also entire passages.[143]

---

connection. On the other hand, the existence of Old Babylonian balags seems significantly to shorten Cohen's evolutionary period.

138 CBC, pp. 8, 13, 33.
139 Caplice, "Namburbi Texts."
140 CBC, p. 12.
141 CSH, pp. 40-41.
142 K-(1) III, cited in CSH, p. 27.
143 Ibid., p. 36, points out that lines 15-22 of eršemma no. 162 are the same as no. 174:11-18. In the latter, they appear to be an integral part of the structure whereas in the former they appear to intrude into the story line. But even more interesting is the occurrence of this same

Another factor complicating an attempt to specify a particular *Sitz im Leben* for the *eršemma* is the variety of themes among the *eršemma*s. Some consist entirely of praise. The difficulty arises when the *eršemma* in question is not appended to a *balag* nor listed in one of the calendars along with a lament liturgy. In either of these cases, it may be assumed that the *eršemma* was probably composed for use in the lament liturgy on the analogy of praise in the classic city-laments. Rather, the *eršemma*s which are cataloged or scheduled apparently independent of a *balag* are the ones which present the difficulty.[144]

2.3.6 Development of the Sumero-Akkadian Lament

All available evidence indicates that the classic city laments were not maintained in any cultic tradition past the end of the Old Babylonian period. There quickly appeared, however, a type of composition that demonstrated a close affinity with the city laments. In fact, there were two distinct types of compositions which could be characterized as laments and which seemed to emulate the classic city laments: the *balag* and the *eršemma*. While the classic city laments were preserved in the scribal schools over the subsequent centuries and did not continue to be used liturgically, the *balag*s and *eršemma*s went through at least two evolutionary periods of liturgical use.

If the *eršemma* is to be identified exclusively with laments in the second millennium (an assumption not certain), they are not exclusively identified with each other in the first millennium. Many, if not most, of the *eršemma*s in the first millennium are appended to *balag* laments. But there are a number of extant *eršemma*s which have nothing to do with lament but rather express joy, and some, called *kidudu*s, which were used during specific ceremonial observances independently of the lament.[145]

A fourth category of *emesal* literature is the *šuilla*: "lifting of the hand." This group of public liturgical prayers had its provenance in the Middle-Babylonian period but flourished in the first millennium.[146] Langdon has described the later *šuilla*s as "honorific hymns to the deities ending in the same refrain and are invariably appeals for cities temples [*sic*] and are sung on behalf of the public welfare,"[147] which is how they

---

passage, not in yet another *eršemma* but an Old Babylonian *balag*, the a-ab-ba hu-luh-ha. See also SKly, pp. 23-24.

[144] CSH, pp. 41-42. Cohen indicates that there is insufficient evidence to "determine the exact purpose and function of the independent ersemma in First Millennium B.C.E. ritual."

[145] See above n.. Cf. CSH, pp. 18, 22-23, 42.

[146] See below, Chapter 3. SKly, p. 25; CSH, p. 2; A. Falkenstein, "Chronologie," pp. 1ff., and *Hymnen und Gebete*, pp. 24ff.

[147] *Penitential Psalms*, p. ix.

are associated with lamentations. Though the *šuilla* psalms are included in several catalogs,[148] only a few have been uncovered.

2.4 Thematic Elements of the Communal Lament

The laments along with a host of other literature depict a hierarchical pantheon. The divine assembly was headed by the seven gods "who decree the fates" and thus bear a sort of suzerainty over the fifty "great gods" and the lesser gods in turn under them.[149]

Thus, there existed a concept of ultimate causality in the world view represented in the laments. And this ultimate causality rested with the assembly, though Enlil and An are by far the most frequently mentioned as the prime cause of the calamity which is being lamented. The causal action of the gods could be expressed in either of two modes: immediate or mediate, or both. One feature which makes it difficult to establish a firm distinction between immediate and mediate activity of the gods is the common practice of assigning divinity to natural phenomena, e.g., Flood, Storm, Ox. The question arises whether a particular event is the direct act of, for example, the storm god or the indirect act of deity through the natural phenomenon of a storm. One might make the distinction on the basis of contextual clues such as the use of the vocative. Thus, if deity is addressed by other names in the context and the devastation of a storm is the subject of the complaint, one might assume mediate action on the part of deity. In either case, both Sumero-Akkadian theology in general and the lament texts in particular would seem to support the notion that the gods were ultimately responsible.

2.4.1 Methodology

In order to collect as many thematic elements as possible, both the classical city-laments and the *balags* and *eršemmas*, I have searched for identifiable recurring motifs. These were then cataloged under relative categories. For example, occurrences of the following terms were listed: how long? until when? abandon, forsake, sleep, lie down, silent, silence, indolent. Those passages in which these terms were used in reference to a deity vis-à-vis a city or people were collected and, if appropriate, put into categories as examples of divine neglect. Likewise, passages which included the terms: anger, angry, soothe, pacify, implacable, inimical, still, and appease were categorized as references to divine anger. In this

---

148 T. Pinches, *Cuneiform Inscriptions of Western Asia*, vol. IV, 2nd ed. (London: British Museum), no. 53; RA 18, pp. 158ff.; et al.

149 Ibid., pp. 13, 18, 35-37.

way, a thematic concordance was developed to be used as an analytical tool. The various laments were then studied individually for their development of various themes. These were then compared, and the composite description which follows was prepared.

2.4.2 The Anger of the Gods

In the treatment of categories of themes or motifs, the data mentioned above was collected from the content of the laments. From the dynamics of the relationships of the various thematic elements it was determined that the arbitrary, capricious anger or wrath of the gods would be a logical starting point for a theoretical ordering of the thematic elements. This anger is represented in many of the laments as the underlying cause of the calamity and suffering commemorated in the laments. It is treated in some depth in most of the laments, and collectively they depict a rather full-blown emotion of extreme displeasure and hostility. It is described in such terms as: anger, wrath, hostility, cursing, inimical posture, evil disposition of heart, and pacification and appeasement which imply great agitation toward the objects of the anger. This would logically be followed by the decision of the gods to act and then a description of the means of such action as well as a description of the effects of such acts upon the target society. The objects of wrath then remonstrate with the responsible party or parties, often protesting their innocence. At last, there is an appeal for restoration for the aggrieved party and retaliation against those instrumental in afflicting the calamity, occasionally accompanied by expressions of praise to the deity.

An analysis of the literature shows the subject of divine anger being treated both explicitly and implicitly. The anger theme is treated explicitly in the form of direct statements about the anger of the gods, e.g., when Enlil is said to have "glared angrily," or the "wrath of [the lord's] heart" is spoken of.[150]

Probably the clearest examples of the implicit treatment of deific anger are the many appeals directed to deity to be pacified and soothed, or directed to one deity to aid in pacifying and soothing another. It should be noted that the frequent use of these appeals for the pacification of divine anger occur almost exclusively in the balags and eršemmas. They seem to be non-existent in the classic city laments. The pacification theme does occur in the major city laments, but it refers not to divine anger but

---

[150] LU:257,258; LSU 24:21-26; LEr24 1:26; SBP24 II:17, XII.5:21-34, XIII:19-20; CSH:10.

rather to grief and anguish either on the part of people and city (LU 430) or on the part of the patron deity (LEr 7:20-22).[151]

2.4.3 The Decision of Deity to Act

Anger is often presented as the prime motive for the gods' deciding to act. There does not seem to be much emphasis on the notion of the gods arriving at such a decision in solemn assembly though there is reference to numerous deities' decreeing in concert vis-à-vis the city or cities in question. I have found only one direct reference to "the verdict of the assembly" of at least certain of the gods: LSU, line 366.

As I shall show presently, even when the cause for lament appears to have been a natural disaster or an act of a human enemy, there seems to be a sense that the real cause is still to be assigned to divine decision or more specifically, the ensuing decree which in those cases is discharged mediately against the given city or cities. There are, however, numerous cases of reference to the immediate action of deity as the basis of lament.[152]

The decrees, orders or utterances of the deity in question are declared to be inexorable, unalterable and irrepressible.[153]

It seems that the decree motif was pervasive in the balags and eršemmas while being virtually absent in the classic city-laments.[154] It was most often expressed by the term "Word" which seems often to have been used to personify both deity and divine decree. And as such it was the subject of many of the causal statements referring to the calamity being lamented. As demonstrated above, the "word" could not be opposed.[155]

One further aspect of the word motif, seen already in some of the examples given, is that of the inscrutability or incomprehensibility of the word, i.e., deity. Deity is called the "Universal Ruler of the unsearchable heart . . . whose thoughts are unfathomable." And this inscrutability is often described in parallel with the "sacred word" or "true word."[156]

---

151 See also SBP X:29-40, rev. 23-36, XXIV rev. 2-19; CBC 2:60-62; CSH 13:22-24, 45:12-13.

152 LU:140-142, 162-164; LSU:21, 55; SBP V:1-3, 15-17, 22-23, XXIII:1-2, 5-6, 13-14; CBC 1:39-42.

153 LU:168-169; LSU:56-57; SBP II:32-34, IV:52-54, X:16-17; CSH 160:2-6; CBC 1:5-6.

154 LSU: 366-367 "The verdict of the assembly cannot be turned back. The word commanded by Enlil knows no overturning."

155 SBP IV rev. 1-19, 21-35, 40-49; CBC 2:1-12, 18-23, 3:61-67, 4:41-81; CSH 35.1:24-26.

156 LSU:166; SBP 24 V:11-13, VII:22-27, rev. 1-4, X:14, 36-39, XX:1-3; BL LXXIII:45-46, rev. 1; CBC 3:1-2, 4:1-2, 24; CSH 163.1:1, 160:3.

2.4.4 The Actions of Deity

The laments tend to focus upon the abandonment and neglect of the cities by one or more of the gods. Often, abandonment by An or Enlil forced a concomitant abandonment by the patron deity of the city in question. In some cases, the immediate patron of the city is identified as not having abandoned its own city, at least for a while, even though a higher god has done so.[157]

The gods are also blamed for sending the ravaging flood and then drought and famine, all of which result in a tremendous upheaval of society and the destruction of its institutions. Though the flood came to be used metaphorically as an appellative, there is doubtless literal reference to the natural phenomenon, sometimes caused by seismic activity and sometimes by torrential downpour and flash flooding.[158] Drought is self-explanatory.[159] But it ought to the noted that famine may be the result of other causes such as a ruined economy or an invading army, etc.

The descriptions of the pervasive and inescapable devastation at the hands of deity tends to be rather detailed,[160] including not only the physical toll but the emotional toll upon the population as well.

The effects of the acts of the gods upon Mesopotamian society as described in the laments fall into two categories: 1) the destruction of material culture, 2) the upheaval of social culture. Although each is distinct, the two notions are often related in the course of human experience. It has been observed that an upheaval of the social culture may itself have the effect of causing destruction or at least decay of the material culture. One reason is that essential public works, such as the irrigation systems, required a stable central government to maintain them. In times of political instability this was lacking.

These laments describe the destruction of the cities, their walls, canals, dikes, houses, and temples.[161] They also describe the despoiling of the flora and fauna of the land.[162]

---

[157] LU:1-377; LSU:68, 249, 375-376; LEr 1:11-12, 5:1-2, 7:10-14; CBC 1:84-92; CSH 166.1:16-17; SBP XVIII:9-12; V rev. 16.

[158] OAS:62-63, 273-280; SBP IV:11-12, 17-31; BL LXXI:5-7, 60-62, CLVIII:1-7, 9, 16, 31-34, 36-39, rev. 23; SBP 24 VII:7, rev. 13-14, 17-24.

[159] LSU:297; SBP III:45-46, XIII:19, XIV:26-27.

[160] SBP XXIV:1-18, XXV:10; BL 24 XVI:14-27.

[161] LU:42-43, 45, 65-66, 77-78, 108-109, 122-132, 208-209, 240, 261-264, 292; LEr 1:25, 2:12-18; CBC 3:56-57, 5:13-21; SBP III:30-38, 47 rev. 8, 40-45, IV:1-15; CSH 79:31-32, 166.1.1-7, 166.2:1-14, 1.2:28-35, 10:13-15.

[162] LSU:6-11, 38, 42-51, 61, 130-135; SBP IV:23-31, 56, rev. 5, 34, 38, IVB:9, 16, VII rev. 20-21, 24; CSH 106:14.

The intensity of emotion, however, seems to be reserved for those passages which describe the rending of the social fabric. The patron god has abandoned or been driven from the city and its temple. What was sacred is now defiled. Religious observance has been overturned.[163] The administration of justice is disrupted.[164] Homes are pillaged and demolished. Both natural relationships and characteristic roles are confounded. Families are driven from their homes. Marriages are rent. Children are torn away from their parents. Mothers abandon their children. Members of a family no longer recognize one another. People become displaced; some are deported.[165] Many go mad from the terror and anxiety which lead to deep depression. Even the gods are subject to terror, anxiety and depression and they too find themselves displaced.[166] In the Sumero-Akkadian world view the metaphysical explanation for this entire range of events is also given in the laments: the "me"—the force or system established at creation for the perpetuation of various phenomena and entities according to divine intent—had been "overturned."[167]

2.4.5 The Identity and Actions of the Political Enemy

As indicated and demonstrated above, the laments overwhelmingly express the sense that deity was ultimately behind the calamity which was the subject of complaint. There is, however, numerous mention of the presence and activities of political enemies who were described as the immediate cause of much of the havoc which had been wreaked upon their society. In the classic city-laments primary enemies are named: Anshan, Elam, Halma,[168] Guti, Subar, the Su-people, and Tidnum.[169] In the *balag*s and *eršemma*s, though political enemies are mentioned, they are usually not specifically identified.[170]

---

163 LU:116-117, 322-323, 393-395; LSU:154-156, 186-187, 194-198, 207-208, 252-253, 325-326, 343-345; SBP II:35-36 rev. 16, IV:5-6, XXI:29-38, XXXII:33; BL:24-35; CSH 106:15-16.
164 LU:231-232, 265-271; LSU:62, 446-447; CBC 1:13-16, 164-166.
165 LSU:12-16; CBC 1:97-102, 3:52-55, 4:53-54; SBP II:20-21, III.2:58-59, III.3:16-24, IV:21, 58, rev. 7-9, V:10, 17-18, VII rev. 19.
166 LU:97-102, 117; LSU:34, 58, 67, 69, 86, 108-110, 181, 205, 219; LEr 1:11-13, 4:1, 7:5-9; CBC 2:10-12; SBP XI.2:46, rev. 10-11, XI.3:29-31, XI.6:32-40, XVI rev. 1-8, XXIII:19-26, rev. 1-4, XXI:1-3, XXVII:12, XXX:9, XXXI:24-25, rev. 8-10, BL LXXI:29-31, 36-38; CSH 32:37; CSH 1.1:30-31.
167 LU:69-70, 171, 386; LSU:1, 3-4, 27-28, 356; LEr 1:16-18.
168 According to A. Oppenheim, this is probably a reference to Elam. "Notes breves 6: ARM 10, 78:23," RA 63 (1969): 95.
169 LU:244-246; LSU:33-36, 75, 153-154, 156, 169, 183, 187, 191, 195, 200, 208, 233, 244, 253, 257-260, 332, 391, 404-414, 426, 450, 456, 495-498; LEr 1:21, 3:17-19, 4:10.
170 SBP XI.2:17, XI.3 rev. 12-47.

2.4.6 Remonstration

Logically, but not necessarily rhetorically, the transition from the descriptive elements of the complaint to the appeal elements is somewhat typically marked by questioning "why?" "how long?" and "until when?" In the passages set off by these questions, the people remonstrate with the responsible deities. Often the questions will contain elements already referred to in the extended complaints: "Why do you terrify the land?" "How long will [PN] stand aside...?" "What are your plans?" etc.[171]

In addition, there are several examples of the complainants' straightforward declaration that the gods should not have done what they are being accused of, or should not have allowed the calamity to have happened. These examples do not occur in the classical city-laments but rather in a few of the *balag*s and *eršemma*s.[172]

2.4.7 Protestation of Innocence

In a sense, the protestation of innocence is closely related to the remonstrations just treated. There occurs in the laments a comparison, either explicit or implicit, of the Sumero-Akkadian society with those of the enemy. The former is claimed to be righteous, like an innocent ewe, like little children without sin. Hence, the calamity is said to be "without cause." The latter are described as hostile rebels. It seems the composer is expressing the notion that the society is marked by a relative righteousness vis-à-vis the foreigners.[173] One possible exception to this claim of righteousness may be what appears to be a confession contained in the Ur Lament.[174]

2.4.8 Appeal

The next element of the lament is the appeal. Once again, this element follows the complaint logically but not necessarily rhetorically. It is not uncommon for the lament to alternate between complaint and appeal. The object of appeal varies. There is appeal for the gods to be

[171] LU:46-47=63-64=71-72, 374-375; LSU, 243-245, 341-342, 401, 459; OAS:1-2, 28-30, 99-102, 153-159; SKly VII:31-39; SBP II rev. 14, V rev. 16-20, XI.2 rev. 22, XI.3 rev. 2-3, 6-7, 10-11, XI.6:18-20 XII.1:1-3, 13, XII.2:3, 41, XII.5:1-20, XIII:19, XIV:26-27, XVI:11; CBC 1:24-29, 118-130, 2:72-73; CSH 164:12.

[172] CBC 1:84-92; CSH 13:30-31.

[173] LU:42, 67-68, 74, 119-125, 243-245, 265-266, 317-318, 324-325, 340; LSU:72-75, 226, 358; SKly I:3-6, 16-17, IV:7-8, IX:8-9.

[174] LU:429, 431-434.

pacified[175] and for rapprochement to be effected.[176] There is both appeal for the gods to receive intercession and to make intercession on behalf of the city or cities.[177] The gods are also requested specifically to cause the calamity to cease,[178] and to cause restoration to take place.[179] Imprecation is also part of the appeal in some cases. The gods are appealed to for retaliation against the enemy—"the inimical lands."[180]

2.4.9 Praise

The theme of praise is virtually non-existent in the classic city laments. However, in the *balags* and *eršemmas* expressions of adulation can be profuse. Occasionally, the praise theme is connected with the invocation.[181] In some cases, the praise is offered in terms of honorific epithets attributed to the deity. In others, there are exclamations of joy.[182]

2.4.10 Summary

The occasion of complaint is by definition some type of pain, grief or discontent. For a complaint to become formalized and institutionalized, one would expect the cause of the pain or grief to be no small matter. An analysis of the Sumero-Akkadian laments indicates just that.

Regarding the antagonist, these laments identify two distinct categories of adversary which in some of the compositions are blended into one. Primary attention is given to those who make up the Sumero-Akkadian pantheon. In addition to the sometimes extended invocations and paeans treated above, the gods are taken to task for their role(s) in the calamity in question. Often the anger of the god(s) as expressed by decree is bewailed as being utterly implacable and described as a great on-rushing flood-wall which cannot be stopped or turned back, nor can it be withstood. It completely devastates all in its path. But there are also mortal enemies whose actions are deplored and cursed. In the face of enemy attack and oppression, the gods are taken to task for ordering it or at the very least for standing by and letting it happen—for abandoning their place and people and looking the other way.

---

175 LEr 7:5-9, 21-23; SBP IX:1-19, XV:12-13.
176 LU:378-384; LSU:490-492; LEr 7:10-20; SBP X:10-15; CSH 1.2:1-27.
177 SBP X.4 rev. 1-14, XXIII rev. 9-26; BL LXXIII rev. 3-47; CSH 13:22-29.
178 LU:145-149, 155-159, 407-414.
179 LU:423-424, LSU:352-356; SBP V rev. 24, XI.5 rev. 65+?, XII.6:77; CSH 13:24-25, 10:20-21.
180 LSU:493-499; SBP I rev. 29-30; BL LXXI:48-49; SBP XXIX:26; CSH 23.1:22-26, 168:33.
181 See Cohen "Analysis," p. 96. Cf. CBC pp. 22-23, 26-27.
182 See OAS, pp. 44-51 on the use of divine and heroic epithets.

The results of the decree are tremendous. The material culture is demolished. Cities are no more and their glorious public works, such as the great river-canal systems, are either destroyed and dried up or else left in such a state of disrepair that they flow with bitter, brackish water and are overrun with weeds and lead into marshlands filled with a stench. The city walls and public buildings are in ruins; streets and courtyards filled with the cadavers.

The social culture obviously cannot survive such circumstances. The basic institutions of society have been crushed. In the family, the husband no longer recognizes his wife and vice versa, should they both have survived. Siblings are separated and do not know each other. Parents no longer recognize their own children. Justice is banished. Law and order have ceased and ethics are subverted so that now the liar is "superior to the honest man." The whole notion of government is made impossible when the gods overturn the *me* of Sumer.

Neither have religious institutions been spared. Temple and shrine have been razed and "light in darkness is overwhelmed." The priestly rites are suspended; the offerings and burnt offerings are cut off; the sanctuary is carried away.

Some of those who have survived the horror find themselves deported: sons and daughters, commissaries, diviners and priests, the women of Baba's house, and in the Lament over Sumer and Ur, Ibbi-Sin himself is carried off by the Elamites thus ending the dynasty of Ur-Nammu.

There is common in the laments a protestation of innocence, the people of the city being compared with an innocent ewe. This is probably to be understood as a relative evaluation on the part of those lamenting as compared with the hostile foreign enemies. The reason for this assumption is that though confession of sin is rare, it does occur.

The thrust of appeal is two-fold. One is that the lament and prayer of appeal will even be heard by deity: that the gods might be pacified and be reconciled to the people. The other is that deity will cause the hostile action to be diverted to the enemies' lands and return and restore the city to its former glory.

The element of praise is common to most of the laments. But the various sub-genre do not use praise uniformly. It is a small segment of the classic city-lament though it may occupy the whole of a given *eršemma*.

A thematic survey of the Akkadian lament must be sketchy because it is based on a single 27-line composition.[183] It seems most of the thematic elements seen in the Sumero-Akkadian laments are missing in this composition. There is no reference to either the anger of the gods or their decree to act against the cities. There is no accusation directed against the gods for their deeds. Elements of complaint are found which the Akkadian composition has in common with its Sumero-Akkadian counterparts: the ruin of the city, removal of the throne, the laying waste of the "house." In this lament, Ishtar complains of her distress, depression and disgrace. She complains that a slaughter has taken place and "the daughter of Nippur weeps, unto the land of the Kutean who has finished his mission."[184]

---

[183] SBP XXV.
[184] Ibid., line 12.

—◦—◦— **3** —◦—◦—

The Lament Phenomenon in the Ancient
Near East as it Relates to the Hebrew
Communal Laments

3.1 *Introduction*

The effort to establish the *Sitz im Leben* of a genre is an effort to describe, not prescribe, how the observable phenomena, which are related to the given class of literary expression, occurred and were practiced in their cultural setting(s) according to the available documentary evidence. Gunkel strongly encouraged the study of the relationship of a given literary genre to the "everyday life" situations in which or out of which it grew. But since human life, individually and collectively, is dynamic and not static, it is not likely that a given genre, unless very narrowly defined, could be delimited to a single situation or circumstance. Those literary categories which are so narrowly defined in terms of situation of origin and of use ought to be considered a sub-genre, e.g., the classic city-laments, within the genre of communal lament.

A genre must have a beginning somewhere, somehow. It is in the attempt to reconstruct an "original, pure" form, however, that one risks stretching the data.[185] It would seem that the pursuit of an understanding

---

[185] See above pp. 11-12.

of a genre would best be served, not by trying to reconstruct a theoretical original, pure form, but by realizing that genres develop as the result of various processes of human life and interaction. In this regard, it may be observed that, while they are neither universal nor identical, human experience and response do seem to demonstrate a remarkable degree of commonality. This seems especially true of the basic relationships and basic experiences of life such as birth, death, kinship units and societal relationships, etc.

Virtually every culture about which data is available possesses some sort of mourning rite. The more closely related two given cultural groups may be, the greater the likelihood that there will be a close "natural" affinity between their cultural conventions and expressions. This affinity is not necessarily due to direct conscious borrowing. It may just as well be the result of various cultural factors held in common. The purpose of this chapter is to survey several aspects of human experience which are treated in the literature and which relate to the cultural phenomenon of communal lament in the Bible, viz., individual lamentation and funereal mourning.

The phenomena of the individual lament and the funeral dirge both hold a place in the background of the communal laments. This can be seen at once in the many elements and features which they hold in common with the communal laments.[186] The genres of individual lament and mourning dirge deal with a range of matters that touch human emotions deeply. They give expression to those emotions. The subject matter and approach taken by the individual laments are similar in many respects to those found in the communal laments.

3.2 *Individual Lament*

Two outstanding features of poetry in general are its tendency toward conservatism and its being an artistic expression of the mind in emotive language. Thus, even more recent poetic compositions tend to exhibit older forms and styles. For example, Krecher has noted that thus far the *šuilla* and *eršahunga* are known only from the Kassite period on.

---

186 Cf. G. Widengren, *The Accadian and Hebrew Psalms of Lamentation as Religious Documents* (Stockholm: Bokforlags Aktiebolaget Thule, 1937); R. G. Castellino, *Le lamentazioni individuali e gli inni in Babylonia e in Israele*, (Turin: Societa Editrice Internationale, 1940); H. Jahnow, *Das hebräische Leichenlied im Rahmen der Völkerdichtung*, BZAW 36, (Giessen: A. Töpelmann, 1923).

But he also notes that in large part they appear to be "composed out of old traditional phrases."[187]

The two classes of literary texts which are related to the communal laments either by subject or style or both are identified as the *šuilla* and the *eršahunga*. A third category which relates to the lament theme is the funeral dirge.

3.2.1 *Šuilla*

The *šuilla*, a prayer of "the raising of the hand,"[188] may be divided into two sub-groups by a distinction of subject matter. Some of the *šuilla* compositions contain penitential elements and thus should be classified as penitential psalms. However, other *šuilla* compositions lack any penitential formulae and would be classified as individual laments.[189]

The famous stele of the "Code of Hammurapi" depicts Hammurapi, in a bas-relief, standing before the sun-god Shamash who is seated on his throne. Hammurapi is standing with his left arm folded against his abdomen and his right hand raised to the level of his head with palm turned inward. T. Meek identifies the scene as showing "the act of receiving the commission to write the law book from the god of justice." The text of the prologue mentions Adad's recognition of the "lifting of hand" prayers.[190]

Most of the extant *šuilla* prayers are in Akkadian rather than Sumerian. A Babylonian catalog cites forty-seven bilingual *emesal*/Akkadian *šuilla*s, but only three of these are extant.[191]

Kunstmann identified the following structural/thematic elements in the individual laments:

I. Address
   a. Invocation of deity with honorific titles
   b. Praise of the deity
II. Prayer
   c. Lamentation
   d. Transition formula
   e. Prayer

---

[187] SKly, p. 25. Cf. A. Falkenstein, *Mitteilungen der Deutschen Orientsgesellschaft in Berlin* 85, pp. 1 ff., and *Sumerische und akkadische Hymnen und Gebete*, pp. 24 ff.

[188] W. Mayer, *Untersuchungen zur Formensprache der babylonischen "Gebetsbeschwörungen,"* Studia Pohl: Series Maior 5, (Rome: Pontifical Biblical Institute, 1976.), p. 7 defines the *uilla* as "*erhobene Hand, Handerhebung*." See also E. Ebeling, "*Handerhebung*," cf. BPP, p. vi.-ix.

[189] Widengren, *Psalms*, p. 16.

[190] ANET, p. 163 ff. See lines iii:50-60. Cf. n. 25.

[191] M.-J. Seux, *Hymnes et Prières aux Dieux de Babylonie et d'Assyrie* (Paris: Editions de Cerf, 1976), p. 27. See ANET, pp. 385-386, 389-390; SAHG, pp. 222-225; Thureau-Dangin, *Rituels accadiens*, pp. 108-111.

66   THE GENRE OF COMMUNAL LAMENT

III. Thanksgiving
   f. Thanksgiving with benediction formula.[192]

3.2.1.1 Invocation and Eulogy

Castellino points out that in some cases the titulary or invocation is structurally separate from the eulogy and, in other cases, the two elements are intertwined.[193] The titulary may run for a number of lines each adding epithets to the vocative and followed with a repetend.[194]

3.2.1.2 Complaint

The complaint and its exposition tends to be brief in the *šuilla*. As the titulary section tends to fade into the eulogy, so the complaint tends to fade into the entreaty. On some occasions it is only implied in the appeal.[195] The complaint often contains a presentation of the plaintiff who speaks in the first person, though in some examples this feature is absent.[196]

3.2.1.3 Entreaty

The prayer of entreaty in which the supplicant importunes the deity for good fortune is in some examples punctuated with the repetends seen so frequently in the *balag* and *eršemma*.[197]

On the other hand, Langdon offers a translation of a text reconstructed from K. 2824 with an insertion from Sm. 336 which exhibits a more creative style.[198]

---

[192] W. Kunstmann, *Die babylonische Gebetsbeschwörung, Leipziger semitistische Studien* N.F. 2 (Leipzig: Hinrichs, 1931). Nine years later, Castellino (*Lamentazioni*, p. 50, cf. pp. 75-78.) offered the following structural analysis which is not substantively changed:
   I. The title or invocation
   II. The eulogy or praise
   III. The complaint and its exposition
   IV. The prayer of entreaty
   V. The promise...
   Seux offered the following structure:
   I. Praise to the invoked god
   II. Presentation and justification of the plaintiff
   III. Complaint
   IV. Petition
   V. Thanksgiving
Hymnes et Prières, pp. 24-25.
[193] *Lamentazioni*, pp. 6-16.
[194] See IV R 9: SAHG no. 44, or F. Stephens, ANET, pp. 385-386.
[195] K.2824: SAHG no. 54, or Ebeling, "*Handerhebung*," pp. 48 ff. Cf. BBP, pp. 82-84.
[196] Seux, *Hymnes et Prières*, p. 24.
[197] IV R. 9, lines 25-39. See above n. 194.
[198] Lines A-C, 15-32, BBP, pp. 83-84.

3.2.1.4 Praise

The last element is that of praise: the promise of praise or hymn of praise. This element characteristically marks the conclusion of the *šuilla* in either one of the two forms just mentioned. Examples of the first type would be:

> I will announce your grandeur to the vast peoples.[199]
>
> By the mouth of the vast peoples your grandeur will be
> celebrated,
> You will respectfully be praised.[200]

The second type, the brief paean to the deity, may be exemplified by the following *šuilla* to Marduk:

> Enlil himself rejoices for you,
> May Ea delight in you.
> The gods of the universe, they bless you,
> The great gods, they delight your heart.[201]

Often, the tablets contain specific prescriptions for the ritual performance of the prayer or else, the summary statement: "You will perform the rite either in a cultic setting or with an incense-burner." Also, several extant *šuillas* show that at least sometimes the *šuilla* was composed for multiple use. This is evidenced by the provisions for inserting one's own name in the text of the prayer.[202]

3.2.2 Eršahunga

The second class of individual lament-type song is that commonly marked by the rubric *eršahunga*, "lament for appeasing the heart," and was identified as a private penitential prayer by Langdon. Both the *eršahunga* and the Sumerian portion of the bi-lingual *šuilla* are composed in the *emesal* dialect identified with the laments. Langdon noted that the terminology used in the *eršahunga* is often identical to that of the *eršemma*.[203] And in form, it is often quite difficult to distinguish the *eršahunga* from the *eršemma*. Seux states that "in this particular literary genre, it is difficult to discern a normative, constant structure."[204] Dalglish analyzed the form of the *eršahunga* thus:

---

199 KM 18, L. W. King, *Babylonian Magic and Sorcery*, cited by Castellino, LIIBE, p. 50.
200 KAR 55, E. Ebeling, *Keilschrifttexte aus Assur religiösen Inhalts*, cited in *LIIBE*. Cf. *SAHG* no. 53.
201 KM 9 et al., BBP, p. 53. Ebeling, "*Handerhebung*," p. 64 ff., *SAHG* no. 42.
202 Seux, *Hymnes et Prières*, pp. 25-26.
203 BBP, pp. vi.-vii.
204 Seux, *Hymnes et Prières*, p. 18.

I. Hymnic Introduction
II. Lamentation
    a. Description of distress
    b. Confession of sin
    c. *Ahulap* formula
III. Prayer
    a. Presentation of self
    b. Specific prayers of forgiveness etc.
IV. Concluding formulae
    a. The thanksgiving formula (Promessa/Gelubde)
    b. Intercession of other deities
    c. Final formula.[205]

3.2.2.1 Introduction

The hymnic introduction tends to be a precative, sometimes of benediction, sometimes of appeal, but in the extant examples, always addressed to deity.[206]

3.2.2.2 Lamentation

The lament which follows is presented in typical lament fashion with all of the characteristic expressions: tears, weeping, moaning, sighing, wailing, distress, woe, full of sorrow, oppressed, etc.

There is in the lament unit a breadth of sin-consciousness expressed in the *eršahunga* ranging from a sense of unspeakable wrong-doing to a claim of ignorant, unwitting transgression. For example:

O my queen, many are my transgression, [great are my sins].[207]

I am unaware of the fault that I have committed,
I am unaware of the infraction that I have committed,
I am unaware of having acted contrary to the prohibition,
I am unaware of the awful thing I treaded upon.[208]

The confession portion of the lament is followed by the *ahulap* formula which often serves as a transition to the actual appeal or prayer.

---

[205] To which he adds: "It should be understood, however, that these elements do not follow a rigid sequence but may vary considerably in their order and prominence. Every formula is not necessarily represented in each psalm. Moreover, there is an individualistic element which so differentiates each composition that it is impossible to define in detail what is normative." E. Dalglish, *Psalm Fifty-One in the Light of Ancient Near Eastern Patternism* (Leiden: Brill, 1962), p. 22.

[206] K. 1296 = IV R. 21* No. 2, lines A-E, 1-5, BBP, p. 1. Cf. IV R. 10, lines 1-17, BBP, pp. 39-40.

[207] K. 3153 rev. line 11, BBP, p. 22.

[208] IV R 10, lines 26-29, Seux, *Hymnes et Prières*, pp. 139-143.

This formula is characterized by three phrases which occur in the inter-linear Sumerian/Akkadian *eršahunga*s: *muš-a* (Akk. *ahulap*), an exclamation used to express or seek compassion;[209] *me-na-se* (Akk. *adi-mati*), "how long?"; and *ib-si* (Akk. *maṣi*), "it is enough." One example from an interlinear text is K. 4623, lines 17-20:

> O my queen, in anguish I have uttered cries in pain to thee;
> Command my release.
> O my queen, for thy servant command, "It is enough,"
> And may thy heart be at rest.

Another example is K. 101, reverse, lines 5-8:

> Command my release,
> May thy passion be stilled.
> How long, O my lady,
> Until thy face be turned?[210]

3.2.3 Hebrew Individual Laments

The Hebrew Bible contains numerous examples of laments of the individual. Both those that complain of personal suffering and those that also include a penitential expression are amply represented.[211] For the most part, the individual laments are quite similar in form to the communal laments. Westermann summarizes the genre of the individual lament as being composed of three main elements: "*address* (often with an introductory call for help), *complaint* in its threefold form, *petition* with motifs and words which express the fact that a reversal of the complaint has occurred."[212] Thirty years ago, he convincingly demonstrated the threefold subject of the complaint proper: God, the plaintiff, and the enemy. Without arguing that all three of the subjects are consistently present in all laments, Westermann concluded that "these three elements or dimensions alone constitute the lament as complete. What a lament is can only be seen in the relationship of these three components to each other."[213] In more detail, he offered the following model of the individual lament:

> I. Introduction
> II. Lament

---

[209] CAD, s. v. "*ahulap*." Langdon, BBP, p. 81, n. 5. translates it "cessation, release." He refers to A. Poebel, PBS V 152 IX, 8-10.

[210] BBP, pp. 29-31, 80-82.

[211] E.g., Pss. 3-7, 11-12, 16-17, 22-23, 25-28, 36, 38-41, 51-55, 57, 61-64, 71, 73, 86, 88, 130, Jer. 11:15-16,18-20, 20:7-11, Job 29-31.

[212] C. Westermann, *The Psalms*, trans. R. D. Gehrke, (Minneapolis: Augsburg, 1980), p. 59.

[213] Idem., "Struktur und Geschichte der Klage im Alten Testament," ZAW 66 (1954): 47.

III. Confession of confidence
IV. Petition
V. Double wish
VI. (Confidence of being heard)
VII. Vow of praise[214]

As the individual laments found their place in the personal devotional and cultic life of the ancient Near East, the adaptation of the developing genre to the public and corporate life of the representative peoples was virtually assured.[215]

3.3 *Funeral Dirge*

Another type of composition which relates to the communal lament in matters of theme and forms is the funeral dirge. The primary emotion common to both is grief: that intense mental anguish and sorrow experienced in the face of loss. In the Sumerian literature there are two types of dirge: the one having to do with the gods and the other with humans.

3.3.1 **Elegy for a God**

The first type I have termed mytho-cultic because of its mythic content and its apparent role in the cult. The precise role seems unclear. This is primarily because of the disagreement over the meaning of the death of Tammuz. A common view is that Tammuz dies and is resurrected each year.[216] Kramer speaks against this "prevalent view" and argues that Tammuz did not die and resurrect annually. Rather, the Sumerians, he argues, believed that once Tammuz died he "stayed dead" in the nether world and never "rose again."[217] This type is exemplified by those examples in which Inanna *et al.*, grieved the departure of Tammuz to the nether world. An example is CT XV 26.[218] It is structured thus:

---

[214] Idem., *Praise of God in the Psalms*, trans. K. R. Crim (Richmond: Knox, 1965), pp. 66-69, 156.

[215] See Gunkel-Begrich, *Einleitung*, pp. 11, 175ff. Cf. also Mowinckel, *Psalms*, vol. II, pp. 18ff., who sees a much greater involvement of the so-called I-psalms in the congregational cultus. The actual distinction between those I-psalms which are indeed individual and those which are representative-congregational is not always easy to make. I must agree, however, with Mowinckel's observation on p. 20 that "there is no contrast between what is cultic and ritual and what is personally felt and experienced. It is not here a question of either/or." Though this is claimed specifically for the Hebrew laments, much the same might be said of the Sumero-Akkadian compositions.

[216] See S. Moscati, *The Face of the Ancient Orient* (Garden City, N.Y.: Doubleday, 1962), p. 26.

[217] S. Kramer, "Sumerian Literature and the Bible," *Analecta Biblica* 12 (1959):198.

[218] = K 23658. See M. Witzel *Tammuz-Liturgien und Verwandtes*, AnOr 10 (1935); SAHG, pp. 185-186.

I. Lamentation for the distant son. 1-6
II. Lamentation for the city and house. 7-8
III. Lamentation for the produce of the land. 9-20
   A. Crops. 9-10
   B. Flocks and Herds. 11
   C. People. 12
   D. Natural resources. 13-20
IV. Lamentation for the palace. 21

It begins: "I raise a lamentation for the distance, For my distant son I raise a lamentation." Sections II through IV demonstrate a great similarity in that most of the lines begin and end about the same:

> This lament is for the barley, he has produced the seed furrow.
> ...
>
> This lament is for mother and child, he has produced man and woman.
> This lament is for the great river, he has produced the 'Carp-stream.'
> ...
> This lament is for the palace, he has produced long life.

3.3.2 Funeral Dirge

The second type is exemplified by the two funeral songs translated by S. N. Kramer.[219] This tablet is assumed to have been copied c. 1700 B.C. at Nippur from a possibly much earlier composition. The first text on the tablet consists of 112 lines; the second, 66 lines. Both are dirges recited by one individual, Ludingirra by name, but each eulogizes a different person. The first is an elegy for his father and the second is for his wife. The structure of the first is much more detailed. It is represented as follows:

I. Prologue, 1-20
II. Lament, 21-62
III. Prayer of appeasement, 63-69
IV. Lament, 70-75
V. Prayer, 76-112
   A. Blessings, 76
   B. Imprecations, 77-84
   C. Blessings, 85-112

The structure of the second lament on the same tablet follows the same general order although shorter:

---

[219] *Two Elegies on a Pushkin Museum Tablet: A New Sumerian Literary Genre*, (Moscow: Oriental Literary Publ., 1960). M. Lambert also lists a dirge to Ur-Nammu he entitles "The Liturgy of the Dead" under the category "liturgical hymns" in his "La Littérature Sumerienne," p. 196.

I. Prologue, 113-121
II. Grief narrative, 122-159
III. Lament, 160-168
IV. Prayer-Blessings, 169-178

3.3.2.1 Prologue

In both examples the prologue describes the setting of the dirge. Both are set in poetic form except that the first begins with what Kramer calls "a relatively prosaic two-line statement."[220]

3.3.2.2 Lamentation

As Kramer translates it, the lament section of the first elegy begins with a vocative address to the deceased and to Nanna and describes the grief experienced by the survivors. There is "what seems to be a brief seven-line prayer for Nanna's welfare" interposed near the end of the lament section. This is followed by a series of imprecations.

3.3.2.3 Curses

The eight-line section of imprecations is preceded by a one-line appeal or prayer: "May the eldest son [establish(?)] for you your...firm foundations." The imprecatory section identifies the object of the curse, viz., the man who killed the deceased. It then attributes vengeance to the king, the shepherd, the (personal) god, Utu. The section closes with a listing of curses.

3.3.2.4 Prayers

The final unit of the dirge begins with a benediction on Nanna/Utu but consists mainly of an extended series of one-line appeals on behalf of the deceased and his family. For example:

May Nanna decree your fate (favourably) on the "Day of Sleep,"
...
[May] Nedu and Etana [be] your allies,
...
May he [annul] for you your promises(?) (and) debts,
May he [erase] the guilt of the household [from] the accounts, . . .
May the children you begot be written(?) down(?) for leadersh[ip](?)

Of the dirges that have been translated and treated in various studies, the majority fall in the category "Elegy for a God." Regarding funeral dirges for people, it should be noted that the two dirges translated by

---

220 Ibid., p. 48.

Kramer may be ideal rather than typical. It is Kramer's conclusion that these were composed by "one of the 'professors' who worked and taught in . . . the e-dub-ba, and . . . the compositions themselves were used as texts to be studied and copied by the students.[221] There does seem to be a logical connection between the funeral dirge and the other forms of lament including the communal lament. It seems that the funeral dirge is more or less a personal lament in that it is generally recited by a select few, primarily relatives and close friends, perhaps accompanied by some hired mourners.[222] If this is so, it is clear that not just one individual is involved in its performance but a select representative community. This is to be expected because death has an unraveling effect on a community, touching not only the family but also upsetting a wider circle of social relationships. Therefore, the matter of the loss is addressed directly both by words and by action. Herzog's studies have indicated that a common first reaction toward the dead is flight. In "primitive" cultures entire villages have relocated to avoid contact, real or imagined, with the corpse. The funeral customs then serve as a secondary reaction on the part of a given community to help deal with the human horror of death and thus are a therapeutic as much as a sacral rite.[223] Statistically, one would assume that human death must impinge upon a culture far more often than does the political demise of a community. Hence, funeral rites are going to exert a significant influence upon the ways a people publicly express grief over the loss or the threat of loss of their communal existence or of significant symbols of that communal existence.

3.3.3 Funeral Ceremony

From the data available in the biblical literature, it seems that the main feature of the funeral ceremony per se was the recitation or chanting of the dirge apparently at the bier begun, as we have seen, by the relatives and close friends. Other symbolic gestures of mourning are reported, such as when David tore his clothes and lay on the ground at the death of Amnon. But this is part of the mourning response; it is not specifically described as part of a funeral ceremony. Other customs include the uncovering of the feet and head and the covering of facial hair which Ezekiel was prohibited from doing at the death of his wife.[224]

---

221 *Two Elegies*, p. 50.
222 E.g., Gen. 23:2, 50:10; II Sam. 11:26. Cf. I Sam. 25:1, 28:3; II Sam. 1:11-12, 3:31.
223 E. Herzog, *Psyche and Death: Archaic Myths and Modern Dreams in Analytical Psychology* (London: Hodder and Stoughton, 1966.)
224 Ezek. 24:16-17, 22-23.

Though proscribed in Leviticus and Deuteronomy,[225] the custom of shaving at least part of the head and lacerating the body as a part of the mourning ceremony seems to have been practiced in Israel as was common in the ancient Semitic world.[226]

3.3.4 Mourners Guild

It seems that in connection with the importance placed upon the funeral rites in the Near Eastern cultures, there arose a professional order of lamenters to whom fell the task of sometimes composing, collecting and rendering the dirges.

Composing was apparently not always done by a professional. For example, David, out of his grief over the deaths of Saul and, perhaps especially, Jonathan, most likely composed his own dirge which is preserved in II Sam. 1:19-27, where (v. 18) it is said to be included in the Book of the Upright. There were, however, those specially trained in the art of keening. This group included both male and female mourners as can be seen from cases such as the lament over the death of Josiah by Jeremiah. He was said to have been accompanied by a group of השרים והשרות "male and female singers" who ויאמרו...בקינותיהם על יאשוהו עד היום "speak in their dirges about Josiah to this day."[227] This combination of male and female mourners parallels the general situation observed in Mesopotamia.[228] Amos speaks of יודעי נהי "those who know mourning song" who are summoned to join in the מספד "wailing."[229]

Although the treatment of the connection of the funeral dirge and the communal lament is yet to come, a passage from Jeremiah is noteworthy at this point. In response to the threat of national disaster, Jeremiah draws from funereal traditions. In the face of massive disaster, he charges the people to call for the מקוננות "mourning women"—those whose job it is to know and chant the dirges—they must hurry and lead the people in wailing. It should also be noted that this term מקוננות is in parallel with the term חכמות "skilled women," perhaps an indication of the skill required in the execution of the mourner's tasks.[230] In the same

---

225 Lev. 19:26-28, Deut. 14:1 ff.
226 See J. Morgenstern, *Rites of Birth, Marriage, Death and Kindred Occasions among the Semites*, (Cincinnati: Hebrew Union College, 1966), pp. 164-166 for a survey of mourning practices in ancient Israel. Cf. T. H. Gaster, *Myth, Legend and Custom in the Old Testament* (New York: Harper, 1969), pp. 590-602, for a survey of this particular aspect of the mourning rites from the perspective of cultural anthropology and comparative religions.
227 II Chron. 35:25.
228 See above p. 27ff.
229 Amos 5:16.
230 Jer. 9:16.

composition, due apparently to the magnitude of this anticipated "funeral," the wailing women are instructed to increase their corps: they are charged למדנה בנותיכם נהי ואשה רעותה קינה "teach your daughters wailing, and each her neighbor a dirge."[231]

The Akkadian term *bikitu* denotes 1) weeping, tears, 2) sorrow, grief, 3) wailing, mourning (over the dead). This third category may refer either to the general experience of mourning over a death or to a cultic ceremony. The texts in which this term occurs indicate that certain symbolic acts accompanied such mourning. For example, in connection with a formal public mourning observance, the text ABL 518: r. 10 speaks of the mourning "and the unkempt hair (that goes with it)." BRM 4, 6:44 says of the priests: "their heads are covered with their rent garments while they sing dirges (*ṣirihtu*), wailings (*nissati*), and laments (*bikiti*)." In the expression *ša bikiti* the term *bikitu* is taken to denote a professional mourner.[232] The term *bakkitu* denotes a "wailing woman" who in one text "circumambulates the city."[233] In other instances there is indication that the mourning rites took place at "the temple where they wail for the one who has been taken away."[234] This mourning may continue for varying periods of time from a full day to six days and seven nights.[235]

Ugaritic literature also provides some testimony to the presence and role of such professional mourners. Cognates of these same two terms occur: *bkyt* and *mšspdt* both in parallel with each other.[236] The former is from *bky* "to weep (for)," hence "weeping women;" the latter is from the causative of *spd* "to wail/mourn," hence "mourning women." T. H. Gaster concludes "that they *lead* the dirge, which is then, apparently, taken up by others."[237] These two passages in close proximity to each other contain the only extant occurrences to either term I have been able to find in the Ugaritic texts.[238]

---

231 See v. 19.
232 See IVR 11:21 ff. CAD, s.v. "*bikitu*."
233 ZA, 51 138:67. Cf. *bakû*, "to wail (over a dead person), to mourn" and *ubkû*, "to be drenched with tears, to commence a wailing."
234 KAV 42 r. 9, RA 14 174 r. 18.
235 CAD, s.v. "*baku*."
236 I Aqht 4.171-2, 183.
237 *Thespis* (New York: Harper, 1950), p. 369.
238 A third term which also occurs only in this passage is suggested by Gaster as having to do with mourning customs. He hypothesizes *pẓgm ǵr* means "*men who tear their skin*," thus indicating male members of the mourner's guild, *Myth*, p. 871, sect. 339, n. 4. This expression is difficult. Gordon does not offer a suggested meaning for *pẓgm* in his Glossary, and Ginsberg leaves the term untranslated, C. H. Gordon, UT (Rome: Pontifical Biblical Institute, 1965), 19:2040, p. 468. Cf. H. L. Ginsberg, "The Tale of Aqht," AQHT C iii, lines 173, 185, ANET, p. 155. Perhaps if *ǵr* is actually a component of the term, it would shed some light on the expression, though in perhaps a somewhat different direction than "tearing skin." Of the

3.3.5 Formal Weeping and Lament

Without much in the way of extended funeral dirges preserved in their primary form in the Bible,[239] it becomes necessary to look for clues to the nature of the formal weeping in the adaptations of the dirge in the prophets. For example, Amos's reference to the saying (chanting?) repeatedly הו הו "Alas!—Alas!" or "Oh no! Oh no!"[240] or the term הוי: "often this interjection was addressed to specific persons:

"Oh no! my brother!"

or the chant could be addressed to the king:

"Oh no! The lord!"

or the idea may occur without the specific interjection:

"Oh my son! Absalom my son!
Oh my son Absalom!
If only I had died in your stead!
. . .
Oh my son Absalom!
Absalom my son! Oh my son!"[241]

At any rate there seems to be a tendency to repetitious ejaculations—whether הוי/הו or any number of other expressions, none of which are uniformly or universally used.[242]

Sometimes there seemed to be merely a howl repeated in perhaps an off-beat cadence. Interestingly enough, the onomatopoeic word ילל occurs only in the hiphil—"to make a yell, cause a howl"—always in stressful situations dealing with destruction either accomplished or

---

three different roots ǵr listed in UT, one, ǵr III is defined as "to groan," or some other similar kind of utterance (UT 19:1985, p. 465, cf. Ba`al and `Anat Cycle, 16:68, 6, 7, p. 180. Cf. RS 19:54 "lowing, mooing." Cf. CRAIBL p. 181, n. 1). Thus this may well be a reference to a third group of this time, male mourners who are called to perform the keening in the courtyard of Daniel's palace.

239 H. Jahnow, *Leichenlied*, p. 2 ff.

240 Amos 5:16.

241 Amos 5:16; I Kgs. 13:30; Jer. 22:18 cf. 34:5. הוי has been especially identified with the lament or dirge. See Jahnow, *Leichenlied*, p. 83 ff. See especially W. Janzen, *Mourning Cry and Woe Oracle* (Berlin: de Gruyter, 1972) who argues that "there can be no doubt that הוי is a term associated with lamentation for the dead." p. 1. But, Janzen argues, though הוי was initially a call to mourning, it "became specialized to express the foreboding and threatening aspect of that call, a function for which the lament-vengeance range that constitutes its background made it immensely suitable." p. 90. It should be noted, however, that the expression is also used in non-lament contexts, e.g., Isa 55:1.

242 E.g., איך/איכה do not always express a lamentation. Sometimes they serve merely as an ejaculatory expression. Nor does every dirge or lament make use of the expressions.

threatened.[243] All the occurrences except that in Joel refer to the political disintegration of a nation; in Joel the threat is natural disaster, but the potential is virtually the same. One clue to the nature of the "howl" is offered by Micah who compares it to the cry of an ostrich.[244]

In connection with the scazonic cadence mentioned above there are two lines of evidence that may indicate that this may well have been a fairly common characteristic.

The first has to do with the so-called qinah, 3:2, meter. As its name suggests, this off-beat meter came to be commonly identified with the dirge especially after Budde's treatment of the meter in the book of Lamentations. Gray posits that Budde's main contribution in this regard was to point out "1.) the nature of the unequal division of the rhythmical periods; and 2.) the extent to which the rhythm characteristic of Lamentations i. - iv. occurs elsewhere in the Old Testament."[245] Budde did recognize, however, that the 3:2 cadence was neither universal nor exhaustive within the book of Lamentation and the other Hebrew lament literature. There were variations, e.g., 4:3 or 4:2, but, he argued, there was always an uneven balance.[246] This does not seem to be borne out by the extant texts, however, e.g. the presence of an apparent 2:2 meter. As Sievers demonstrated, there is a substantial number of lines in the book of Lamentations which contain balanced cola rather than an off-beat pattern. He also pointed out that the so-called qinah appears in other kinds of poetry which do not deal with lament themes.[247] The point is, however, that the uneven meter is indeed apparent.[248]

The second line of evidence would connect the choliambic effect of the off-beat meter with a funereal dance, though admittedly from a different milieu, both historically, geographically, and culturally. Herodotus reports the funeral practices of the Egyptians in the fifth century B.C.

---

243 Of its thirty-one occurrences, all in the latter prophets, eleven are in Isaiah, nine in Jeremiah. The rest are scattered.

244 Mic. 1:8.

245 G. B. Gray, The Forms of Hebrew Poetry (London, 1915; reprint ed., New York: KTAV, 1972), p. 91.

246 K. Budde, "Das Hebräische Klagelied," ZAW (1882): 4 ff.

247 E. Sievers, Metrische Studien, vol. 1, sect. 1 pp. 120-123, sect. 2, pp. 550-563, cf. sect. 1, p. 116. See D. Hillers' survey of the qinah in his Lamentations, Anchor Bible 7a (Garden City, N.Y.: Doubleday, 1972), pp. xxx-xxxiii. See also W. Rudolph, Klagelieder, KAT 17 (Gütersloh: Mohn, 1962), pp. 192-193.

248 J. Lundbom, Jeremiah: A Study in Ancient Hebrew Rhetoric, Dissertation Series, no. 18 (Missoula, Mont.: SBL, 1975), notes that "the canons [of Hebrew meter] are still as obscure as they were in the time of Lowth." Note, however, the versatility of the "off-beat" meter in Ugaritic: UT 13:110, 112. The 3:2 cadence is not uncommon, and one function suggested by Gordon is to induce a "climactic effect," which may occur even in administrative texts. See UT, p. 133 n. 1.

without any specific reference to a limping dance.[249] The point of connection is drawn by E. Lane, who describes the funeral practices observed in the last century in Egypt along the Upper Nile. There, for three days groups of both male and female mourners bewail the death. The description of the female mourners' performance is remarkably close to that described by Herodotus. But what Lane observed that Herodotus at least did not report was how the women would "dance with a slow movement, and in an irregular manner; generally pacing about, and raising and depressing the body. This dance is continued for an hour or more, and is performed twice or three times in the course of the day."[250]

Gaster suggests this limping dance is witnessed in the *Aqht* myth by the word he reconstructs as *mrqdm*. The idea is suggestive but the state of preservation of the text in question leaves only *mr[ ]d[ ]* from which to reconstruct the word. The Hebrew רקד which he cites seems exclusively to denote a skip or leap of joy. In fact, it is used in antithetic parallelism to ספד "wail, mourn" in Eccl. 3:4. There is no doubt, however, that a skipping gait would, especially in slow motion, produce a limping effect. Gaster argues that,

> this is also the normal meaning of Accadian *raqadu* and of Arabic *r-q-ts* and *r-q-z*. But the Accadian syllabary (B.M. 83-1-18, 1846, rev. i, 6-7 = Pinches, PSBA 18 [1896], 253) lists *ru-qu-ud-du* [sic] as a term meaning "professional mourner" (equivalent of Sumerian *LU.TU.IGI.GUGU(?)*, "one who weeps with troubled eye"), while in Arabic and Syriac, the corresponding nouns *raqtsath* and *marqodeta* denote a special kind of hopping or limping dance performed at funerals.[251]

Gaster also cites I Sam. 15:32, the Agag incident where מעד used: מערנות "tottering, shaking"[252] to describe his movement or gait as he recites a kind of dirge: "Surely the bitterness of death is past."[253]

3.4 *Sitz im Leben*

There seems to be a connection between the various forms of lament: funeral dirge, individual lament, and communal lament. As already suggested, the occasion of a death would bring the clan and close friends

---

[249] Book II, sect 85.

[250] *An Account of the Manners and Customs of the Modern Egyptians*, 5th ed. (London: Murray, 1871), p. 528.

[251] T. H. Gaster, *Thespis*, pp. 370. Note: should read *ra-qu-ud-du* above. Note also that Pinches cited a Syriac meaning of "bitter weeping." Cf. Jahnow, *Leichenlied*, p. 75, n. 6, refers to the staggering, reeling, lamenting women.

[252] Note that the LXX understood מערנות mean τρέμων, "tremble, quiver," and the Vulgate, *tremens* "tremble, shudder."

[253] Gaster, *Thespis*, p. 371.

together to deal with the loss of this individual to that societal group. There were various roles to be played by the various individuals, depending somewhat on the level of the previously held relationship. Without a doubt, the response to the death began within a rather limited circle: the one(s) who witnessed the death or found the body of the individual and the immediate family. Much of the evidence mentioned above indicates that the funeral activities seldom, if ever, remained limited to this group. Soon the larger community would become involved and with apparent regularity, a special troupe of mourners were brought in to lead in the keening. It became a community event.

Meanwhile, the phenomenon of the individual lament per se makes its appearance. It is amply attested in the extant literature, especially Hebrew. It finds its role in the cult in the ancient Near East as the devout take their personal calamities—be they sickness, persecution, economic reversal or guilt—to their god(s).[254] These expressions formed an integral part of the practice of Hebrew religion as well. Often, in the individual laments, the given issue of suffering was linked to the question of sin. Widengren shows that this was common also in the Sumero-Akkadian individual laments and cites numerous examples. There, especially, it seemed that personal calamity was integral to an awareness of sin. For "in Babylonia the criterion of sin was to be overtaken by misfortune. Not until this happened did anyone begin to think of his sins."[255] His point is that he feels that this is the natural chain of events in the case of unwitting sin. The problem is, at least in the Hebrew literature, to establish that unwitting sin was the prime focus of the lament response. The case seems to be that the lamenter sometimes protests his innocence and hence, the apparent inappropriateness of the calamitous events.[256] The psalmists occasionally refer to "unknown" or "hidden" sins, but these references are relatively rare and are not included in the laments.[257] Just as often, the lamenter acknowledges that indeed he has sinned and pleads forgiveness as a necessary step to reconciliation with God and relief from the pressures of the misfortune, or more properly, chastisement, in view.[258] Little wonder then, that in the face of impending calamity—whether the harbingers of drought, famine, or pestilence, or the threat of military attack by the enemy—or in the aftermath of such a calamity, the lament was put into service. Likewise, especially in the lat-

---

254 See Mowinckel, *Psalms*, vol. II, pp. 1 ff.
255 Widengren, *Psalms*, p. 177.
256 Cf. Pss. 5, 17, 26.
257 Cf. Ps. 19.
258 E.g., Pss. 51, 130.

ter case when the capital city was destroyed and the socio-political structure had undergone great convulsion, the adaptation and utilization of
the funereal traditions seems most natural.

What is clear, however, is that while there are similarities that
demonstrate lines of probable influence, the community rarely, if ever,
arbitrarily pressed these forms into service without adaptation. After a
most extensive study of the "folk poetry" of the Hebrew Bible, focusing
on funeral customs and dirges, etc., Jahnow concludes that there is a
marked distinction between the actual funeral dirges and the other
laments which display certain affinities with them. She states that the
funeral dirge can be found, e.g., in the book of Lamentations "only in
modified form . . . from an originally completely secular type into a religious poem."[259] While the point made of the clear distinctions is significant, one wonders if the classification of secular [profan] can accurately
be applied to the bulk of ancient Near Eastern funeral customs and
especially the Hebrew customs.

At any rate, the cultural phenomenon of lament in the face of
impending calamity or its results is well attested. The appropriation of
these means of expression by the community seems to have been facili-
tated by existing structures. The existence and role of the so-called
"professional" mourner's guild was mentioned above. On the broader
community—or national—level, there was already in place the necessary
structure to perform the same role, viz., the cult. The role, e.g., of the
priests and/or prophets in composing, maintaining, and performing the
laments has been understood for some time.[260] This is borne out in
Mesopotamian literature as well. Referring to the occurrence of *gala*
(UŠ.KU) = *kalû* in a royal inscription,[261] Langdon infers that it denoted
those who were professional chanters of the dirge but were not
"consecrated priests, at least not in the early period." He suggested that
the term "probably describes him [the lament psalmist] as a man in the
temple service who chants songs to appease the gods. In fact we shall
find that public temple services originated from the desire to pacify the
gods whose anger manifests itself in causing all human woes."[262] These

259 *Leichenlied*, p. 170.
260 Gunkel-Begrich, *Einleitung*, p. 124 identifies a *Vorbeter* "prayer leader" who leads in
the cultic recitation of the lament.
261 F. Thureau-Dangin, *Die Sumerischen und Akkadischen Königsinschriften*, vol. 1 VAB
(Leipzig: Hinrichs, 1907), p. 50, X:22-30.
262 BL, pp. vii-viii, where he cites the syllabary published by Hrozný in ZA 19, p. 363.

official liturgical psalmists were sometimes joined by a *naru* "professional singer" in the chanting of the liturgical laments.[263]

In later periods, the guilds, which had earlier been composed of generally lower class individuals,[264] came to be a somewhat elite group—"a learned community, a kind of college which studied and edited the official liturgical literature."[265] They apparently became the sole custodians and liturgists of the laments and other liturgies. Their function came to be limited to the temple liturgy where they served alongside the priests. The *kalû* did not participate in funerals per se. This was taken over by the *naru*.[266]

There is also the feature of the fast. The fast might be the occasions for the observance of any of the forms of lament. Often in the Hebrew setting, the fast was the occasion for making an inquiry of the LORD for wisdom and direction regarding some, usually weighty, situation. But the fast was also a part of the funeral ceremony when they would fast in mourning for a period of seven days.[267] The fast is found mentioned in connection with community or national events associated with the lament as well. The passage in Joel mentioned above is a graphic example.[268] Here the prophet seems to imply that fasting may serve as a link between the two elements he is dealing with: sin and calamity, which are bound in a causal relationship. The fasting is both expressive of reaction to woe in the face of the calamity and expressive of remorse and repentance in the face of the sin with which they have been indicted. A parallel example may be found in Jeremiah where drought and famine have brought great discomfiture. The heads of Judah lead out in lamentation by assuming the posture of mourning—sitting on the ground with heads covered,[269] whereupon the LORD tells Jeremiah: "When they fast, I am not about to hear their cry." The fast was connected to a communal lament

---

[263] See Hartmann, "Musik," pp. 147 ff.

[264] See RTC 17 from J. A. Craig, *Assyrian and Babylonian Religious Texts* (Leipzig: Hinrichs, 1895-7), translated in ZA 25, p. 212, deals with the sale of the son of a poor man who was a temple psalmist. Langdon also cites a text, DP 99, rev. I, where one "Hensa, an inferior *kalû* is one of the mule-herds of the temple estate." See also DP 100, rev. I, in BL, p. x, n. 3. Langdon notes other professions pursued by the *kalû*, viz.: beer merchant(?), and notary public.

[265] Langdon, BL, p. xii. Cf. CAD "*kalû A*" s.v.

[266] Ibid., p. xxx-xxi.

[267] E.g., I Sam. 31:13 refers to a seven-day mourning-fast after the burial of Saul and his sons. Gen. 50:3, while not directly specifying a fast, speaks of a seventy-day period of weeping ceremonies. This does not appear to be the rule, however. It seems best understood in the context of the Egyptian culture, and it seems almost to bear some of the marks of a state funeral. Note the late, more normal mourning period of seven days in v. 10. Cf. also Jdt. 8:5-6, 16:24, Sir. 22:12.

[268] Joel 2:12, 15.

[269] Jer. 14:2-3. Cf. Gunkel-Begrich, *Einleitung*, pp. 117-119.

making complaint and appeal to the LORD, and the fast and lament are set in the cultic context by the reference to the burnt offering and grain offering made at this time.[270] Similarly in the Psalm laments, there is ample indication that the lament was often accompanied by a fast.[271]

Fasting in this regard does not seem to play much of a role, if any, in the Mesopotamian lament rituals. This may be due in part to what appears to be a somewhat different view of sin. Krecher posits that:

> the basic tenor of the lament songs does not question the guilt of the people who might have deserved the divine punishment. In this regard, the lament songs fit themselves into the framework of the other Sumerian religious texts which . . . do not recognize the problem of personal guilt.[272]

Even so, there are expressions contained in some of the laments which do seem to indicate a consciousness of perhaps at least a collective sense of culpability. One such example may be found in the eleventh *kirugu* of the "Lament over Ur" where Nanna is addressed:

> Verily thy black-headed people who have been cast away,
>   prostrate themselves unto thee!
> Verily thy city which has been made into ruins set up a
>   wail to thee!
> . . .
> Undo the sins of its . . . !
> . . .
> May every evil heart of its people be pure before thee!
> May the heart of those who dwell in the land be good
>   before thee![273]

Another is in the "Lament to Ištar" in which the "goddess of goddesses" is implored:

> Look at me, my mistress, accept my entreaty,
>   Look at me in mercy and hear my prayer!
> Speak my pardon and may your mind be soothed!
> . . .
> I am begging you, yes you! Undo my spell!
> Undo my guilt, my offense, my misdeed, my sin,
>   Forget my offense and accept my entreaty![274]

---

[270] Jer. 14:12.
[271] Pss. 35:13; 69:11, 12; 109:24.
[272] SKly, p. 49.
[273] LU, lines 421-422, 429-430, 433-434.
[274] E. Ebeling, "Klagelied an Istar," *Altorientalische Texte und Bilder zum Alten Testament*, ed. H. Gressmann (Leipzig: de Gruyter, 1926-7), pp. 257-260, lines 43-45, 80-82.

But both in the Hebrew Psalms and Lamentations and in other references to the communal laments contained in the pre-exilic historical and prophetic narratives, there does not seem to be any indication that these communal mourning ceremonies were practiced on any regular basis. Rather, they were used at "called meetings," assemblies that were convened in response to a given course of events, or as Mowinckel calls them: ad hoc festivals.[275] The Book of Esther indicates, however, that at least by the Persian period there had developed a prescribed scenario to be followed. The successful machinations of Haman against the Jews prompted just such a public lamenting as described above with the sackcloth and fasting and weeping and the wailing of the dirges. But later, as Purim is established as a regular festival, it is said that there had also been established דברי הצמות וזעקתם "the instructions/or the manner of their fasts and lamentation."[276]

As with the Hebrew laments, so with the Sumero-Akkadian laments, Langdon notes that "in later times it became customary to fix the public lamentation service."[277] This is borne out by the extant "ritual calendars."[278] Whether we have fixed services per se in the Hebrew Bible may be debated. Those Hebrew laments which deal with the fall and destruction of Jerusalem came to be recited at the observance of the anniversary of the occasion(s) they treat on the ninth of Ab.[279] This practice of anniversary observation of major events in the life of Israel-Judah came to be a fairly common custom in post-exilic times. From pre-exilic times, the most graphic portrayal of the conduct of one such national lamentation is found in Joel.[280] The priests, dressed in lament garb, would call the leaders and the people to the temple for a convocation to utter a lament to the LORD between the porch and the altar.[281] Obviously, after the fall of Jerusalem and the destruction of the temple, for at least the next eight or nine decades, this was not the locus of the rites of lamentation. While there is no reference to a lament at the dedication of the restored temple in Jerusalem, the discouraged mood of the

---

[275] I Kgs. 21:9, 12; Joel 1:14. Cf. Mowinckel, Psalms, vol. I, p. 193.
[276] Est. 4:1-3; 9:31.
[277] SBL, p. xii.
[278] S. Langdon, "Calendars of Liturgies and Prayers," AJSL 42 (1926): 110-127.
[279] See below, Ch. 4, "Sitz im Leben."
[280] Following A. Kapelrud's argumentation for a pre-exilic date, Joel Studies (Uppsala: Uppsala Universitets Årsskrift, 1948), pp. 191 ff.
[281] Joel 2:17, cf. Jdt. 4:9-15.

occasion may well have lent itself to a ritual bemoaning of the loss of the former glory which had not been restored.[282]

3.5 Musical Instrumentation

Certain aspects of the recitation of the lament ritual have already been treated in the section on the guild. There is yet another aspect related to the performance, viz., instrumental accompaniment.

Regarding the Hebrew laments, the information available does not indicate whether, for the most part, the laments were performed with accompaniment. However, they probably were not recited a cappella. There is just no explicit evidence to indicate how the accompaniment was effected for any given composition.

Jeremiah refers to a public lament for Moab as a result of the doom pronounced upon it by the LORD. He says: על כן לבי למואב כחללים "יהמה ולבי אל אנשי קיר חרש כחלילים יהמה "therefore, my heart shrills like the flutes for Moab; my heart even shrills like the flutes for the men of Kir-Heres," indicating the appropriateness of such a sound in lamentation.[283] Similarly, in another lament for Moab, Isaiah says: על כן מעי למואב ככנור יהמו "Therefore my insides sound like a lyre for Moab."[284] The fact is that these instruments, the חליל "flute" and כנור "lyre," are cited in almost every instance as accompanying some usually joyous celebration. This would lead one to believe that there is nothing necessarily inherent in the instruments which would identify them with the dirge.[285] The point must be either that the pitch or tone of the חליל "flute" was the closest to describing how the "heart felt," or that the flute could be played in such a way as to express the mournful mood of the lament rather than the lilting notes of joy. Similarly, the type of sounds emitted by the כנור "lyre" may have seemed to fit by analogy either the sounds or the feelings (or both) of one's insides in turmoil.

---

[282] Cf. Hag. 2:2-4, Zech. 1:12, "Oh LORD of hosts, how long will you not be compassionate toward Jerusalem and the cities of Judah, which you have sentenced these seventy years?"

[283] Jer. 48:36, cf. Isa. 15; 16:7. The translation value of המה is affected by the context. KB, s.v. "המה," indicates the meaning "to make noise, groan, growl, bark." Of a musical instrument it indicates the denotation of making a sound, presumably of that instrument. Therefore, when predicated by a lyre, the value of "sound" is most appropriate. Of the flute, the English verb "to shrill" might be appropriate.

[284] Isa. 16:11.

[285] On the contrary, Mowinckel posits that the occurrence of the אל הנחילות "to the flutes" notation in the title of Ps. 5, a protective Psalm, and על מחלת "to the flute" in the titles of Pss. 53 and 88, individual laments, "and the analogy from the Babylonian seems to indicate that the flute belonged to the rites of the psalms or lamentation, cf. Jer. 48:36; Matt. 9:23." Psalms, vol. II, p. 210. The question seems to be whether belong is the appropriate term when the same instrument is used so frequently under quite opposite conditions.

However, there does not seem to be any direct evidence pointing to any special instrumentation unique to the Hebrew laments. The data does, however, support the idea that the laments were accompanied. This may be inferred from two different lines of evidence. First, there is the ample evidence of the use of instrumentation in other aspects of Israel's cultic practice. Amos, e.g., though in a negative way, cites the use of songs accompanied by harps during the sacrifice of burnt offerings and grain offerings.[286] Second, there are the notations in a number of the Psalm titles already mentioned.[287]

The case is somewhat different when we turn to the Sumero-Akkadian laments. On the one hand, there are certain parallels with the Hebrew laments, e.g., the use of a fairly broad range of instruments in cultic observances as well as in general entertainment. By broad range I mean that stringed, percussion and wind instruments are all represented in both the literary and graphic documentation from the times of the Sumerians on.[288] And there are a number of specific lamentation texts from the Sumero-Akkadian corpus which themselves make direct reference to their being accompanied by instrumentation.

For example, one temple foundation-laying ceremony prescribes: "You shall chant [the piece] ešabhungaeta to the accompaniment of the halhallatu in the direction of the temple."[289]

Another text dealing with the refurbishing of a ruined temple prescribes: "Facing the temple, you shall sing [the pieces] 'ezi gulgullude,' 'nibišu,' and 'er imšeše.' After this, accompanied on the halhallatu, you shall sing for the gods Ea, Samas, and Marduk [the pieces] 'nitug niginna,' 'utu lugalam,' and 'ešabhungata.'"[290] CT XV, 10, a hymn to Enlil, closes with the colophon nigin 25 mu-bi-im, er-šem-ma, which Langdon translates: "total of 25 lines, a wail of the flute."[291]

---

[286] Amos 5:23.

[287] Cf. J. B. Peters, The Psalms as Liturgies (New York: Macmillan, 1922), p. 44.

[288] F. W. Galpin, The Music of the Sumerians and Their Immediate Successors the Babylonians and Assyrians (Cambridge: University Press, 1937).

[289] Thureau-Dangin, Rituels Accadiens (Paris: Geuthner, 1921), pp. 42-44, cf. ANET, pp. 339-342.

[290] Ibid., p. 34.

[291] SBP, pp. 278-9. Langdon understands eršemma to refer to a flute and is supported by Galpin, who understands the instrument to which it refers, the ŠEM, as a single-pipe (Sumerian Music, p. 17). However, there lacks any scholarly consensus regarding the identification of many of the instruments. Langdon (BL, p. xxxii.) relates the em to the halhallatu, which he identifies as a double flute. CAD, "halhallatu," s.v. describes the instrument as a metal drum covered with a skin head belonging to the tympanum class along with the uppu, manzu, and lilissu. Cohen (CBC, p. 33) identifies the halhallatu as a drum. H. Hartmann, "Die Musik der sumerischen Kultur," (Ph.D. dissertation, Johann Wolfgang Goethe Universität, 1960), points out that the em in the older translations is taken to mean a flute, whereas in the

Another instrument associated with the laments is the *ME-ZU* / *manzu*. It occurs, e.g., in the colophon of both the obverse and reverse sides of the *am-e barana-ra* series over Nippur (SBH 22). The *manzu* is said by Galpin to be some sort of timbrel or tambourine.[292] There are numerous instances, however, where the *manzu* appears to be grouped with other types of drums thus favoring its being identified as a drum.[293]

A third type of instrument, the *balag*, is mentioned so often as to lend its name to a particular sub-genre of the communal lament. This was not the case in the neo-Sumerian period, but Krecher notes four Old Babylonian texts which bear the subscript title *balag-GN* to which Cohen added one more.[294] It was particularly the first millennium copies of the laments which bore the title *balag*. E.g., the series *muten-nu-nunuz gim* contains the colophon in tablet five: "he who sits in thraldom sighs upon a *balag*."[295] Another text includes in the poetic narrative the statement: "Unto the temple god upon a *ba-lag-gu* let us go with a song of petition. The *kalû* psalmists a chant shall sing."[296]

The *balag* is taken to refer to a harp or lyre. This is based on the pictogram published by Deimel.[297] It seems that the primary reason for designating the *balag* a lyre is its association with the voice of a bull in the Gudea cycle (28:17) and the lyre found in the Ur III tombs with a bull on the sound box. The *balag* is depicted as a large, double-barreled, hourglass shaped instrument in the pictograms. The *balag* came to be perhaps the most common designation of a "type" of communal lament so that by the time of Assurbanipal in the mid-seventh century B. C. when the great catalogs were compiled, one[298] lists the incipits of forty-nine different *balag* laments from which the *kalû* could choose. Contenau states that the

---

more recent works it is taken to mean a percussion instrument (p. 216). The term *halhallatu* he equates with *tigi*, which he takes to be a "concussion instrument" or drum (pp. 56, 86). Cf. CAD, s.v. "*halhallatu*," "a kind of drum." It is beyond the scope of this work to deal with the identification of the various instruments. I simply want to point out the presence of instrumentation in given laments. There is agreement that the ŠEM and *halhallatu*) are used to accompany the *eršemma* laments. Cf. SKly, pp. 25 ff.

292 Galpin, *Sumerian Music*, pp. 7, 9 ff., 55-56.
293 CAD, s.v. "*manzu*".
294 SKly, p. 30, n. 60. CBC, p. 6, n. 10.
295 SBP, pp. 166-7.
296 Ibid., pp. 68-69.
297 No. 41 in *Die Liste der archaischen Keilschriften*. See Hartmann, "Musik," pp. 52-67, 210-211. See also discussion in CAD, "*balaggu*" s. v. Cf. The Ebla lexical texts attest the use of balag, *Testi Lessicali*, p. 264 #572: balag = gi-na-ru-$_{(x)}$-um, gi-na-lum, gi-na-rum = כנור 'zither.' Cf. #571: balag-di = na-ti-lu-um.
298 R IV2 53.

catalogs altogether list fifty-seven laments which were accompanied by the *balag* and forty by the *halhallatu*.[299]

Whether or not a definitive identification of each instrument is possible, it is most significant that two of the technical terms of the Sumero-Akkadian lamentations take their name from their association with instrumentation. In spite of the uncertainties of specific identification, it also seems clear that the laments in Mesopotamia were led by people, both men and women, who were specially trained to perform the lamentations.[300] It seems equally clear that this was a musical presentation accompanied by various kinds of instrumentation but probably predominantly percussion instruments. Given the parallels between the Sumero-Akkadian cultures and the Canaanite-Hebrew cultures, and given the role of music and musical instruments in other aspects of the social and religious life of the latter, it seems reasonable to infer that the Hebrew communal laments were likewise accompanied by musical instrumentation.

---

[299] G. Contenau, *Everyday Life in Babylonia and Assyria* (London: Arnold, 1954), p. 282.

[300] See above, Ch. 2, p. 25, n. 90, pp. 27ff., pp. 74ff.

4

Basic Forms of Communal Lament in the Hebrew Bible

4.1 Introduction

This investigation of the Hebrew communal lament begins with the Psalter as the major collection of laments and other hymns. Perhaps more than any other, it was Gunkel's work with *Formgeschichte* and *Gattungsgeschichte* that focused attention in Psalms studies on the content of the Psalms as a significant factor in indicating its function in the cult when he suggested that the Psalms be classified by content much as a modern hymnal.[301]

4.2 The Structure of the Communal Lament in the Psalter

When the people needed to express their deepest emotions over some grievous set of circumstances, a lament would be composed or adapted. The works which appear to have been composed and used on such occasions do not in their present form appear to be quiteas stereotypical as, for example, Mowinckel has argued. He does, however, make an important point when he states that:

---

301 Cf. H. Gunkel and J. Begrich, *Einleitung in die Psalmen. Die Gattungen der religiösen Lyrik Israels* (Göttingen: Vandenhoeck und Ruprecht, 1928, 1933).

the content was determined by the aim, and the aim, again, was dictated by the situation.

In the same way the situations also determined the form. The form is the one which, in each case, was felt to be the most natural and most suitable means of expressing the word to be said and of reaching the goal to be attained. This consideration consciously or unconsciously decides the choice of the details to be included, the expressions and imagery employed, the fundamental mood, and the composition as a whole into which the details have been fitted.[302]

A significant liturgy developed in Israel and the laments were a part of it, as Solomon's reference to the practice of national mourning in his temple dedication prayer seems to indicate.[303] Liturgy in Israel, as in most any other culture, had a developed a rich heritage from which to draw. There are specific instances of the use of a prescribed liturgy in the narrative sections of the Bible.[304] Such liturgies are normally rich in formulaic language. Often, specific formulae appear to be reserved for specific types of composition. It must be noted, however, that the laments do not seem to allow a rigid ordering of either form or formulae. For example, הוי "Ah! How?" used so characteristically in other laments[305] is never used in either the Psalm laments or the book of Lamentations. Likewise אוי "woe" is notable for its absence from the Psalm laments. It does occur only once in Lam. 5:16 and there it is used reflexively. This is also the case with אלה, ארר and קלל "curse,".[306] In this connection, Mowinckel makes an important point when he notes that in Israel an attitude existed toward this whole issue which may not have been common in the surrounding cultures, viz., the conviction that the lament observance was not merely the recitation of some magical formula that would effect the desired outcome vis-a-vis the calamity or the enemy. "Rather more frequently than the directly cursing word, we find the prayer for Yahweh to stay the enemy by means of his 'ban': his operative word, his 'threats' shall destroy them."[307] The point is that the

---

[302] Mowinckel, *Psalms* vol. I, p. 28.

[303] See below, sect. 4.4.4.1 Cf. I Kgs. 8:22-52, esp. vv. 33-34, 44-45.

[304] E.g., II Chr. 29:30 where the Levites are commanded to "sing praises to the LORD in the words of David and of Asaph the seer." Cf. Joel 2:17.

[305] E.g., I Kgs. 13:30, otherwise in the Latter Prophets, e.g. Jer. 22:18. See Jahnow, *Leichenlied*, p. 83 ff; G. Wanke, "אוי und הוי," ZAW 78 (1966):215-218; H. -J. Kraus, "hoj als prophetische Leichenklage über das eigene Volk im 8. Jahrhundert," ZAW 85 (1973):15-46; W. Janzen, *Mourning Cry and Woe Oracle*, BZAW 125, (Berlin: de Gruyter, 1972).

[306] Mowinckel, *Psalms* vol. II, pp. 50 ff. does indicate that the formulaic curses are "less prominent in the Psalms." But the point needs to be made that they are indeed absent from the communal laments.

[307] Ibid., vol. 1, p. 203. Cf. Pss. 69:25;109:15.

LORD is seen by Israel to be the operative factor and not the formula per se. So the cursing appeals generally take the form of prayers. As with the complaints and the appeals for deliverance, so with theappeals for cursing: the prayers are usually both detailed in their specifications and they correspond directly to the calamity being lamented.

Mowinckel presents the following structural form for the communal laments:[308]

> I. Invocation of Yahweh's name
>   A. Hymnal attributes
>   B. Hymnal introduction
> II. Lamentation
>   A. Description of distress
>   B. Evil and audacious words of enemies
> III. Prayer
>   A. Wish
>   B. Prayer for revenge
> IV. Motive for response
>   A. Honor of Yahweh
>   B. Hymnal motive
>   C. Covenant
>   D. Innocence
> V. Vow of thanksgiving and praise
> VI. Confidence of being heard[309]

C. Westermann offers basically the same structural scheme:[310]

> I. Address (and introductory plea)
> II. Lament
> III. Turning to God (confession of confidence)
> IV. Plea
> V. Vow of praise

I would suggest the following model:

> I. Invocation
> II. Hymn of praise
> III. Expression of confidence and trust
> IV. Lament
> V. Appeal and motivation for response
>   A. for deliverance

---

308 *Psalms* vol. I, pp. 195-239.

309 *Gewissheit der Erhörung.* See Gunkel, *Psalms* vol. I, pp. 35-36, cf. Mowinckel, *Psalms* I, 217-218, 234-235. There are numerous direct expressions of this motif in the Psalter, e.g., Pss. 4:4; 5:4; 10:17; 17:6; 20:7; 38:16; 55:18, 20; 145:19 but they are not common in the communal laments.

310 "Struktur," p. 48 where he describes his structural representation as "*stark stilisiert*" considerably stylized.

B. for cursing
VI. Protestation of innocence
VII. Expression of confidence and hope
VIII. Vow of praise

When the actual structure of these elements is charted and the form
is analyzed, it becomes clear that although there emerges a discernible
body of what appear to be essential elements, they fall in no formal order
(See fig. 3). The structural elements are variously represented and variously placed from composition to composition. The structure of the
laments is notably flexible and is subject to the issues being treated and
all the emotions which are brought to bear upon their being brought
before the LORD. The national laments refuse a formal structure to which
they must conform.

4.2.1 Invocation

The invocation, the lament proper, and the appeal are the elements
found in all the communal laments. The lament Psalms characteristically
address God directly. Usually, they begin with either אלהים or יהוה in
the vocative case: "O God!"[311] or "O LORD!"[312] Two variant addresses are
found: רעה ישראל " O Shepherd of Israel,"[313] and אל נקמות יהוה " O LORD
God of vengeance."[314] Four of the Psalms, 77, 89, 137, and 142, although
containing the direct address, do not begin with it. The vocative occurs
after an opening hymn.[315]

Regarding the opening forms, Mowinckel, following Gunkel, argued:

> The fixed form elements will usually begin to appear in the opening words
> of the psalm. Any one could at once classify a piece of writing that began:
> "Once upon a time," or "Dear Friend," or "We are in receipt of your
> favour." . . . In the same way we find that a certain group of psalms, a
> "psalm-type", quite regularly starts with "Praise Yahweh," or "Let us
> praise," and so on. Another starts with a mention of Yahweh's name (the
> "invocation") and a supplication, "LORD (i.e. Yahweh), I cry unto thee," and
> so on.[316]

---

311 Pss. 42:2; 44:2; 56:2; 59:2; 60:3; 69:2; 74:1; 79:1; 83:2; 109:1.
312 Pss. 31:2; 35:1; 85:2; 102:2.
313 Ps. 80:2.
314 Ps. 94:1.
315 Westermann does not recognize these as communal laments or at least not pure
communal laments. He argues that the "lament or petition follows directly after the address,
and these are never introduced or anticipated by detailed praise." (*Praise*, p. 37). Of these
four, Gunkel places only part of Ps. 89 in the communal lament category (RGG sect. 5).
316 *Psalms* vol. I, p. 26. Cf. Gunkel-Begrich, *Einleitung*, pp. 25 ff.

FIGURE–3

Main Structure of Communal Laments

	31	35	42/3	44	56	59	60	69	74	77	79	80	83	85	89	94	102	109	137	142	LAM 1	LAM 2	LAM 3	LAM 4	LAM 5
INVOCATION	x	x	x	x	x	x	x	x	x	x	x	x	x	x	x	x	x	x	x	x	x	x	x		x
HYMN OF PRAISE	6			1					2	2				1	1		3								
EXPRESSION OF CONFIDENCE/TRUST	1	1	1	2	2			1	1	1	1	1	1	2b	3	1									
LAMENT PROPER	3	4	2	3	1 3	2a	1a	3 5	1b 3	1	2	2	2	2a	2	2	1	1 3	1	1	1	1	1 4	1	1
APPEAL & MOTIVE: DELIVERANCE	2 5	1b 4b	1b 4b	5	4	1	1b 3a	2 4 7				1 3			3		2 4	2		2			3 7		
APPEAL & MOTIVE: CURSING		2b	2b			3 5	6	6					3						3		3				
PROTESTATION OF INNOCENCE		2		4		2b	2 3b														[2]*				[2]*
EXPRESSION OF CONFIDENCE/HOPE	4				5	4								3		3	5						2		
VOW OF PRAISE		3 5	4		6	6		7b			3				4			4							

numbers indicate order of components

*confession

Yet, of the sixty-five Psalms which contain a vocative of God in the opening lines, only forty-four are classified by Gunkel as either individual or
communal laments.[317] But that leaves twenty-one exceptions. 68% does
indicate a majority trend, but does not make the form a certain identifier.

Occasionally the invocation is accompanied by a preliminary appeal.
For example:

80:2	O Shepherd of Israel,	רעה ישראל האזינה
	give ear! . . .	
80:3	. . . Stir up Your might	עוררה את גבורתך
	and come to save us!	ולכה לישעתה לנו
83:2	O God, do not stay silent	אלהים אל דמי לך
	do not be speechless,	אל תחרש
	and do not be quiet, O God	ואל תשקט אל

This feature at the beginning of the composition foreshadows the
occurrence of the vocative at the beginning of the appeal.[318]

4.2.2 Hymn of Praise

Though as we shall see later, the praise forms are usually located at
or near the end of the laments, three of the laments include a hymn of
praise at or near the beginning: Pss. 44, 85, 89. These hymns, addressed
to God in the second person, recount some aspect of His prior saving
acts. In Pss. 44 and 85, thereis an introduction stating that the fathers had
passed this information along to the next generation (v. 2). This is followed by a listing of God's acts in the time of the conquest and settlement. For example:

44:3	You drove out the nations	אתה ידך גוים הורשת
	with Your hand,	
	Then You planted them;	ותטעם
	You broke the peoples,	תרע לאמים
	Then you sent them away.	ותשלחם
	For it was not by their sword	כי לא בחרבם
	they possessed [the] land;	ירשו ארץ
	And their arm did not save them;	וזרועם לא הושיעה למו
	But Your right hand, and Your arm,	כי ימינך וזרועך
	and the light of your face,	ואור פניך
	Because You favored them.	כי רציתם

This hymn seems to be placed here preparatory to the confession of
confidence which follows and then the appeal.

---

[317] RGG, sects. 4, 13; 7, 15, *Einleitung*, sects. 4, 6.
[318] Cf. Pss. 44:24; 74:22; 80:4, 8, 15, 20; 83:14.

4.2.3 Expression of Confidence and Trust

The elements of praise and confidence are occasionally treated with a somewhat different emphasis and at distinct locations within the composition. Therefore, in the model I have indicated both the hymn of praise and the vow of praise, and the expression of confidence which occurs early in some of the compositions, prior to the complaint, and the expression of confidence which occurs near the conclusion.

There are two forms of this expression. The first is the confession of trust that God is able and will hear.[319] This occurs in several laments at or near the beginning of the composition. The expression is not so straightforward as "I know that He will hear," rather, it tends to be a more oblique reference to trust in God and His victory or deliverance.[320] A similar unit occurs later in some of these and other laments.[321] Sometimes this unit is combined with the invocation and opening appeal as in the case of Psalm 31:

31:2	O LORD, I have taken refuge in you	בך יהוה חסיתי
	let me never be ashamed	אל אבושה לעולם
. . .		
31:4	Because You are my hiding-place and my fortress;	כי סלעי ומצורה אתה
	For the sake of Your name, You will lead and guide me.	ולמען שמך תנחני ותנהלני
31:5	You will pull me out of the net which they have hidden for me;	תוציאני מרשת זו טמנו לי
	For You are my stronghold.	כי אתה מעוזי
	Into Your hand I commit my spirit;	בורך אפקיד רוחי
	You have ransomed me, O LORD, God of faithfulness.	פריתה אותי יהוה אל אמת

4.2.4 Lament

There are basically two elements composing the lament proper. The first is the description of the external circumstances aboutwhich the complaint is being made. The second is the description of the concomitant mental anguish. These elements usually occur in this order. The exception is Psalm 80. (E.g., see fig. 4 below).

There are parallel forms of expressing the physical trauma:

44:10	But You have rejected us and humiliated us;	אף זנחת ותכלימנו

---

319 See above, n. 308, 309.
320 Pss. 31:1-9; 42/3 (refrain); 44:5-9; and 56:4-5.
321 See sect. 4.2.7 below.

	And You do not go out with our armies.	ולא תצא בצבאותינו
60:12	Have You not rejected us, O God?	הלא אתה אלהים זנחתני
	Will You not go out with our armies[322]	ולא תצא אלהים בצבאותינו

However, it seems the formulae occur more in the descriptions of the emotional trauma inflicted. For example:

חרפה לשכנינו		reproach to our neighbors	44:14
		79:4	
		(79:12)	
		89:42	
לעג וקלס		a scoffing and a mocking	44:14
לסביבותינו		to those around us	79:4 cf. 80:7

These examples are noteworthy in that in the Psalter, שֵׁכֶן "neighbor" is used only in the laments. The same is true of both the noun and verb form of חרף " reproach" when applied to Israel, with the exception of Ps. 119:22, 39, 42.

FIGURE 4

	Psalm				
Subject	44	60	74	79	80
Military defeat	10-13, 20, 23	3-4, 12	1, 3-11, 22	1-3, 7	13-14
Emotional trauma	14-17	5	21	4, 8c	5-7

Westermann has pointed out that one way of looking at the structure of the lament is to recognize the three subjects of the laments: subject 1, Thou, God; subject 2, we; subject 3, the enemy.[323] He argues convincingly that the primary focus of the complaint seems to be on God. The verbal forms of the complaint proper are most frequently in the second person. The term " reject" used of God's action toward people occurs only in the laments.[324] Many of the terms for God's anger so prominent in the Prophets and the "prophetic liturgies"[325] occur as well in the laments, e.g., אנף "be angry," אף " anger," חמה "wrath, rage," חרר "burning anger." This is to be expected inasmuch as calamity had been identified

---

322 Cf. 60:3 with 80:13; 74:3, 7 with 79:1.
323 "Struktur," p. 50 ff.
324 Pss. 43:2; 44:10, 24; 60:3,12 (cf. 108:12); 74:1; 77:8; 88:15; 89:39.
325 E.g., Ps. 78:21, 38, 49, 50.

as a by-product of God's anger.[326] God is seen to be ultimately responsible for the calamity whether by immediate or mediate action.

4.2.5 *Appeal and Motivation for Response*

Apart from any notion of national culpability, there exists a tension between Israel's theology and her circumstances. The penitential Psalms address this issue differently. Rather, in the laments there is occasionally a protestation of innocence.[327] The people respond with the remonstrant interrogatives למה "Why?" or עד מתי "How long?"[328] In the Psalter, these forms as directed to God are common to the laments. They are rarely used outside the laments.[329] "They approach the borderline between accusation and judgment. But they never quite reach a point where God is judged; for never are these sentences objective statements; they always remain personal address."[330] The shift from complaint to appeal is often marked by these remonstrant adjectives. The questions contain elements of the complaint but imply a request for a reversal of the circumstances.

The appeal unit may take one of two directions or a combination of both. The one is the plea for God to deliver His people from the calamity. The other is the appeal for God to curse the means of the calamity—the enemy.

4.2.5.1 *Appeal for Deliverance*

The primary appeal is for deliverance, occurring exclusively in twelve of the twenty laments. Four additional laments contain both kinds of appeal. Formally, the appeal is expressed in the imperative or אל with the jussive. Characteristic to the introduction of an appeal is the use of terms such as:

---

[326] See, e.g., Solomon's dedication, I Kgs. 8:46.

[327] Cf. Pss. 44:18-22; 59:4.

[328] Gunkel, "What Remains," p. 82.

[329] עד מתי occurs in Pss. 6:4; 74:10; 80:5; 90:13; 94:13 as well as in Pss. 101:2 and 119:82,84. Though למה addressed to God, occurs only in the laments within the Psalter: 10:1; 22:2; 42:10; 43:2; 44:24, 25; 74:1, 11; 79:10; 80:13; 88:15, there are

[329] parallel uses, e.g., Ex. 32:11 "O LORD, why does Your anger burn against Your people . . . ?"

[330] Westermann, "Struktur," p. 53.

44:27 74:22	"rise up"	קומה
35:23 44:24 59:5 80:3	"awake"	עוררה עורה
35:23 44:24 59:6	"awaken"	הקיצה
80:2	"give ear"	האזינה
74:20 80:15	"look"	הבט
74:2,18,22	"remember"	זכר
44:25 74:19,23	"do not forget"	אל תשכח
44:27 69:19	"redeem us"	פדנו
44:27 60:13 79:9	"help us"	עזרנו
79:9	"deliver us"	הצילנו
79:9	"atone"	כפר
31:17 59:3 60:7 69:2	"save"	הושיעה
80:4,8,20	"restore us"	השיבנו

The phenomenon in the Psalter of imperatives directed at God occurs mostly in the laments.

4.2.5.2 *Appeal for Cursing*

Mowinckel identified in the laments a feature he called "the ancient *formula of cursing.*"[331] This, not surprisingly, occurs in the form of the jussive: "may the nations be destroyed," etc. These expressions are a calling upon God to avenge His covenant people against the enemy who had injured and humiliated them and who, in so doing, had attacked His

---

331 *Psalms* vol. I, p. 202.

name. This practice does not appear to have had any magical over-tones[332] but was a genuine prayer to the LORD to intervene.

4.2.5.3 Motivation for Response

Again, Mowinckel argues convincingly that the lament may be seen as an exercise intended to arouse the LORD's compassion and hence move Him to action on behalf of the people.[333] The motivations may be summarized as follows: God's reputation ("for Your name's sake"), His covenant ("Consider the covenant"), consistency with God's past actions ("we have heard . . . our fathers have told us the work that You did in their days . . ."), innocence of the plaintiffs ("we have not forgotten . . . dealt falsely . . . turned back . . . deviated from Your way"), trust of the plaintiffs ("As for me, I trust in You, O LORD"), promise of praise ("to all generations we will tell of Your praise").[334] The first three point to salient features of Israel's history in which God's honor and covenant with His people are tied up with His works. Thus, the laments accompany an appeal with what Mowinckel calls the "hymnal motive"[335]: citations of the exodus (80:9), the conquest (Ps. 44:3), the settlement (80:10-11), etc.

4.2.6 Protestation of Innocence

Actually this unit is rare in the Psalm laments, occurring only in Pss. 44 and 59. It is countered in some of the laments by a recognition that the calamity is connected with the people's iniquity.[336] One example has just been alluded to in the discussion of motivation: innocence of the plaintiffs. Psalm 44 declares:

44:18	All this has come upon us	כל זאת באתנו
	but we have not forgotten You,	ולא שכחנוך
	and we have not dealt falsely with Your covenant.	ולא שקרנו בבריתך
44:19	Our heart has not backslidden	לא נסוג אחור לבנו
	and our steps have not turned aside from Your path.	ותט אשרינו מני ארחך
...		
44:21	If we had forgotten the name of our God,	אם שכחנו שם אלהינו
	Or spread our hands to a strange God,	ונפרש כפינו לאל זר
44:22	Would not God examine this?	הלא אלהים יחקר זאת
	For He knows the secrets of the heart.	כי הוא ידע תעלמות לב

---

332 See above p. 90.
333 Psalms, vol. I, p. 204 ff.
334 See Westermann, Praise, pp. 55-60.
335 Psalms, vol. I, p. 205.
336 Any significant attention accompanied by a confession would classify such a peni-tential Psalm. Cf. Ibid., pp. 214 ff.

4.2.7 Expression of Confidence and Hope

The invocation, complaint or lament proper and the appeal are the only virtually universal elements in the lament. Most of the laments do contain an expression of confidence. And most of these make such expressions at or near the close of the laments. As mentioned above, three of the laments, Psalms 31, 42/3, 56, include this expression of confidence both at or near the beginning and the end.[337] Westermann argues that this unit belongs between the complaint and the appeal where it does occur a number of times.[338] However, as with many of the other units, the laments refuse a fixed order for the expression of confidence and hope in the resolution of the calamity also follows the appeal. Sometimes, it is woven into the appeal itself. Sometimes, it is intertwined with the praise unit at the end. Psalm 31 is an example of this last case. Verses 20-25 move back and forth between expressions of confidence in what God has "stored up for those who fear" Him, and praise, "Blessed be the LORD!" and it closes:

31:24	O love the LORD, all you His loyal ones!	אהבו את יהוה כל חסידיו
	The LORD preserves the faithful,	אמונים נצר יהוה
	and fully rewards the proud.	ומשלם על יתר עשה גאוה
31:25	Be strong and let your heart take courage,	חזקו ויאמץ לבבכם
	All you who hope for the LORD.	כל המיחלים ליהוה

4.2.8 Vow of Praise

As mentioned above, a few of the laments include a paean to the LORD at or near the beginning of the composition. Most, however, do not. Rather, they include a call to praise or a vow to praise God at or near the end. Psalm 31 is the exception. It closes with the hymn just mentioned. Psalms 35, 42/3, 56, 59, 69, 74, and 109 contain the call or vow. In 35, the psalmist promises that upon vindication "my tongue shall declare Your righteousness and Your praise all day." The refrain which occurs three times in 42/43 is what closes the song: "Wait expectantly for God, for I will yet give Him thanks, the deliverance of my countenance and my God."

4.3 The Structure of the Communal Lament in Lamentations

Though Gunkel and his disciples worked primarily with the Psalter, their work touched on Lamentations as well.

See p. 92.
338 Praise, p. 57. See above, fig. 3.

Again a problem becomes evident when the formal stylistic criteria set forth by Gunkel *et al* is applied to Lamentations. Indeed, by such criteria, Gunkel proposed that the book consisted of three types of lament: the *Klagelied des Einzelnen* "lament of the individual," *Klagelied des Volkes* "lament of the people," and the *Leichenlied* "funeral dirge." By virtue of the formal typology, Gunkel classified chapter 3 as an individual lament, and chapters 1, 2, and 4 as funeral dirges. Yet the content of the latter did not leave him comfortable with this classification without qualification, so he felt constrained to specify that these were *national* funeral dirges, not personal, thus opening up a new category.[339]

It is in the face of such difficulties that Gunkel offers a catch-all category, that of the *Mischungen* "mixed" type,[340] which is where he places the book of Lamentations. But as far as the genre issue is concerned, Gunkel classified the primary *Gattung* as the *Klagelied des Volkes*. In his *Introduction*, Eissfeldt summarizes some of these issues, indicating the positive contributions of the *Formgeschichte* and *Gattungsgeschichte* schools while pointing up some of the problems as well: "In none [of the chapters of Lamentations] does the type appear in its *pure form* [italics mine]. They all reveal influences from other types, mixture of styles, and the recognition of this is just as important as the recognition of the type itself."[341] Similarly, Gottwald concludes:

> Thus the outcome of our investigation suggests that the formal literary types are useful as descriptions of the *approximate* categories into which the Hebrew poetry divides but they are incapable of providing us with *ironclad rules*. Basic to the analysis of any particular *Gattung* must the the *historical standpoint*, the *motivation* and *thought* of the author. *They* were after all the decisive factors in the writer's mind. It is always the danger of literary criticism that it will becontent with a survey or history of the formal literary types. Sheer arbitrariness with respect to the types is not to be expected, and the very mixture of *Gattungen* in Lamentations is ample evidence of the freedom which the poet felt to adopt and adapt any form that might further his avowed purpose.[342]

The formal features are indeed significant but they are features; their categorization is descriptive in function, not normative.

One feature which has contributed to the confusing categorizations is that of the apparent changing of the speaker throughout the book and

---

339 Gunkel-Begrich, *Einleitung*, p. 136. Cf. "Klagelieder Jeremiae," RGG 2d ed., vol. 3, col. 1049-52.

340 Ibid., pp. 397-403.

341 Eissfeldt, *Introduction*, p. 501.

342 N. K. Gottwald, *Studies in the Book of Lamentations*, rev. ed. (London: SCM, 1962), p. 41. Italics mine.

even within individual poems.[343] Much of the difficulty in this regard is constructively dealt with by the approach suggested by Lanahan as he addresses the question of *persona*, that "mask or characterization assumed by the poet as the medium through which he perceives and gives expression to his world."[344] Such a device is not to be seen as fantasy or fiction but a poetic broadening of perspective from individual to panoramic. Lanahan identifies five distinct *personae* in Lamentations: 1) the city of *Jerusalem* (1:9c, 11c-22, 2:20-22);2) a more objective *reporter* (1:1-11b, 15a, 17, 2:1-19); 3) a *defeated soldier* (ch. 3—with echoes of the voice of Jerusalem); 4) the *bourgeois* (ch. 4—with echoes of the voice of the reporter); 5) choral voice of Jerusalem as a *community* (ch. 5). This "variety of voices sketches the topography of a unique spiritual consciousness which can realize itself only by projecting its grief in its constituent phases by adopting different *personae*."[345]

In a somewhat superficial manner, the structure of the songs which make up the book of Lamentations is determined by the alphabetic acrostic device used in the first four songs and perhaps reflected in the twenty-two lines of the fifth.[346] The function of this particular formal feature has long been debated. Some have suggested it served as a pedagogic device.[347] Others suggest its purpose is mnemonic.[348] Perhaps the most likely is the suggestion offered by W. deWette that its intent is to underscore the immensity and range of the suffering—from A to Z as it

---

343 The difficulties in identifying the subjects by formal criteria and the lack of scholarly consensus at the time led Lohr to postulate that two separate poems make up the third chapter. He concluded it was an individual lament. "Threni III und die jeremianische Autorschaft des Buches der Klagelieder," ZAW 24 (1904):1-6. But such an approach puts the modern scholar in a most tenuous position as critic of the literary skills of the Hebrew poet.

344 W. F. Lanahan, "Speaking Voice in the Book of Lamentations," JBL 93 (1974):41-49.

345 Ibid., p. 42.

346 Acrostics are known from Mesopotamia. However, as would be expected, they are not alphabetic acrostics. The largest is a 297 line composition known as the "Babylonian Theodicy" and dated c. 1000 B.C. The initial syllables of each stanza create a sentence. There are four other extant Akkadian acrostic compositions: A hymn to Marduk (DT 83), a hymn to Nabu in honor of Nebuchadnezzar II (BM 55469), a prayer to Nabu (K 8204), and a hymn of Ashurbanipal to Marduk (KB VI/2. 108-17). W. G. Lambert, *Babylonian Wisdom Literature*, (Oxford: Clarendon, 1960), pp. 63-67. See R. Sweet, "A Pair of Double Acrostics in Akkadian," Or NS 38 (1969):459ff.

347 To help students learn the funeral dirge style, so P. Munch, "Die alphabetische Akrostichie in der jüdischen Psalmendichtung," ZDMG 90 (1936): 703-710, followed by W. Rudolph, *Das Buch Ruth, Das Hohe Lied, Die Klagelieder*) (Gütersloh: G. Mohn, 1962), p. 191.

348 R. Lowth, *Lectures on the Sacred Poetry of the Hebrews* trans. G. Gregory (Boston: Buckingham, 1815), pp. 39, 318; S. Oettli, *Die Klagelieder* (Munich:n.p.,1889), p. 199.

were.[349] To the notion of completeness, Gottwald adds the purpose of inducing an "emotional catharsis."[350]

A. Condamin noted an interesting feature in the first song, in which terms seem to be repeated in a chiastic order, leading him to see a structural division between the eleventh and twelfth verses. These he then divided into symmetrical strophes: 1-3, 4-6, 7-11, 12-16, 17-19, 20-22.[351] There does appear to be some pattern, but it is not clear how it fits the development of the content of the song other than the fact that vv. 9 and 11 end with the vocative/imperative appeal.

In conclusion, it must be observed that an analysis of the formal characteristics of these compositions, both in the Psalter and in the book of Lamentations, indicates that form isinsufficient as a means to establishing a genre. As far as the communal laments are concerned, it is the nature and the use of the themes found in a composition which are the more determinative.

4.4 Sitz im Leben

4.4.1 Historical Setting

A search of these Psalms for incontrovertible evidence of a specific historical setting is an exercise in frustration. While concrete terms are used to describe this calamity or that, they are for the most part only general terms. With few exceptions, P. Miller correctly observes that "the very nature of the psalms and the language with which [the enemies or evildoers] are described both obscure the immediate identification of the enemies and at the same time suggest that they may have many identities."[352] The exceptions are, of course, those laments which specify the oppression of the exile and the destruction of Jerusalem: Psalms 42/3, 69, 74, 79, 89, and 137.

That musical expression was common in the life of the Israelite is not a debated matter. This is not the place to develop the data but to recount that both vocal and instrumental music show up in numerous settings.[353]

---

349 Lehrbuch der historischkritischen Einleitung in die kanonischen und apokryphischen Bücher des Alten Testamentes, 7th ed. (Berlin, 1852), p. 532, followed by C. Keil Lamentations of Jeremiah, Biblical Commentary (Grand Rapids: Eerdmans, 1950), p. 339.

350 Lamentations, p. 30.

351 "Symmetrical Repetitions in Lamentations I and II," JTS 7 (1906):137-140.

352 "Trouble and Woe: Interpreting Biblical Laments," Int 37 (Jan. 1983): 34. Contra Mowinckel who tries to authenticate specific historical circumstances, Psalms vol. I, pp. 243-246.

353 E.g., I Sam. 18:6; II Sam. 19:35; I Kgs. 10:12, etc.

Both were also used in Israel's worship[354] which included the singing of psalms.[355]

4.4.2 Temple Singers

In addition to references to the popularity of music in Israel, a guild of professional Levitical singers was established. Only in the last forty-five years or so has sufficient evidence been available to answer the theory that any reference to a musicians' guild in the Davidic period was anachronistic. Albright concluded,

> a priori there is nothing to be said against the Davidic origin of temple music. Syria and Palestine were noted for their musicians in the ancient Near East, as we know both from Egyptian and from Mesopotamian sources. . . .
> . . . There is, accordingly, no reason why the institution of temple musicians migth not go back to an early date.[356]

Their bailiwick was the temple. According to the Chronicler, David had appointed them, ‏להזכיר ולהודות ולהלל ליהוה אלהי ישראל‎ " to invoke, to thank, and to praise the LORD, the God *of Israel*." Elsewhere,their duties are described as "to thank and to praise the LORD" on a prescribed schedule.[357] This practice is perpetuated in Israel as indicated, e.g., by the Chronicler's description of worship in Hezekiah's day:

> When the burnt offering began, the song to the LORD also began with the trumpets accompanied by the instruments of King David of Israel, and the entire assembly worshiped, and the singers sang, and the trumpets blew; all this until the burnt offering was consumed . . . . Then King Hezekiah and the princes told the Levites to sing praises to the LORD with the words of David and Asaph the seer.[358]

As seen above, the verb ‏זכר‎ " remember" is used in its hiphil infinitive form: "to cause to remember, to bring to remembrance, to mention,"[359] which in the jussive and imperative may imply entreaty or exhortation. Thus, the term is used in the qal in the laments[360] and other Psalms[361] which contain some lamentation. This usage in lament and the

---

354 Num. 10:2, 10. Cf. Ps. 81:3-5; II Sam. 16:6; I Chr. 25.

355 E.g., I Chr. 16. Cf. Amos 6:5.

356 W. F. Albright, *Archaeology and the Religion of Israel* (Baltimore: Johns Hopkins, 1956). See also J. M. Meyers, *1 Chronicles* (Garden City: Doubleday, 1965), pp. 119-123, 160-161, 171-173.

357 I Chr. 23:30.

358 II Chr. 29:27b, 30. Cf. II Chr. 7:1-6; 31:2.

359 KB, s.v. "‏זכר‎."

360 Pss. 74:2, 18, 22; 89:48, 51; 137:7; Lam. 3:19; 5:1.

361 Cf. Pss. 25:6-7; 106:4; 119:9; 132:1.

use of להזכיר in the title of Psalms 38 and 70, "individual laments," seems to indicate at least one motif of the laments. This leads to the possibility that one of the elements of the singers' task mentioned in I Chr. 16:4 may be the performance of laments.

4.4.3 Liturgical Terms in the Psalms

Another possible clue to the *Sitz im Leben* of the lament Psalms may be found in the titles.[362] Psalms 31, 42/3, 44, 56, 59, 60, 69, 77, 80, 85, and 109 each carry the prefatory inscription למנצח "to the choirmaster"—the "prominent" one appointed as overseer or superintendent or leader of the temple singers.[363] If a logical connection can be made between the use of the term in the Psalm prefaces and in the historical narratives, then one must conclude that these were intended for public worship.

Similarly, the use of מזמור in the preface of Psalms 31, 77, 79, 80, 83, 85, and 109 from זמר "to praise, sing with an instrument," indicates something of the setting. The lxx translates as $\psi a\lambda\mu\acute{o}s$ "song of praise." Such a meaning, and the use of מזמור with למנצח in a number of the laments indicates these may have been sung or chanted in public worship.

The remaining Psalms give no special clues in their prefatory lines. Two have no preface: 94 and 132. One is simply marked לדוד: 35. One has a notation indicating it is a prayer of or for the afflicted: 102. The others are noted as a משכיל: 74, 89, and 142. Although משכיל is sometimes associated with מנצח, it probably indicates a contemplative composition (following the lxx rendering $\sigma v v\acute{\epsilon}\sigma\epsilon\omega s$ "intelligence, understanding") and does not indicate any particular liturgical rendition.

4.4.4 National Mourning Rites

Early in Israel's history, there is indication of the practice of fasting and mourning in the face of trouble. For example, when Israel was massacred at the hand of Benjamin, the people wept and fasted and offered both burnt offerings and peace offerings. When Saul died, a seven day fast was proclaimed: again, a time of national mourning and lamenta-

---

[362] See H. -J. Kraus, *Psalmen*, 4th ed. (Neukirchen:,1972), p. 30 and sect. 7a. Cf. B. Childs, "Psalm Titles and Midrashic Exegesis," JSS 16(1971):137-150; L. Delekat, "Probleme der Psalmenüberschriften," ZAW 76 (1964):280-297; Mowinckel, *Psalms* vol. II, pp. 207-217; J. Enciso, "Los titulos de los Salmos y la historia de la formacion del Salterio," *Estudios Biblicos* 13 (1954):135-166; B. D. Eerdmans, *The Hebrew Book of Psalms*, Oudtestamentische Studien IV, (Leiden: Brill, 1947), pp. 51-90.

[363] Cf. II Chr. 34:12; I Chr. 15:21. *Contra* Mowinckel, *Psalms*, vol. II, p. 212 who sees it as a benediction: to make Yahweh's face to shine.

tion.[364] The roots of such practices are found early, but the background
for the *Sitz im Leben* of the Psalm laments and the book of Lamentations
is probably best understood as being in Solomon's dedicatory prayer.[365]

4.4.4.1 Occasion of the Service

At the completion of the temple, Solomon had the ark of the
covenant brought into the Holy of Holies and led a celebration of the
LORD's entrance into His temple.[366] On this occasion, he then offered a
dedicatory prayer in which he outlined seven specific kinds of situations
for which prayer might be offered in the temple.[367] Of the seven, four had
to do with some aspect of national calamity. They were:

Defeat in battle	8:33-34
Drought	8:35-36
Other natural disaster	8:37-40
(famine, plague, blight, locusts, etc.)	
Captivity	8:46-50

On such occasions, the people were instructed to התפללו "pray" and
התחננו "make supplication" to the LORD at the temple.[368]

Thus, in the face of mounting enemy pressure, Jehoshaphat proclaims a fast to seek the LORD at the temple.[369] A look at the prayer
offered on that occasion shows that he follows the Solomonic pattern.
Also apparent are the main elements of the communal lament: invocation
(v. 6a), praise (v. 6b), expression of confidence in the form of a reiteration
of His past acts (v. 7-9), lament proper (v. 10), appeal for deliverance and
curse (v. 11-12b), and expression of confidence (v.12c).[370]

Moore has noted that public fasts were also observed as an
apotropaic rite in the face of impending natural calamity such as drought
or plague, citing Joel as an example.

Public fasts were appointed by the authorities in other perils or calamities,
or when for any reason the Jews believed themselves to be under divine

364 Jud. 20:26; I Chr. 10:12.
365 I Kgs. 8.
366 I Kgs. 8:1-21.
367 I Kgs. 8:22-53, esp. vv. 31 ff.
368 8:33.
369 II Chr. 20:3 ff.
370 See also the account of Hezekiah's "day of distress, rebuke, and rejection" in the face
of the Assyrian threat. Hezekiah offers a prayer following much the same pattern and containing many of the elements of the communal lament: II Kgs. 19:15-20.

displeasure, after such biblical examples as Judges 20,26; I Sam. 7,6; 2 Chron. 12,5-8; Neh. 9,1, etc.; and this custom has continued to modern times.[371]

Granted, the setting of some accounts is that of transgression, and the lament called for is of a penitential nature,[372] or at least ought to have been so.[373] On one occasion, a fast is called to appeal to the LORD for journey mercy in the face of potential trouble from an enemy as Ezra prepares to return to Jerusalem.[374] The clearest reference to the fact that over time a regular schedule of national days of mourning had developed is found in Zech. 7:5 and 8:19 which state that such observances were held in the fourth, fifth, seventh and tenth months.

4.4.4.2 Description of the Service

When a disaster threatened or had occurred, the following procedure was put into motion:

1. A public fast day was proclaimed.
> Jud. 20:26
> Joel 2:15
> Jer. 36:9
> II Chr. 20:3
> Est. 4:3, 16

2. All the citizens were expected to gather before the LORD.
> Jud. 20:26
> I Sam. 7:5
> Joel 1:14
> Jer. 36:6, 9
> II Chr. 20:4,13
> Est. 4:16

3. Various acts of mourning were performed:
> *fasting
> Jud. 20:26
> I Sam. 7:6
> Isa. 22:12
> Jer. 14:12

---

371 G. F. Moore, *Judaism*, 3 vols. (Cambridge: Harvard, 1950), 2:68. Cf. M. Ta`anit 3 (Ta`anit 19a); I Macc. 3:47; II Macc. 13:12.

372 Isa. 58:3,4; Joel 1:14; 2:12-15; Neh. 9:1 ff.

373 Jer. 36:6 ff.

374 Ezra 8:21 ff.

*donning sackcloth
> Isa. 22:12
> Isa. 58:5
> Jer. 6:26
> Jer. 32:11

*rolling in ashes
> Isa. 58:5
> Jer. 6:26
> Est. 4:3

*weeping
> Jud. 20:23,26

4. Acts of sanctification were observed.
> Joel 1:14; 2:15

"They had to abstain from certain things during the time of humiliation: food and drink, anointing with oil, sexual intercourse, and other manifestations of normal life."[375]

5. Prayer was offered expressing the distress.
> Josh. 7:6 ff.
> I Sam. 7:5
> II Kgs. 19:14,15
> II Chr. 20:5
> Joel 2:17

These prayers reflect the salient thematic elements found in the laments.[376]

4.4.5 Summary

As we have seen, although a certain number of laments specify the exile and destruction of Jerusalem, the others tend toward an ambiguous though detailed description of the calamity. Songs in both categories contain notations which seem quite strongly to indicate liturgical intentions. Together, this would seem to support a conclusion that the communal laments were used both by and on behalf of the community on national days of mourning which could either be specially called or regularly scheduled.

---

375 Mowinckel, *Psalms*, vol. I p. 193.
376 See Gunkel's detailed description, *Einleitung*, pp. 118-120.

4.5 Thematic Elements of the Communal Lament Psalms

In the application of the form-critical method to a text or corpus of texts, one must be cautious not to force the notion of "characteristic formal language."[377] Empirical evidence will not support any insistence upon a stereotypical opening for the laments, e.g., consistently beginning with הוֹי "Ah! How!,"[378] as the criterion for genre identification. For example, a survey of the Psalter for consistent usage of key lament terms in the communal laments uncovers no discernible pattern. Only four[379] of the following terms occur frequently enough to determine even if their usage is in a key formulaic phrase:

tear	דִּמְעָה	to mourn	אָבַל
to sigh, moan	הָגָה	mourning	אֵבֶל
moaning	הֶגֶה	mourning rites	אֲבֵל
to grieve	יָגָה	woe	אוֹי
grief	יָגוֹן	trouble, sorrow	אָוֶן
lamentation	מִסְפֵּד	to curse	אָלָה
mourning feast	מַרְזֵחַ	to lament	אָנָה
to lament, wail	נָהָה	to sigh, lament	אָנַח
lamentation	נְהִי	sigh	אֲנָחָה
to bemoan	נוּד	sorrow, mourning	אֲנִיָּה
to wail, lament	סָפַד	to weep	בָּכָה
to dress for mourning	קָדַר	weeping	בֶּכֶה
to chant dirge	קִין	languish	דָּאַב
elegy	קִינָה	to weep	דָּמַע

As with the Mesopotamian laments, we are looking for compositions which concern themselves primarily with some issue or event which has caused or is causing grief in the community. Though the rites of mourning may vary from culture to culture, they serve as an instrument of expressing, and hence, accepting and adjusting to, a real or perceived loss. It may be the loss of identity or integrity, morally, ethically, socially, politically. The loss may be due to a "natural" disaster or to a political or military onslaught either threatened or accomplished. It is the expression

---

377 Gunkel-Begrich, Einleitung, p. 11.

378 H. Gunkel, "Fundamental Problems," p. 60.

379 אָוֶן, nine times: Pss. 10:7, 14:4, 53:5, 56:8, 59:3,6, 90:10, 94:4,16; דִּמְעָה, six times: Ps. 42:4, 56:9, 80:6, Lam. 1:2, 2:11,18; הָמָה, five times: Ps. 42:6,12, 43:5, 77:4, 83:3; יָגָה five times: Lam. 1:4,5,12, 3:32,33. On מַרְזֵחַ see M. Pope, Song of Songs), AB (Garden City: Doubleday, 1977), pp. 214-221. Cf. B. Porten, "The Marzeah Association" in Archives from Elephantine, Berkeley: University of California, 1968, pp. 177-186; E. Y. Kutscher, Words and Their History (Jerusalem: Kiryat-Sefer, 1965); O. Eissfeldt, "Etymologische und archaeologische Erklärung alttestamentlicher Wörter," Oriens Antiquus 5 (1966):167-171; O. Eissfeldt, "Kultvereine in Ugarit" in Ugaritica VI, ed. C. Schaeffer (Paris: Paul Geuthner, 1969), pp. 187-195.

of this grief by or on behalf of the community that becomes the focus of attention here.[380] As argued in the first chapter, the thought and mood content of a composition must be given priority as a determining factor in the process of identifying and comparing the communal laments. As we shall see, the formal factors vary somewhat, whether by the deliberate purpose, poetic device or apparent whim of the author. However, matters of form per se will not suffice as distinguishing criteria.

A study of the Psalter based on this approach yields nineteen or twenty Psalms which have the content of complaint or lamentation and which permit communal expressions of such lamentation.

Of the eight primary thematic elements identified in the communal laments, the most common are:

> 1. direct address,
> 2. the complaint/lament, and
> 3. the appeal.

There are other motifs, however, which are important to note as one analyzes the thematic elements of the communal laments. These other motifs are: praise, confidence or trust, innocence, hope, deliverance, imprecation. It is immediately apparent that none of these motifs are inherently communal. In fact, they are themes for the most part held in common with individual laments and penitential Psalms.[381] Some of them are also commonly to be found in Psalms of Confidence.[382]

4.5.1 Direct Address

Most of the laments in the Psalter address God directly throughout the given lament, using either or both אלהים and יהוה and the second person, rather than using a structurally distinct invocation proper.[383] For this reason, I conclude that there seems to be a distinct awareness of the addressee, God, on thepart of the Israelite represented in these Psalms. The grief expressed is done in direct address throughout the lamentations.

---

380 As indicated above, sect. 3.2.3, there is another category of Psalm which expresses a type of lament or complaint but which, by its content and purpose, is properly considered a penitential Psalm because the apparent intent of the composition is to express contrition or repentance and then to ask for relief. Thus, they fall outside the focus of this work.

381 See Castellino, Lamentazioni, pp. 81-142; Westermann, Praise, pp. 64-75; id., "Struktur," pp. 56-66.

382 E.g., Pss. 23, 121, etc. See Gunkel, Psalms, p. 35.

383 See Pss. 35:1,17,22,24; 42:2,7; 43:1,4; 44:2,5,24; 56:2,8,13; 59:2,4,6,9,12; 60:3,12-13; 69:2,6,7,14,17,3 0 ; 74:1,10,18,22;77:1 4 ,1 7 ; 79:1,5,9,12;80:2,4,5,7,15,2 0 ; 83:2,14,1 7 ; 85:2,5,8; 89:6,9,16,47,50,51; 94:1,2,3,5,12,18; 102:2,13,25; 109:1,21,26; 137:7; 142:6.

For example:

31:2	In You, oh LORD, have I sought refuge. Never let me be ashamed. By your righteousness, cause me to escape.	בך יהוה חסיתי אל אבושה לעולם בצדקתך פלטני
31:10	Be gracious to me, oh LORD, for I am distressed . . .	חנני יהוה כי צר לי
31:15	But as for me, In You have I put my trust: I have said, "You are my God."	ואני עליך בטחתי יהוה אמרתי אלהי אתה

The direct address is expressed not only with the vocative but also by use of the second person as the psalmists importune their God to survey the matter at hand and to address Himself to it in His power and righteous judgment. Begrich pointed out that there is an assumption in these laments of a special relationship between the parties. This seems evident by the frequency with which God is directly addressed."[384] Rather than allowing the calamity completely to overwhelm them and undermine this relationship so that they now merely talk about God in the third person: "Why did He let this happen?" or "Why did God do this to me?", the lament psalmists seem to recognize that the covenant relationship called for a different approach. The Hebrew laments demonstrate an assumed dialog with God.[385]

In summary, although a formal invocation which is structurally distinct is not a feature of the communal laments, the motif of direct address is a classic feature. It seems clear that the communal laments are not to be seen as having been a collective groan or moan, but rather a direct corporate dialogical expression of grief to God.

4.5.2 Complaint or Lament Proper

The actual poetic development of the substance of the lamentations varies from a simple to a more complex treatment of the issue in question.

The complaint is generally expressed as a description of the results of physical or emotional trauma or both.

For example:

---

384 J. Begrich, "Die Vertrauensäusserungen im israelitischen Klagelied des Einzelnen und seinem babylonischen Gegenstück," ZAW 46 (1928): 250.

385 W. Brueggemann, "From Hurt to Joy, From Death to Life," Int 28 (Jan. 1974): 6. Cf. C. Westermann, Psalms, pp. 39-40.

31:10	Be gracious to me, oh LORD for I am distressed.	חנני יהוה כי צר לי
	My eye has wasted away with vexation,	עששה בכעס עיני
	My throat and my belly as well.	נפשי ובטני
31:11	For my life is exhausted by grief, And my years by groaning.	כי כלו ביגון חיי ושנותי באנחה
	My strength has staggered because of my iniquity,	כשל בעוני כחי
	And my bones have wasted away.	ועצמי עששו

This lament then turns to an impassioned appeal to God for deliverance and for a curse on the enemy. For example:

31:16	My times are in your hands,	בידך עתתי
	Oh deliver me from the hand of my enemies and from my persecutors.	הצילני מיד־אויבי ומרדפי
31:17	Make your face to shine upon your servant.	האירה פניך על עבדך
	Deliver me with Your covenant loyalty.	הושיעני בחסדך
31:18	Oh LORD, let me not be ashamed, for I proclaim You.	יהוה אל אבושה כי קראתיך
	Let the wicked be ashamed,	יבשו רשעים
	Let them be silent to Sheol.	ידמו לשאול

The impassioned complaint may be occasioned by several different circumstances or any combination of them. In attempting to identify certain marked distinctions observable in the Psalms, it is noted that some concepts overlap and therefore, need to be defined for the sake of discussion. As used in this study, the term "political" as describing an "enemy" or "calamity" will refer to that which has a bearing on what would normally be understood as the governmental institutions of a people: its king or other duly recognized leadership, the machinery of civil and social administration, the national existence, etc.

On the other hand, while moral and ethical issues do have a bearing upon political institutions as seen through the eyes of the prophets and surely even of the psalmists, I will use this term when the primary focus of the lament appears to be on a moral or ethical cancer which has evidenced itself in the social fabric of Israel. In these cases, the psalmist will be concerned as well with the covenant relationship of the people with their God, hence, religious ramifications are also perceived.

4.5.2.1 Political Enemy

First, we will look at the complaint concerning the political enemy. The terminology of the thirty-fifth Psalm indicates that a political threat and/or present disaster is in view. The LORD is entreated, ריבה "'contend' with those who contend with me." But here it is not a legal controversy which is of concern, but a politico-military battle that is envisioned. For example, the LORD is asked to:

35:2	Seize buckler and shield	החזק מגן וצנה
	and rise up to my aid!	וקומה בעזרתי
	Draw out the spear and javelin...[386]	והרק חנית וסגר

Psalm 42/43, apparently speaking from an exiled perspective, mourns:

42:10	... because of the enemy's oppression.	בלחץ אויב

as part of a refrain repeated in 43:2. Psalm 44 again uses the terminology referring to a politico-military adversary:

44:5	You are my King, O God,	אתה הוא מלכי אלהים
	Command victories for Jacob.	צוה ישועות יעקב
44:6	By You, our foe we will push back,	בך צרינו ננגח
	By Your name, we will trample our adversary.	בשמך נבוס קמינו

But then the psalmist complains to God:

44:10	You do not go out with our armies.	ולא תצא בצבאותינו

In the fifty-ninth Psalm, the enemy is generalized:

59:2	Deliver me from my enemies, O God.	הצילני מאיבי אלהי

where the enemy is plural and further referred to as כל הגוים "all the nations" in vv. 6, 9. The 83rd Psalm follows something of the same approach to the theme but, instead of broadening its scope by generalizing, it does so by multiple specific references, e.g., naming the co-conspirators: Edom and the Ishmaelites, Moab and the Hagrites, Gebal, Ammon, Amalek, Philistia with the inhabitants of Tyre and Assyria, thus, covering the gamut of their political adversaries.[387]

4.5.2.2 Moral, Ethical and Spiritual Enemy

The substance of the conflicts shifts in these Psalms from what is clearly a primarily political confrontation to an issue over a moral or ethical question. This conflict may have repercussions upon the relationship between the subject and his God. In these cases, it is sometimes difficult, if not impossible, to ascertain just who the enemy might be. That is, it becomes difficult to determine whether the enemy attacks from

---

[386] Following Y. Yadin's suggested vocalization, סְגֹר, based on its occurrence in 1QM5:7,9. *The Scroll of the War of the Sons of Light against the Sons of Darkness* (London: Oxford, 1962), p. 137, n. 3. Cf. K. Galling, *Biblisches Reallexikon*, (Tübingen: Mohr, 1937), p. 353 ff.

[387] Cf. Ps. 60:2.

within the community and harasses the pious or is an enemy alien to Israelite society.

Examples of enemy action on the moral or ethical front would be:

31:18-19	lying lips of the wicked	רשעים...שֹפתי שקר
31:21	strife of tongues	מריב לשנות
35:10	robbing the poor	ועני ואביון מגזלו
35:11	malicious witness	עדי חמס
59:3	those who do iniquity	פעלי און
59:8	swords are in their lips	חרבות בשֹפתותיהם
69:5	those who hate without cause	שֹנאי חנם
94:4	the wicked who speak arrogantly	ידברו עתק
94:5-6	those who crush, afflict, slay the widow, the stranger, and the orphan	ידכאו...יענו...יהרגו...ירצחו
94:20	throne of destruction which devises trouble by statute	כסא הוות יצר עמל עלי חק
109:2	wicked and deceitful mouth	פי רשע ופי־מרמה
109:2-3	lying tongues, words of hatred	לשון שקר ודברי שֹנאה
109:16	persecuted the poor and afflicted	וירדף איש־עני ואביון

4.5.2.3 Political Calamity

There are two major categories of political calamity. The first, though serious enough, is the lesser of the two. It is a defeat in battle which threatened the integrity of the nation. A classic example of a lament over such a calamity is Psalm 60, which describes the plight of Israel as having been זנח "rejected" and פרץ "broken," made to see קֹשה "hardship," and made to drink wine that made them רעל "reel," all apparently at the hand of Moab, Edom, and Philistia. I call this the lesser calamity because the defeat, as devastating as it may have seemed, was not as great as what appeared to be the ultimate devastation wreaked upon Judah and the disintegration of the nation at the hands of the Babylonians in the early sixth century B.C. It is this series of events which gave rise to the mournful expressions such as Psalm 42/43, 69, 74, 79, 89, and 137. The nation grieves over the loss of its national integrity, its homeland, the national identity of its capital, the special loss of the locus of the cult, its temple in Jerusalem. Thus the dirge goes:

42:5	These are what I remember	אלה אזכרה
	And I pour out my soul upon me.	ואשפכה עלי נפשי
	For I used to go along in the throng	כי אעבר בסך
	And lead them in slow procession	אדדם עד בית אלהים

> to the house of God
> With a voice of joy and thankfulness,   בקול רנה ותודה
> A great throng making a pilgrimage   המון חוגג

and the במעה "tears" and the קדר "mourning" are marked by the refrains:

42:10	Why must I go mourning Because of the oppression of an enemy?	למה קדר אלה בלחץ אויב
43:2	Why must I continually go mourning Because of the oppression of an enemy?	למה קדר אתהלך בלחץ אויב
42:6	Why are you despairing, O my soul, And murmuring against me? (repeated in 42:12 and 43:5)	מה־תשתוחחי נפשי ורהמי עלי

Psalm 89 is a recitation of the LORD's covenant with David followed by a lament over the demise of the Davidic throne in Jerusalem:

89:39	But you have spurned and rejected; You have become furious with Your anointed.	ואתה זנחת ותמאס התעברת עם־משיחך
89:40	You have spurned Your servant's covenant; You have dishonored his crown into the dirt.	נארתה ברית עברך חללת לארץ נזרו
89:41	You have breached all his walls; You made his fortification a ruin.	פרצת כל־גדרתיו שמת מבצריו מחתה
89:42	All who pass along the road plunder him; He is a reproach to his neighbors.	שסהו כל־עברי דרך היה חרפה לשכניו
89:43	You have exalted his adversaries' right hand; You have caused all his enemies to rejoice.	הרימות ימין צריו השמחת כל־אויביו
89:44	You have even caused the edge of the sword to bounce back; And you have not let him hold his ground in battle.	אף־תשיב צור חרבו ולא הקימתו במלחמה
89:45	You caused his splendor to cease; And you have hurled his throne to the earth.	השבת מטהרו וכסאו לארץ מגרתה
89:46	You have cut short the days of his youth; You have wrapped him with shame.	הקצרת ימי עלומיו העטית עליו בושה סלה
89:47	How long, O LORD?...	עד־מה יהוה...

4.5.2.4 Spiritual Calamity

It should be clear that given the notion of covenant and theocracy, it would be impossible to divest political or even natural disasters such as drought and famine of spiritual or religious significance. Jerusalem was not just the capital. It was also the special locus of the cult. Therefore, it is not just the loss of kingship that is grieved but the destruction of the temple as well. This was apparent in Ps. 42:5 in the reference to the pilgrim throngs. The seventy-fourth Psalm laments that the enemy has destroyed and desecrated the sanctuary and set up their own standards, and the seventy-ninth cries:

| 79:1 | O God, the nations have entered
Your property;
They have defiled Your holy temple;
They have made Jerusalem a heap of ruins.
... | אלהים באו גוים בנחלתך

טמאו את־היכל קדשך
שמו את־ירושלם לעיים |
| 79:5 | How long O LORD?
Will you be angry forever? | עד־מה יהוה
תאנף לנצח |

Regarding the issue of a spiritual or religious calamity, it must be noted that this notion of Israel's estrangement from her God is so prevalent throughout the laments. In this connection the penitential Psalms occurred as well.[388] But even apart from the formal Psalms of penitence, there is strong expression of the notion of broken relationship, of the feeling of the heat of God's anger and the strong desire for reconciliation—the normalization of relationships between the parties of the covenant, which strong desire, as we shall see later, was also a confident expectation that their God would both hear and deliver, heed and restore.

4.5.2.5 Scope of Complaint

In the treatment of the addressee, the directness of the complaint was noted—the dialogical nature of lament in Israel. Here, I want to note also the specificity of the complaints. They were not generalized and amorphous. Rather, they seem to be quite detailed in their description of the issue of the complaint: either the calamity in question or the effects of the calamity upon the community, or both.

Abandonment/Isolation

The sense of abandonment and isolation is bewailed in the laments: abandonment by God and isolation from society. The matter of abandonment is broached somewhat obliquely and generally does not occur in the complaint proper but in the appeal. For example, Ps. 35:22-23:

---

[388] Note Mowinckel's treatment of the penitential Psalms in this same context indicating that even those Psalms which have been singled out as "pure" laments (as vs. penitential Psalms) were used as part of the cultic ceremonies on public fast-days. "All these *penitential rites*, originally intended perhaps for the purpose of averting the disaster or protecting against it, and atoning for and cleansing from impurity, in Yahwism became a token of penitence and 'self-humiliation' before Yahweh in order to temper his wrath and rouse his compassion." *Psalms*, vol. I, p. 193.

35:22	You have seen, O LORD, do not keep silent,	ראיתה יהוה אל־תחרש
	O LORD, do not be far from me.	אדני אל־תרחק ממני
35:23	Rouse Yourself, awake to my right	העירה והקיצה למשפטי
	And to my case, my God and my Lord.[389]	אלהי ואדני לריבי

The theme of isolation or estrangement is expressed, e.g., in Psalm 44, with parallel synonyms like חרפה " reproach," לעג " derision," קלס "scoffing," משל "by-word," מנוד ראש "head-shaking," and on. Granted, this may be explained in part as normal poetic expression in which the parallel synonyms are used. But the point must be made that the Israelites did not just casually state their problem but, rather, were at no loss for words when it came to detailing the occasion for their lament. Others explain, for example:

31:12	I have become a reproach	הייתי חרפה ולשכני מאד
	especially to my neighbors	
	And a dread to my friends.	ופחד למידעי
69:9	I have become estranged from my brothers,	מוזר הייתי לאחי
	And a foreigner to my mother's sons.	ונכרי לבני אמי

Shame/Humiliation

Psalm 69:19 laments of חרפתי ובשתי וכלמתי "my reproach and my shame and my humiliation." Psalm 44 speaks to the matter of shame and humiliation as indicated above and further complains:

| 44:16 | All day my humiliation confronts me | כל־היום כלמתי נגדי |
| | And my shame overwhelms me.[390] | ובשת פני כסתני |

Despair/Depression

I have mentioned above[391] the refrains of Psalm 42/43. They use the *hithpo'el* of שחח to describe that experience of soul we call despair or depression. This is the only time I can find this verb used this way in the biblical literature. The verb המה "murmur, be in commotion, be turbulent" is used in parallel. In 77:4 המה is used in parallel with תתעטף רוחי "my spirit faints away."

Danger from the Enemy

Various Psalms refer to the jeopardy which confronts the people by means of an enemy. For example, the psalmist appeals the case to God:

---

389 See also Pss. 69:17-19; 80:15.
390 For other examples, see Pss. 31:2,12,18; 35:4,26; 44:8,14,16,17; 69:7,8,10,20,21; 74:18,22; 79:4,12; 109:25.
391 See p. 112.

83:2	O God, do not be silent,	אלהים אל־דמי־לך
	Do not be speechless,	אל תחרש
	And do not remain quiet, O God.	ואל־תשקט אל
83:3	Because now Your enemies are creating an uproar,	כי הנה אויביך יהמיון
	And those who hate You have become arrogant.	ומשנאיך נשאו ראש
83:4	Against Your people they make shrewd plans,	על־עמך יערימו סוד
	And they consult together against Your prized ones.	ויתיעצו על־צפוניך
83:5	They said 'Come, let us annihilate them as a nation,	אמרו לכו ונכחידם מגוי
	That the name of Israel will be remembered no more.	ולא־יזכר שם־ישראל עוד
83:6	For they consulted together with one heart . . .	כי נועצו לב יחדו

This theme is represented fairly widely in the Psalm laments.[392]

Physical Impairment

Physical maladies may seem to be related more closely to the laments of the individual and penitential psalms.[393] However, since the circumstances complained of in the communal laments often have physical implications, it should not be surprising to find descriptions of physical impairment there as well. Certain, perhaps even most, of these symptoms may be considered psychogenic in that they are linked to a calamity in such a wayas to imply that the physical malady is not the direct result of a battle wound or terrorist's act. Rather, they are often described as the result of one's pondering the overwhelming nature of the circumstances. For example:

31:10	Be gracious unto me, O LORD, because of my distress.	חנני יהוה כי צר לי
	My eye is wasted away with grief,	עששה בכעס עיני
	My throat[394] and my belly [as well].	נפשי ובטני
31:11	For my life is exhausted with grief, And my years with groaning.	כי כלו ביגון חיי ושנותי באנחה
	My strength has staggered because of my iniquity	כשל בעוני כחי
	And my bones have wasted away.	ועצמי עששו

---

392 See 31:9,16; 35:19; 42:10; 43:2; 4 4:17; 5 6:10; 59:2; 69:5,19; 74:3,10,18; 80:7; 83:3; 89:2,3,11,43,52.

393 See, e.g., Pss. 22, 38, 51, 88. Cf. Castellino, *Lamentazioni*, pp. 93-96.

394 This translation is both supported by the parallelism with other body parts, and by internal and external documentary evidence. See M. Dahood, *Psalms*, Anchor Bible, vol.I, (New York: Doubleday, 1966), p. 189. Cf. Jonah 2:6; UT 67:II:18-19. Cf. Dahood's review of Kraus' *Psalmen*, Bib 42 (1961): 384.

The psalmist recognizes that these pressures occasioned real grief, and he continues to describe the symptoms of acute grief response as if one had lost one's own friend or brother or even mother (35:14): the profusion of tears (42:4, 56:9, 69:4, 80:6), the fainting spirit and speechlessness (77:4,5), the loss of appetite and severe weight loss (102:5-8), the premature aging (89:46, 102:24).[395]

Death

In the Hebrew literature, the notion of death encompasses more than the biological termination of life. The death motif exhibits a range of connotative meaning depending on the context in which it is used. "The Bible's metaphoric usages of the term [death] correspond, roughly, to such modern perceptions as psychological death, social death, and 'spiritual' death."[396] The motif is used as a metaphor of illness, persecution, great trouble and despair. For example, Bildad's speech to Job includes the expression:

| Job 18:13 | He eats parts of his skin, | יאכל בדי עורו |
| | Maveth, the first-born, eats his limbs. | יאכל בדיו בכור מות |

Jonah 2:3-7 offers another example. This time, the שאול בטן "belly of Sheol," and שחת, the "pit, grave" are used as metaphors of Jonah's watery plight. Still another example of a metaphoric use of death is found in the expression כלב מת "dead dog" meaning aninsignificant person, a "nobody."

The occurrence of "death" as a chthonic spirit or deity is not common in the Hebrew Bible. However, vestiges of this usage seem to be preserved in the proper names of חצרמות "Hatsarmavet ben Yoqtan"[397] and אחימות " Ahimot ben Elqanah."[398]

---

395 A large body of literature has developed on the psychological effect of grief indicating a genuine pathology connected with severe or abnormal grief. The symptoms may on occasion be so severe as to contribute to the apparently premature death of the mourner himself. See E. Lindemann, "Symptomatology and Management of Acute Grief," *American Journal of Psychiatry* 101 (1944): 141-148; See also M. Young, et al., "The Mortality of Widowers," *Lancet* 2 (1963): 454-456 in which the authors show through a study of a sample of 4,486 widowers a 40% increase in the mortality rate during the first six months after the death of a spouse. See also H. Archibald, et al., "Bereavement in Childhood and Adult Psychiatric Disturbance," *Psychosomatic Medicine* 24 (1962): 343-351. Note especially their treatment of biogenetic vulnerability as well as psychiatric vulnerability as a result of grief. See also G. Krupp, "The Bereavement Reaction: A Special Case of Separation Anxiety—Socio-Cultural Considerations," *Psychoanalytic Study of Society* 2 (1962): 42-74, dealing with the symptomatology, pathology, and significance of extreme grief crises.
396 L. Bailey, *Biblical Perspectives on Death* (Philadelphia: Fortress, 1979), p. 98.
397 Gen. 10:26, I Chron. 1:20.
398 I Chron. 6:10.

Tromp observes that most expressions in the Hebrew Bible which deal with death "conceal the existential aspect we expect to find. It occurs, but generally in descriptions of serious illness and the like, which were considered as an anticipation of death."[399] As might be expected, the treatment of various aspects of the death motif is common in the laments of the individual, but they occur as well in the communal laments. For example, the psalmist details in his complaint the potentiality or actuality of death at the hand of the enemy. For example, the complaint in 56:7:

They fight, they hide,	יגורו יצפינו
They watch my footprints	המה עקבי ישמרו
Like those who lie in wait for my life	כאשר קוו נפשי

or in 59:4, ארבו לנפשי "they have lain in wait for my life." The significant thing to note here is that in the communal laments we are not dealing with an individual death, but rather an expression of Hebrew idiom in which, as Eissfeldt pointed out, the downfall or overthrow of the community or nation is thought of as death.[400]

4.5.3 Appeal

It would seem that the purpose of the lamentation was not merely to be cathartic in the current sense—to unload feelings in order to feel better. The laments had as their purpose the resolution of the crisis or calamity, and so an essential component of the lament compositions is the appeal. In most of the Psalms, there is an actual direct appeal to God, but in a couple, the appeal is more implicit than explicit. In these cases, the appeal seems to be assumed by virtue of the expression of confidence and trust.

For example, in the seventy-seventh Psalm one finds expressions such as:

77:2	With my voice I will cry out unto God;	קולי אל־אלהים ואצעקה
	My voice unto God and He will hear me.	קולי אל־אלהים והאזין אלי
	In the day of my distress I sought the Lord	ביום צרתי אדני דרשתי

---

399 N. Tromp, *Primitive Conceptions of Death and the Nether World in the Old Testament*, Biblica et Orientalia 21 (Rome: Pontifical Biblical Institute, 1969), pp. 122, 36.

400 *The Old Testament: An Introduction*, trans. P. Ackroyd (New York: Harper, 1965), p. 95. Note the personification of cities in the ancient Near East. E.g., the motherly aspect of the city-state vis-à-vis her populace or "daughters: בת ציון. Cf. Zech. 2:14, 3:10, Lam. 1:15, 2:1 etc.; בת בבל Isa. 47:1, Jer. 50:42, Ps. 137:8, Zech. 2:11, etc.; בת ירושלם Lam. 2:15; בת אדום Lam. 4:21. On the use of the singular in the communal lament see the discussion of persona below, sect. 4.7.1.

While this Psalm lacks the direct request for specific action common to most of the laments, yet they are marked by the declaration of appeal and by a confidence of being heard. Thus, even this example must be considered to contain this third characteristic component, the appeal.

Of the remaining laments wherein the appeal is direct and specific, there are two kinds of appeal to be found: one positive and the other negative. One is directed toward the plight of the people and calls for deliverance.[401] The other is directed toward the agency of the plight and calls for a cursing of one sort or another.[402] Occasionally, both kinds of appeal are to be found in the same lament.[403] It would seem that behind the appeal aspect of the lament lies a principle of justice that is tied to the notion of covenant. Thus, there is an expectation of God's vindication, sometimes accompanied by a protestation of innocence,[404] sometimes by a recognition of guilt,[405] but always the appeal is made in the context of the covenant and with the principles of justice just mentioned in mind. A most obvious example is Psalm 89:

89:31	If [David's] sons forsake My law	אם־יעזבו בניו תורתי
	And walk not according to My judgments;	ובמשפטי לא ילכון
89:32	If they violate My statutes	אם־חקתי יחללו
	And observe not My commandments,	ומצותי לא ישמרו
89:33	I will punish their rebellion with a rod	ופקדתי בשבט פשעם
	And their iniquity with strokes.	ובנגעים עונם
89:34	But my covenant loyalty[406] I will not take away from them,	וחסדי לא־אפיר מעמו
	Nor will I deal falsely in My faithfulness.	ולא־אשקר באמונתי
89:35	I will not profane My covenant	לא־אחלל בריתי
	Nor will I alter what comes from My lips	ומוצא שפתי לא אשנה

---

401 Pss. 31:3,16-18a; 43:1-3; 44:24-27; 60:3d,4b,7,13; 74:2-3,18-23; 79:8-12; 80:2-4,8,15-20; 85:5-8; 89:51; 102:2-3,25; 142:6-8.
402 Pss. 56:8; 94:1-2; 109:6-20; 137:7-9.
403 E.g., Pss. 35:1-8; 59:2-3,5b-6,12-16; 69:2,17-19,23-29; 83:2,10-18.
404 Ps. 59.
405 Pss. 69, 79.
406 Reading with the Syriac and following II Sam. 7:15 אסיר. Re חסד, see K. D. Sakenfeld, *The Meaning of ḥesed in the Hebrew Bible*. Harvard Semitic Monographs, vol. 17. (Missoula, Mont.: Scholars Press, 1978) who traces its use diachronically and concludes that it refers to the responsibility of the stronger to act on behalf of the weaker, but due to the position of strength, the former cannot be coerced but acts freely toward the helpless party. She offers no English translation but summarizes: "The term *ḥesed* thus proves to be the one which throughout the tradition was remarkably rich in its theological meaning. Here the sovereign freedom of God and his strong commitment to his chosen people were held together in a single word. A single word expressed the utter dependence of the people upon Yahweh and his willingness and ability to deliver them . . ." p. 238.

which echoes Nathan's words to David in II Sam. 7:14: The LORD "will be as a father to him and he will be like a son to me. When he rebels I will correct him with the rod of men and the strokes of the sons of men, but my covenant love will not be removed from him. . . ."

As one might expect, the more overt confessions are to be found in the penitential Psalms. But even in some of the communal laments, as the above passage from Psalm 89 indicates, there seems to be an underlying assumption of some responsibility in the estrangement and corresponding calamity.

79:8	Do not remember our former iniquities	אל־תזכר לנו עונת ראשנים
	. . .	
79:9	Deliver us and atone for our sins	והצילנו וכפר על־חטאתינו
	for Your name's sake.	למען שמך

God's anger understood in the Hebrew context is not aroused capriciously, but for cause. Thus, appeals for its abatement seem to allow the inference of some degree of responsibility on the part of the people.

80:5	How long will you be angry	עד־מתי עשנת בתפלת עמך
	with the prayer of Your people?	
85:5	Cause Your anger toward us to cease.	והפר כעסך עמנו
85:6	Will You forever be angry with us?	הלעולם תאנף בנו
	Will You prolong Your anger	תמשך אפך לדר ודר
	from generation to generation?	

It is the facing of this responsibility which allows for the dialogical nature of the laments and prevents them from being a diatribe against some capricious spirit. It is important to note here that special trust evidenced by the recurring use of the possessive as a vocative: "my God," "my Rock," etc.

4.5.3.1 Appeal for Deliverance from Calamity

The first category of direct, overt appeal is that which petitions the LORD to deliver from the effects of the calamity. There is characteristically a direct correlation between the appeal and the cause of the lament, as would be expected given the specificity of the complaint. The aspects of this appeal cover abandonment and isolation, shame and humiliation, depression and despair, danger from the enemy, physical impairment and death.

Abandonment and Isolation

As the appeals are examined, where the complaints were over a sense of abandonment and isolation, the psalmist appeals for a renewal

of the former relationship. Thus, Psalm 31 laments this sense of abandonment and begs the LORD to "Incline your ear unto me" (v. 3), "Deliver
me with your covenant loyalty" (v. 17). Psalm 69 pleads:

69:17	Answer me, O LORD, for Your covenant loyalty is good; According to the magnitude of Your compassion, turn unto me.	ענני יהוה כי טוב חסדך כרב רחמיך פנה אלי
69:18	And hide not Your face from Your servant; Because of my distress, answer me quickly.	ואל־תסתר פניך מעבדך כי־צר־לי מהר ענני
69:19	Draw near to my soul and redeem it; Because of my enemies ransom me.	קרבה אל־נפשי גאלה למען איבי פדני

Shame and Humiliation

In the sixty-ninth Psalm, it is, at least in part, from חרפה "disgrace,"
בושה "shame," and כלמה "insult," משל "mockery," and the נגינות שותי
שכר "drunkards' mocking song" that the appeal is made for deliverance.

Depression and Despair

From the depths of depression and despair the psalmist appeals for
hope as indicated by the refrain of 42:6, 12; 43: 5 and specifies that that
hope be borne out in God's vindication of Israel against an ungodly
nation (43:1). The Psalmist cries out for God's "light" and "truth" to lead:

43:3	Let them bring me unto Your holy mount Unto Your dwelling places	יביאוני אל־הר־קדשך ואל־משכנותיך
43:4	And I will go to God's altar, Unto God, my great joy.	ואבואה אל־מזבח אלהים אל־אל שמחת

The depression is countered by the confidence of God's strength and
light and truth, and the despair is expected to be turned into great joy at
the renewed sense of God's presence.

Danger from the Enemy

There are really two approaches to this need. One will be dealt with
here, the other will be treated in the next section.[407]

The pattern which calls for a correspondence between the complaint
and the appeal continues. The fifty-ninth Psalm which complains of the
enemy who lies in wait and stirs up strife, pleads:

59:2	Deliver me from my enemies, O my God; From those who rise against me, make me inaccessible.	הצילני מאיבי אלהי ממתקוממי תשגבני

---

[407] See sect. 4.5.3.2.

Again in Psalm 83, God is appealed to to interject Himself on behalf of the oppressed community, to cease His silence and avert the impending danger.[408]

Physical Impairment

Basically, the appeal is for healing or restoration from the physical results of the calamity in question, be it plague or siege or battle.[409] The appeal may be expressed as in Psalm 35:17: השיבה נפשי משאיהם "restore my life from their ravages." In 69:30, the appeal, ישועתך אלהים תשגבני "may Your salvation protect me, O God," comes following the cry אני עני וכואב "I am afflicted and in pain."

Death

Related to the appeal for reversal of physical impairment is the similar approach taken to the threat of death in Psalm 59. But it is Psalm 56 that is perhaps the most interesting in its response to life-threatening oppression.[410] The appeal begins with a call for God's חן "favor" in light of the claim of Israel's consistently having put her trust in Him. Thus, the psalmist proclaims: זה ידעתי כי אלהים לי "This I know: that God is for me!" In the fourteenth verse, there is the anticipated answer to the assumed appeal:

For You will have delivered my soul from death,	כי הצלת נפשי ממות
Keeping my feet far removed from stumbling,	הלא רגלי מדחי
So I may walk before God in the light of life.	להתהלך לפני אלהים באור החים

As already indicated, the references to the death motif may point to the threat of psychological and social death as well as physical death.[411]

4.5.3.2 Appeal for Cursing the Cause of the Calamity

Most of the communal laments are not concerned with imprecations in the appeal theme. However, of the twenty treated in this study, there are three which include imprecations against the enemy along with the appeal for deliverance[412] and three which contain only an imprecatory appeal.[413] Though infrequent, the imprecation does have a primary

---

408 See above, p. 115. Cf. Ps. 35:1-3, 10, 17, 22, etc.
409 See above p. 115.
410 See above p. 117.
411 See p. 116.
412 Pss. 59, 69, 83.
413 Pss. 56, 109, 137. Ps. 56 was used above to illustrate the response to the threat of death. The appeal for deliverance is assumed, however, and not actually expressed.

connection with the lament. That connection has two aspects, both related to the principle of divine justice. On the one hand, there is the positive expectation just mentioned that justice will prevail. On the other, the curse seems clearly to be directed toward the removal of the *cause* of the calamity which is being lamented.

In response to an alleged injustice, the LORD God of hosts is called upon to arouse Himself:

59:6	Awake to punish all the nations! Be not gracious to all who are treacherously wicked.	הקיצה לפקד כל־הגוים אל־תחן כל־בגדי און סלה
59:12	Do not slaughter them, lest my people forget; By Your power, make them homeless and lay them prostrate . . .	אל־תהרגם פן־ישכחו עמי הניעמו בחילך והורידמו
59:14	Destroy in wrath, destroy! and they will be no more	כלה בחמה כלה ואינמו

The imprecation in Psalm 69 perhaps comes closer to a "curse formula." In quite some detail, the psalmist asks that when the enemy feels secure and at peace, may the very locus of the customary enjoyment of that peace and hospitality be turned against them; may physical calamity overtake them and their corporate identity be destroyed. And then the ultimate:

69:29	May they be erased from the Book of Life And with the righteous may they not be enrolled.	ימחו ספר חיים ועם צדיקים אל־יכתבו

Likewise, the protracted use of the jussive in a detailed request for divine judgment is found in Psalm 109.[414]

109:6	Appoint a wicked man to oversee him And let an adversary stand at his right hand.	הפקד עליו רשע ושטן יעמד על־ימינו
109:7	When he is judged may he come out guilty; May his prayer become as sin;	בהשפטו יצא רשע ותפלתו תהיה לחטאה
109:8	May his days become few; May another take his office;	יהיו־ימיו מעטים פקדתו יקח אחר
109:9	May his sons become orphans,	יהיו־בניו יתומים

---

414 There lacks a consensus about the subject and object of the curse of this Psalm which Gunkel thought to be the only "pure" imprecatory Psalm. That is, is the malediction of vv. 6-20 directed against the psalmist, hence Israel, by its enemy, or is it directed against the enemy by the psalmist? It is my judgment that the latter is the case, assuming continuity throughout the fifteen verses. The complaint of the earlier verses is reflected in the reasons for the curse given in v. 16, *viz*, the lack of חסד and the active persecution of the איש עני ואביון "poor and afflicted man." Also the point made in vv. 17 ff. regarding how the subject loved קללה "cursing."

	And his wife a widow;	ואשתו אלמנה
109:10	May his sons continually bum around and beg;	ונוע ינועו בניו ושאלו
	And let them seek far from their desolate places;	ודרשו מחר בותיהם
109:11	May the creditor take aim at all his belongings;	ינקש נושה לכל־אשר־לו
	And may strangers plunder his property;	ויבזו זרים יגיעו
109:12	May there be no one to prolong kindness to him;	אל־יהי־לו משך חסד
	May there be no one gracious to his orphans;	ואל־יהי חונן ליתומיו
109:13	May his posterity be cut off.	יהי־אחריתו להכרית
	In the next generation let their name be blotted out.	בדור אחר ימח שמם

As the curses are subjected to formal analysis, there appears only vaguely what Mowinckel called the "ancient formula of cursing."[415] Although the jussive is used extensively, the actual content of the curse varies so that the common feature is a grammatical-syntactical one rather than a set verbal formula. Such a standard linguistic feature of expression probably should not be called formulaic.

The point also needs to be made that in the appeal units there is a significant admixture of imperative clauses and jussive clauses, thus, precluding any standardization of form. For example:

35:4	Let them be ashamed,	יבשו
	Let them be dishonored,	ויכלמו
	Let them be turned back,	יסגו אחור
	Let them be humiliated.	ויחפרו
35:5	Let them be like chaff;	יהיו כמץ
35:6	Let their way be dark and slippery.	יהי־דרכם חשך וחלקלקות
	...	
35:8	Let destruction come;	תבואהו שואה
	Let them fall [in net].	יפל בה
56:8	Put them down in anger.	באף עמים הורד
59:6	Awake to punish;	הקיצה לפקד
	Do not be gracious.	אל־תחן
59:12	Scatter them;	הניעמו
	Bring them down.	הורידמו
59:13	Let them be caught in their pride.	ילכדו בגאונם
59:14	Destroy them in wrath.	כלה בחמה
69:23	May their table become a trap;	יהי־שלחנם לפניהם לפח
69:24	May their eyes grow dim;	תחשכנה עיניהם מראות

415 Mowinckel, *Psalms*, vol. I, p. 202. He cites as examples: "may the gentiles be put to shame," "be destroyed," "may the culprit go to Sheol" (Hades), "may Yahweh cut off all flattering lips," and so on.

	May their loins continually shake.	ומתניהם תמיד המעד
69:25	Pour out Your curse upon them;	שפך־עליהם זעמך
	May Your burning anger overtake them.	וחרון אפך ישיגם
69:26	May their camp be desolate;	תהי־טירתם נשמה
	May none dwell in their tents.	באהליהם אל־יהי ישב
69:28	Add to their punishment;	תנה־עון על־עונם
	May they not come into Your righteousness.	ואל־יבאו בצדקתך
69:29	May they be blotted out of the book of life;	ימחו מספר חיים
	May they not be registered with the righteous.	ועם צדיקים אל־יכתבו
83:10	Deal with them like Midian.	עשה־להם כמדין
83:12	Make their princes like Oreb.	שיתמו נדיבמו כערב
83:14	Make them like the tumbleweed.	שיתמו כגלגל
83:16	Pursue them;	תרדפם בסערך
	Terrify them.	תבהלם
83:17	Fill their faces with dishonor.	מלא פניהם קלון
83:18	Let them be ashamed,	יבשו
	Let them be terrified,	ויבהלו עדי־עד
	Let them be humiliated,	ויחפרו
	Let them perish.	ויאבדו
109:6	Appoint a wicked one over him.	הפקד עליו רשע
109:7	Let him come out guilty;	יצא רשע
	Let his prayer become sin.	ותפלתו תהיה לחטאה
109:8	Let his days be few;	יהיו ימיו מעטים
	Let another take his office.	פקדתו יקח אחר
109:9	Let his children be fatherless;	יהיו בניו יתומים
109:10	Let his children wander and beg.	ונוע ינועו בניו ושאלו

However, in at least one case, as we shall see, we find merely a non-verbal clause expressing an imprecation by Israel. This occurs in Psalm 137:

137:8	Oh daughter of Babel, you devastator,[416]	בת־בבל השדודה
	Blessed is the one who will reward you	אשרי שישלם לך
	With the equivalent of your dealing with us.	את גמולך שגמלת לנו
137:9	Blessed is the one who will seize,	אשרי שיאחז
	And dash your little ones to pieces against the cliff.	ונפץ את־עלליך אל־הסלע

Here, the intent of the imprecation is clear. There is a brief "prayer" in verse 7, expressed with the imperative זְכֹר יהוה "Remember, O LORD!"

---

416 Unless this is to be understood as so confidently expected that it is spoken of as a foregone conclusion, hence, the passive "devastated one," it seems to suit the context best to treat השדודה as having a metathesis and following T and S, read השודדה "devastator" upon whom it is wished that it shall be returned in kind.

but the form of the imprecation per se lacks the expected imperative or jussive.

4.5.3.3 Motivation

An element which is often an integral part of either form of appeal is the citation of certain reasons why Israel is thus entreating her God. The presence of such a feature serves to support the observation made above that lamentation in Israel was dialogical in nature.

God's Reputation

At the heart of the appeal is the apparent conflict between the prosperity of the wicked and the suffering of the righteous in the face of which the wicked become emboldened in their practice of evil, blatant in their overt expressions of pride, and devoid of any notion of God in their thinking. This is set over against the wonders of the Most High God. There is concern expressed that God's reputation not be tarnished among men. For example, Ps. 74:18:[417]

Remember this O LORD:	זכר זאת אויב חרף יהוה
the enemy has reproached;	
Impious people have reviled Your Name.	ועם נבל נאצו שמך

In Psalm 89 it is God's reputation for His "covenant loyalty" that elicits the psalmist's trust, the basis of appeal.[418] Elsewhere, He is appealed to as "a rock of refuge," "a stronghold," "my fortress" (31:3, 4), and it is concluded that:

For the sake of Your name	למען שמך תנחני ותנהלני
You will lead and guide me[419]	

In Psalms 35, 77 and 89 one finds the confession:

89:9	O LORD God of hosts,	יהוה אלהי צבאות
	Who is like You, O mighty LORD?[420]	מי כמוך חסין יה

And His enduring and immutable nature is appealed to in Psalm 102:25-28.

---

[417] Cf. Pss. 59:14; 79:9, 10; 83:19. This is an example of the use of the motif of the honor of God in the Hebrew Bible in which appeal is made on the basis of a slightly veiled threat against God's reputation should He not respond positively. See, e.g., Gen. 18:23-25; Ex. 32:11-14; Num. 14:13-19; Isa. 48:11; Ezek. 36:22-32.

[418] Cf. Pss. 69:14, 17; 89:2, 3; 109:21, etc.

[419] Cf. Pss. 79:9; 102:13.

[420] Cf. Pss. 35:10; 77:14.

God's Previous Acts

Closely connected with the notion of God's reputation is the idea that as a living God who has acted in the past, His character and nature call for action in the present and future which will have continuity and consistency. Thus, the appeal is often accompanied by a recital of God's might acts in history as a basis for both entreating Him now and confidently expecting that He will act true to form.

Psalm 77 is a good example of this feature. The psalmist muses:

77:12	I will remember the LORD's dealings;	אזכיר מעללי יה
	Certainly I will remember	כי אזכרה מקדם פלאך
	Your miracles from olden times.	
77:13	I will recite all Your doing[s],	והגיתי בכל פעלך
	And consider Your deeds.	ובעלילותיך אשיחה

Throughout the laments one finds numerous references to God's past actions. Against Israel's enemies God is asked:

83:10	Do to them as [You did] with Midian,	עשה־להם כמדין
	Sisera and Jabin by the wadi Kishon.	כסיסרא כיבין בנחל קישון

Much of Psalm 89 is taken up with the recital of God's covenant dealings with David which serves as a basis for the appeal.[421] God's past actions have been recited in testimony by one generation to another—a practice institutionalized in the Passover as well as other occasions in the normal course of Israelite life.[422]

Repentance of Israel

A third category of motivation sometimes offered as the basis of appeal or at least the basis for expecting God to respond is the recognition and confession of responsibility—guilt before God, and an expressed desire for restoration. Although this may be more common in the individual laments, it is not totally absent from the national laments. For example, in Psalm 31, while the focus of the lament is on the adversaries who have caused such oppression, there is also a hint of a moral and ethical responsibility on Israel's part. Thus, the LORD is entreated to show His graciousness unto them in light of the great devastation that has taken place. Psalm 60 recognizes that God, acting and speaking out of His holiness, has been angry with His people and has rejected them and broken them in pieces. Psalm 69 confesses:

---

421 Cf. Pss. 74:12-17; 80:9-14.
422 See Ex. 12:26, 27; Dt. 6:20; Jud. 6:13. Cf. Ps. 78, especially v. 3.

69:6   Oh God, indeed You know my folly   אלהים אתה ידעת לאולתי
       And my offenses from You are not hidden.   ואשמותי ממך לא־נכחדו

And Psalm 79 asks not to have to experience the effects of the sins of a previous generation but accepts responsibility for its own:

79:9   Help us, Oh God of our deliverance,   עזרנו אלהי ישענו
       For the sake of glory of Your name;   על־דבר כבוד־שמך
       And deliver us, and atone for our sins   והצילנו וכפר על־חטאתינו
       For Your name's sake.   למען שמך

Claims of Innocence

The next category claims real or assumes judicial innocence.[423] In these cases the psalmists protest that the oppression is inappropriate, at least at the time. The lesson has been learned. It is time for relief—deliverance. It would seem that the majority of the laments use this type of motivational appeal. One common approach to this appeal is the frequent rhetorical use of למה:

42:10   Why have You forgotten me?[424]   למה שכחתני
44:24   Why do You sleep, Oh Lord?   למה תישן אדני
44:25   Why do You hide Your face   למה פניך תסתיר
       and forget our affliction and oppression?   תשכח ענינו ולחצנו
74:1   Why, Oh God, have You rejected forever?   למה אלהים זנחת לנצח
74:11   Why do You withdraw Your hand?   למה תשיב ידך

In the light of all You have done to establish Your vineyard:

80:13   Why have You broken down its walls   למה פרצת גדריה
       So each one traveling may pluck [from] it?   וארוה כל־עברי דרך

The answer assumed is that at least at this time there is no good reason. Of course, this is only an oblique denial of guilt or responsibility and protestation of innocence. Others are more straightforward.

One way of making the claim was to argue that this calamity had befallen them without cause. That is to say, they were not responsible.

35:7   For without cause they   כי חנם טמנו לי שחת רשתם
       concealed their snare for me;
       Without cause they spied for my life.   חנם חפרו לנפשי
69:5   More numerous than the hairs of my head   רבו משערות ראשי
       Are those who hate me without cause.   שנאי חנם
69:8   Because I have borne reproach on Your account   כי־עליך נשאתי חרפה
       Ignominy has covered my face.   כסתה כלמה פני

---

[423] By judicial innocence is meant that case where the liability of actual guilt has been paid for and the "defendant" released from the penalty.

[424] Cf. Psalm 43:2.

109:2	Because a wicked and deceitful mouth have they opened against me; They spoke [against] me with a lying tongue.	כי פי רשע ופי־מרמה עלי פתחו דברו אתי לשון שקר
109:3	With words of hate they have surrounded me; And they fought me without cause.	ודברי שנאה סבבוני וילחמוני חנם
109:4	In exchange for my love, they accuse me; But I am in prayer.	תחת־אהבתי ישטנוני ואני תפלה
109:5	And they laid upon me evil in exchange for good, And hate in exchange for my love.	וישימו עלי רעה תחת טובה ושנאה תחת אהבתי

Another approach taken by the psalmist was to posit a contrast between the appellant and the enemy/accuser. At least there must exist a relative innocence. Thus, the appellant may boast:

31:7	I hate those who revere vain idols; But in the LORD have I put my trust.	שנאתי השמרים הבלי שוא ואני אל־יהוה בטחתי

The enemy, the one who has "secretly laid the net," is identified as one who reveres vain idols in contrast to the appellant who boasts of his trust in the LORD. In numerous ways in Psalm 44 it is explained how appellants have trusted in Him.[425] Other examples would be:

44:9	In God have we boasted all the day, And Your name we will thank forever.	באלהים הללנו כל־היום ושמך לעולם נודר סלה
44:10	Yet You have spurned and humiliated us. . . .	אף־זנחת ותכלימנו
44:18	All this came upon us, But we have not forgotten You, Nor have we dealt falsely with Your covenant.	כל־זאת באתנו ולא שכחנוך ולא־שקרנו בבריתך
44:19	Our heart has not backslidden, And our steps have not turned aside from Your way,	לא־נסוג אחור לבנו ותט אשרינו מני ארחך
44:20	Though You crushed us in a place of jackals, And covered us with the shadow of death.	כי דכיתנו במקום תנים ותכס עלינו בצלמות

A sense of innocence is implied in Psalm 58:11. The appellant is called the צריק "righteous" who will delight to see God's נקם "vengeance" upon the "wicked," "lying" "workers of unrighteousness." Then, in Psalm 59, a most explicit declaration:

59:3	Deliver me from workers of iniquity...	הצילני מפעלי און
59:4	For now they have lain in wait for my life. Strong men stir up strife against me, *Not for my rebellion* *Nor for my sin*, Oh LORD.	כי הנה ארבו לנפשי יגורו עלי עזים לא־פשעי ולא־חטאתי יהוה

---

425 Vv. 4, 6, 15, 18, 19.

It is of more than passing interest that Psalm 69 possibly contains examples of both the claim of innocence or non-responsibility and the admission of guilt. Though it is difficult to date this Psalm, its expressions are appropriate to the period around 535-515 B.C. This was a period of tension. The return was made possible by Cyrus' decree in 538, yet only some 50,000 chose to return. The restoration of Israel to her homeland was indeed a sign of God's favor and an indication that He had forgiven their sins. The prophets Haggai and Zechariah indicate, however, that the exuberance that may have accompanied the return was short-lived. They interpret the pressures of thenext decade and a half as clear signs of God's displeasure at their misplaced priorities and loyalties. Haggai calls on the people to take these issues to heart. Zechariah pleads for the returnees to "turn from their evil ways and wicked deeds."[426]

In the mean time, Psalm 85 lays claim to a judicial innocence. This lament begins by laying claim to judicial innocence and the evidence of its validity in the LORD's restoration of the fortunes of Jacob:

85:3	You bore the guilt of Your people;	נשאת עון עמך
	You covered all their sin;	כסית כל־חטאחם סלה
85:4	You withdrew all Your fury;	אספת כל־עברתך
	You turned back from Your flaming anger.	השיבות מחרון אפך

But the psalmist continues by asking for God's grace apparently in the face of recurring signs of God's discipline.

85:5	Restore us, O God of our salvation,	שובנו אלהי ישענו
	and cause Your anger toward us to cease.	והפר כעסך עמנו
85:6	Will You be angry with us forever?	הלעולם תאנף־בנו
	Your anger from generation to generation?	תמשך אפך לדר ודר

Then the psalmist implores God to restore and to remove the evidences of His anger. They have had enough. It need not be prolonged. It is time for them to be brought to life again, to experience His חסד and ישע because the issue has been settled. In acquired innocence, they appeal their case. The psalmist relates the deliverance sought to a restoration of כבוד " glory" to the land.[427]

Object of Israel's Trust

This category of motivational argument is logically related to the previous one. Throughout the prophetic literature misplaced trust was a problem addressed by the prophets and was cited by the prophets as

---

[426] Hag. 1:5,7; Zech. 1:3-4.
[427] Psalm 85:10.

reason for calamitous judgment.[428] This data provides an adequate reason for the declarations found in certain of the laments that Israel's trust is in the LORD and therefore, they appeal to Him to act.

The two major issues treated here are the one of trusting objects—tangible or intangible—other than the LORD, and the other of response to fearful situations. In the first instance, the psalmists make it plain:

31:7	I hate those who observe empty vanities;	שנאתי השמרים הבלי־שוא
	But in the LORD have I put my trust.	ואני אל־יהוה בטחתי
44:7	Because I have not trusted in my bow	כי לא בקשתי אבטח
	And my sword cannot deliver me.	וחרבי לא תושיעני

Whereupon, the psalmist continues to laud the salvation of the LORD and to claim to have been boasting in Him all the while.

In the second instance, one finds the confession of Psalm 56:

56:4	The day I am afraid,	יום אירא אני אליך אבטח
	In You will I trust.	
56:5	In God, His Word I praise,	באלהים אהלל דברו
	In God I trust, I will not fear.	באלהים בטחתי לא אירא
	What can flesh do to me?	מה יעשה בשר לי

4.5.4 Expression of Confidence/Hope

W. Brueggemann makes an important point when he says:

"It will be seen that a great many of the psalms [both individual and community laments] are to be understood and interpreted around the turn from distress to relief. The crucial structural question is the relation between these contrasted parts. How does the speaker get from distress to relief and what transforms the mood? It will be immediately apparent that this is not simply a literary question but cuts to the heart of the theological issue for faith. Since we deal only with the extant texts we cannot give a clear answer to the question but we simply observe that the "action" of the lament form lies between the two parts."[429]

Claus Westermann makes the same point: "This transition is the real theme of the Psalms which are being discussed here. They are no longer mere petition, but petition that has been heard. They are no longer mere

---

428 Examples are too numerous to treat here. Hosea offers perhaps the most graphic example in his scathing denunciation of misplaced trust—going after idols and other gods—as a violation of a sacred covenant. So the LORD proclaims that He will be "unto Ephraim as a moth, and to the house of Judah as rottenness;. . . For I will be unto Ephraim as a lion and as a young lion to the house of Judah. . ." 5:12,14. Haggai also cites God's claim of responsibility for the calamities confronting the repatriates as a result of their misplaced priorities, 1:6,9-11; 2:16-17. Cf. Jer. 17:5-11.

429 "Hurt to Joy," p. 9.

lament, but lament that has been turned to praise."[430] No fewer than ten of the twenty laments contain some expression of confidence/hope.[431]

Psalms 31 and 42/3 begin the entire lament with just such an expression of confidence. Prefaced by a claim of trust and abbreviated appeal, the first strophe of Psalm 31 declares:

31:3	Be to me as a rock of refuge,	היה לי לצור מעוז
	A stronghold to deliver me.	לבית מצודות להושיעני
31:4	Because You are my rock and my stronghold.	כי־סלעי ומצודתי אתה
31:8	I will rejoice and be happy in	אגילה ואשמחה בחסדך
	Your covenant loyalty.	
31:15	But I trusted in You, O LORD.	ואני עליך בטחתי יהוה
31:16	My times are in Your hands.	בידך עתתי
31:25	Be firm and let Your heart show strength;	חזקו ויאמץ לבבכם
	All who wait expectantly for the LORD.	כל־המיחלים ליהוה

Psalm 42/3 opens with an expression of commitment of desire and in the depths of despair yet confesses:

42:9	By day, the LORD will command	יומם יצוה יהוה חסדו
	His covenant loyalty	
	And by night, His song will be with me,	ובלילה שירה עמי
	A prayer to the God of my life.	תפלה לאל חיי

Throughout the lament, a refrain recurs, which expresses both turmoil and despair on the one hand, and just as clearly on the other:

42:6-7	Wait expectantly for God	הוחילי לאלהים
	For I will yet give Him thanks,	כי־עוד אודנו
	The deliverance of my countenance and my God	ישועות פניו אלהי

Next to the complaint and the appeal, the expression of confidence/hope is the most common feature of the lament.

---

[430] *The Praise of God in the Psalms* (Richmond: John Knox, 1965), p. 80. Cf. also Harvey Guthrie, *Israel's Sacred Songs* (New York: Seabury, 1966). Brueggemann gives a good summary of the variety of explanations regarding this change that have been put forward by modern scholars. Although each of the theories has something to commend itself, none fits all the laments. He concludes by stating "The question of how the changed mood and changed situation is effected cannot be definitively answered, but that it was changed is beyond doubt. And that is the central conviction of Israel about the structure of reality. Life is transformed, health is restored, enemies are resisted and destroyed, death is averted, *Shalom* is given again. The structure of the poem expresses this change." "Hurt to Joy," pp. 9-10.

[431] Pss. 31:3-4,8,15-16,25; 42:6,9; 43:5b; 44:5-9; 56:4,5,10,12; 59:9-11; 60:8-10,14; 74:12; 94:14,17-23; 102:23-28. See also Gunkels' treatment of the *Gewissheit der Erhörung* motif, *Einleitung* sect. 6, pp.19 ff., 23. See above, p. 92.

4.5.5 Thanksgiving and Praise

The last identifiable element to be treated is that of the expression and/or vow of thanksgiving and praise. Six of the twenty laments include a hymn of praise which recites God's divine attributes and/or His mighty deeds. Ten of the twenty include vows to praise God in the days to come, thanking Him for His mighty intervention on behalf of Israel.

However, more notable than the opening expressions of praise are those which close the laments. As with what have been called the "expression of confidence/hope," so with the vows of praise, they mark a significant shift of focus and attitude. For example, the frightening calamity of Psalm 56 is concluded with the exclamation: "This I know: that God is for me!" followed by the refrain:[432]

56:11	In God, Whose word I praise,	באלהים אהלל דבר
	In the LORD, Whose word I praise.	ביהוה אהלל דבר
56:12	In God I trust,	באלהים בטחתי
	I shall not fear!	לא אירא
	What can man do to me?	מה־יעשה אדם לי
56:13	Upon me, Oh God, are Your vows;	עלי אלהים נדריך
	I will give thank offerings to You.	אשלם תודת לך

Likewise, Psalm 59 closes:

59:17	But as for me, I will sing of Your might;	ואני אשיר עזך
	I will cry out loud of Your covenant loyalty in the morning	וארנן לבקר חסדך
	Because You have been my security,	כי־היית משגב לי
	And a refuge in the day of my distress,	ומנוס ביום צר־לי
59:18	Oh my Strength, unto You I will sing praise.	עזי אליך אזמרה
	For God is my security,	כי־אלהים משגבי
	My God of covenant loyalty.	אלהי חסדי

4.5.6 Summary

A theological analysis of the laments shows that even in the face of gross calamity there is a virtually unshakeable conviction in Israel that she is dealing with the almighty God: a God Who has the wherewithal to address the problem and Who, by virtue of the covenant He has made with Israel, is concerned with their plight. Out of that relationship and that concern He can be expected to act on her behalf.

The elements of the national lament are: 1) direct address, 2) the lament proper—the complaint, 3) the appeal for deliverance and/or 4)

---

[432] Cf. v. 5.

the cursing of the enemy, 5) the reasons why God should act, 6) an expression of confidence/hope and 7) an expression and/or vow of praise and thanksgiving.

There also seems to be an underlying attitude that marks the laments—one of steadfast hope. This optimism remains firm even in the face of circumstances which appear to be humanly impossible. This too seems to have its basis in the theology of Israel. There one finds basic convictions about God and about His concern and His accessibility.[433] At least for the devout in Israel, there is no need to maintain that inner turmoil and despair which would seem only natural to the circumstances. There is no need to foster the depression by griping and exchanging bitterness by merely talking about the plight to others equally affected and equally powerless to do anything about it. There is no need to merely talk *about* God and what He has apparently allowed. Israel can talk *to* God and *with* Him.

4.6 *Thematic Elements in the Book of Lamentations*

We now turn to the other collection of communal laments in Israel: the book of Lamentations. The book consists of five chapters, each a separate lament poem, the first four of which use the alphabetic acrostic device seen in the Psalms. Scholars seem unanimous in viewing the book as a lament. But from there, opinion is divided.

As we look to Lamentations for details of its thematic content, care must be taken not to assume an identity with the Psalms and thereby impose the characteristics observed in the laments of the Psalter upon these here. However, for the sake of comparison and analysis, it will be useful to see if there is a compatibility with those features. But, at the same time, we must note any additional features not found in the Psalms and vice versa.

4.6.1 Direct Address

In Lamentations there is not a dominant addressee. In these five poems, the author makes use of a literary device, whereby he assumes various characters through which he expresses himself in more breadth than would be possible by means of a single viewpoint. Thus, as the specific subject and the treatment of that subject changes, so do the "speaker" and the "audience." For example, the author assumes the personified character of the city of Jerusalem in 1:9,11-22, 2:20-22; that of a

---

433 See Deut. 7, II Chron. 7:13-18 etc.

reporter in 1:1-11,15,17, 2:1-19; that of a defeated soldier in chapter three echoing the voice of Jerusalem; that of the bourgeois in chapter four echoing the voice of the reporter; and that of the community of Jerusalem in chorus in chapter five.[434] Furthermore, Lamentations does seem to include substantially more of what was described above as "talking about God" with reference to the complaint. By means of the various personae, the covenant people appear to talk the issues over among themselves as they recount their former glory in light of their current grief. At least, it is often reviewed in public, and God is referred to in the third person a great deal more than in the Psalm laments.[435] The book of Lamentations begins:

1:1	Ah! How the city sits isolated,	איכה ישבה בדד העיר
	The Lady of the people.[436]	רבתי עם
	She has become like a widow,	היתה כאלמנה
	[who was once] Lady among the nations.	רבתי בגוים
	Princess among the provinces,	שרתי במדינות
	She has become a corvee laborer.	היתה למס

and continues through some thirty-one *stichoi* to delineate in the third person the grief of the city and its causes, her loneliness and despair. But this recitation is not overtly addressed to anyone specifically. Given the response of v. 9c and vv. 11ff., we can only conclude that the account is intended for those directly involved—those who had been a part of the devastation and despair.

In a similar manner, chapters two and four describe with an almost detached tone the calamity that has overwhelmed the daughter of Zion. Chapters three and five speak in the first person of the effect of the LORD's judgment. In the main, the indications are that the exiled "victims" are the audience, not so much as formal addressees but as reflective addressees in a series of soliloquies.

There are, however, interwoven throughout these laments, some statements or requests addressed directly to the LORD:

1:9	Witness, O LORD, my affliction	ראה יהוה את עניי
1:11	Look, O LORD, and give attention,	ראה יהוה והביטה
1:20	Look, O LORD! For I am distressed;	ראה יהוה כי צר לי

---

434 See W. Lanahan, "The Speaking Voice."

435 Lam 2:1-19 and 4:1-22 use the third masculine singular in referring to God, amounting to 38% of the line-volume of the book.

436 Translating as fem. of רב n. m. "chief;" hence, "lady" after the use of *rbt* "lady, mistress" in Ugaritic, Phoenician and Punic honorific appellatives also noting the apparent parallelism between רבית and שרתי "princess." Cf. T. F. McDaniel, "Philological Studies in Lamentations: I," Bib 49 (1968):29-31.

1:21 Listen, because I am groaning!   ...שמעו כי נאנחה אני
       O bring the day You have proclaimed,   הבאת יום קראת...
       And let them be like me.   ויהיו כבוני
1:22 Let all their wickedness come before You,   תבא כל רעתם לפניך
       And deal severely with them..   ועולל למו...
2:20 Look, Oh LORD and give attention   ראה יהוה והביטה
       To whom You have thus dealt severely..   למי עוללת כה...
2:21 You killed [them] in the day of Your anger;   הרגת ביום אפך
       You slaughtered [them]; You had no compassion.   טבחת לא חמלת

In the third chapter the afflicted one considers the boundlessness of
the LORD's covenant loyalty and compassion and cries to the LORD:

3:23 Great is Your faithfulness!   ...רבה אמונתך

and then enjoins his compatriots to repent, to lift heart and hand to God
in heaven to whom they say in unison:

3:42 We have rebelled and disobeyed,   נחנו פשענו ומרינו
       You have not forgiven.   אתה לא סלחת
3:43 You have clothed Yourself with anger   סכתה באף ותרדפנו
       and pursued us;
       You have killed, You had no compassion   הרגת לא חמלת
3:44 You have covered Yourself with a cloud   סכותה בענן לך
       So prayer could not get through.   מעבור תפלה
3:45 You have made us an offscouring and refuse   סחי ומאוס תשימנו
       Among the peoples.   בקרב העמים
3:55 I called Your name, Oh LORD   קראתי שמך יהוה
       From out of the lowest pit.   מבור תחתיות

For the next twelve verses, the lament is addressed in the second person directly to the LORD, thus making the third lament poem the one
with the most extensive direct address. The fourth does not address God.
But only the fifth lament opens with a direct address to the LORD. Even
here, however, it is not a formal invocation but an appeal:

5:1   Remember, Oh LORD, what has happened to us;   זכר יהוה מה היה לנו
       Look and see our reproach!   הביט וראה את חרפתנו

Thus, it appears that, while there seems to be more recital of the
calamity among and for the sake of the afflicted community, there
remains ample evidence of the dialogical nature and function of the
lament. And the poet's use of different personae to portray the various
facets of the calamity and its effects upon the community and its
covenant relations with its God seems to be the main reason for the more
limited use of direct address.

4.6.2 Complaint or Lament Proper

Three of the five chapters of Lamentations open with the expression that has come to be considered a hallmark of lament: איכה "How? Ah how!"[437] However, the use of this term seems better to be explained as simply one of those which suits a sigh and/or exclamation rather than as a *"characteristic* expression ... which *normally* stands at the beginning"[438] [emphasis added] of a funeral dirge—both the prototypical and the dirge adapted to a communal or political expression. The data just does not support this.[439] However, of the seventy-eight occurrences of איך, איכה in the Bible, the vast majority have nothing to do with formal lamentation. Rather, it merely serves as an adverbial interrogative.[440] It is used seventeen times in the book of Jeremiah, more than any other single book. And even there, although it is used as an exclamation in the context of lament in 9:18,[441] the majority occur in regular narrative or discourse.

4.6.2.1 Enemies

In contrast to the Psalm laments, the book of Lamentations is not nearly so concerned with the role of the enemy—either political or moral and ethical. For the most part, this is due to the perspective of the book. Given the subject and theme of Lamentations, one would not expect as much attention. The internal machinations of the proud and rebellious and the life-threatening confrontations of her political enemies have since become a foregone conclusion. It has happened. Judgment has come, and the Holy City lies in ruin. The efforts to negotiate survival with surrounding nations so avidly denounced by the prophets had failed.[442] Judah's sovereignty has been exchanged for slavery.

1:3	Judah has gone into exile under affliction,	גלתה יהודה מעני
	And under great servitude.	ומרב עבדה
	She dwells among the nations,	היא ישבה בגוים
	[But] she found no rest.	לא מצאה מנוח
1:5	Her foes became her masters,	היו צרוה לראש
	Her enemies be at ease.	איביה שלו

---

437 Jahnow, *Leichenlied,* p. 136.
438 As Eissfeldt summarizes the somewhat popular view of the significance of איכה, *Introduction,* pp. 94-95, 97.
439 E.g., II Sam. 1:19,25,27 includes the refrain: איך נפלו גבורים "How the mighty have fallen!"; Jer. 9:18 איך שדדנו "How we are ruined!; Ezek. 26:17 איך אבדת "How you have perished!"; Mic. 2:4 איך ימיש לי "How he removes it from me!"
440 Gen. 26:9, 39:9, 44:8,34; I Sam. 16:2 etc.
441 Cf. the *mashal* in Isa. 14:4,12.
442 Cf. Lam. 1:2, 19; 5:6 with Jer. 2:13, 18, 33, 36, 37, etc.

Likewise, her sanctity has been violated and profaned. And the nations are not to be blamed alone. The writer of Lamentations makes specific point of the fact that:

2:14	Your prophets have seen for you	נביאיך חזו לך
	A worthless whitewash;[443]	שוא ותפל
	And they have not exposed your iniquity	ולא־גלו על־עונך
	In order to reverse your captivity;	להשיב שביתך
	But they have seen oracles for you	ויחזו לך משאות
	That were worthless deceptions.	שוא ומדוחים
4:13	By reason of the sins of her prophets,	מחטאת נביאיה
	The iniquities of her priests	עונות כהניה
	Who shed in her midst,	השפכים בקרבה
	The blood of the righteous.	דם צדיקים

Those who were to have been leaders are thus accused as foes who tore away at the moral/ethical and spiritual fabric of the nation.

4.6.2.2 Calamity

As indicated above, the calamitous ruin of the nation is of special concern here. The effect is overwhelming. Granted, the treatment varies somewhat from chapter to chapter, but throughout the five chapters, one finds the political and the moral and ethical and spiritual ramifications intertwined. The widow is grieving, the princess banished, the noble made slave, and:

1:4	The roads of Zion are mourning	דרכי ציון אבלות
	Because no one comes for the appointed festivals.	מבלי באי מועד
1:10	She saw gentiles	...ראתה גוים
	Had entered her sanctuary.	באו מקדשה

The combined effect of the political and moral devastation is virtually beyond description. The impact of the calamity on Judah was overwhelming. But there is still much more data which points to the subjective impact of the situation. It was not just "bad luck." It was not merely the reversal of good fortune. The enemy in focus in Lamentations is not just one or another of the גוים "nations."

4.6.2.3 Divine Adversary

Lamentations speaks of Judah's circumstances and their causes in a way somewhat different from those Psalm laments which appear to be treating the same or similar circumstances. I am referring to the role of the divine adversary. This is true especially of chapters two and three.

---

443 Or "worthless and tasteless sayings."

The subsequent poems (chapters) develop the theme struck in chapter one: יהוה הוגה "the LORD caused her to suffer" as the rage of His anger is poured out upon them. He beclouds, יעיב, them in His anger, He casts down, השליך, Israel's glory, He swallowed, בלע, them up without sparing. He has הרס torn down, חלל profaned, גדע cut off, בער burned, הרג killed, שפך poured out (anger), איב become hostile to, and the verbs multiply as a scan of these chapters will show.[444]

This feature has a marked effect on the whole tenor and treatment of the book of Lamentations. God is indeed cast as adversary as Deuteronomy indicated.[445] Indeed, the prophets who rebuked in no uncertain terms that syncretism which could not and would not be tolerated have been vindicated. Token allegiance to the LORD was worse than inadequate and the fact of this mere observance of the cult in Jerusalem, rather than bringing the security that was assumed, was an abomination to the LORD and cause for the severest judgment.

4.6.2.4 Scope of Complaint

These laments outline in characteristic detail just what is troubling the people. But the historic frame of reference is more limited, and hence the elements just discussed are somewhat more limited or otherwise modified from the Psalm laments as a whole. And so the specific foci of complaint are also more limited, and the balance of treatment shifts.

Abandonment and Isolation

These laments, as we have seen above, are largely concerned with the sense of rejection by God and isolation from Him and hence, from the normal means of His providential grace. The impact on Judah's society is lamented too, as all the normal relationships break down, even to the

---

444 The issues raised in Lamentations are undeniably theological ones. Several have offered treatments of this issue: H-J. Kraus, *Klagelieder* (Threni), BKAT vol. 20, 2d ed. (Neukirchen: Neukirchener Verlag, 1960), cf. Section 5 "Zur Theologie der Threni"; N. Gottwald, *Lamentations*, cf. ch. 3 "Key to the Theology of Lamentations," ch. 4 "The Theology of Doom," and ch. 5 "The Theology of Hope;" B. Albrektson, *Studies in the Text and Theology of the Book of Lamentations* (Lund: Gleerup, 1963). These last two prove to be the most helpful on the background and issues of the theology of Lamentations as they interact with each other. Gottwald raises some important questions and makes some significant contributions to Lamentations study. Albrektson's treatment of the theology of Lamentations offers a helpful critique particularly in addressing data which Gottwald avoids, which avoidance skews his conclusions. Albrektson argues convincingly that the role of the Zion tradition and the theology of Deuteronomy are both pivotal in the study and understanding of Lamentations.

445 Cf. the close parallels between Lamentations and Deuteronomy, especially chps. 28 and 32.

extent of mother-love's being perverted to cannibalism practiced on off-spring.[446]

Shame and Humiliation

The utter humiliation of Judah is a concern as well, but, relative to the other issues addressed in the laments, not a major one. To be sure, there was a sense of betrayal at the hands of erstwhile friends[447] and the chagrin of having one's severe misfortune cheered on by those watching on.[448]

1:8   All who honored her, make light of her   כל־מכבדיה הזילוה

Depression and Despair

Also, a sense of helplessness and hopelessness is described. The pain is indescribable; the mind לב is miserable; the heart כבד is poured out; the tears are interminable; and the soul is bowed down.[449]

Danger from the Enemy

As with the Psalm laments, there is some expression given in response to past successes and the continuing threat of the enemy. The victor is presented as having vaunted itself and rejoicing over the calamity.[450] The LORD Himself, by His actions, comes to be identified with the enemy.[451] Though the devastation has already taken place, the continued ability of the enemy to act apparently with impunity is of concern.

4.6.3 Appeal

As in the Psalter, there are two aspects of the appeal. The first and the predominant one in Lamentations is the appeal for deliverance and restoration. Although each of the five chapters is a self-contained poem, they still build toward a climax in the fifth poem. This is seen especially in light of the essential elements of the lament. The earlier chapters articulate the nature and effects of the calamity and build toward an impassioned appeal in the last chapter.

In each of the poems and in all five taken together, the attention given to the matter of appeal is not very great. Nor are the appeals which

---

[446] Lam. 2:20; 4:10.
[447] Lam. 1:2, 19.
[448] Lam. 1:21; 2:15; 3:14.
[449] Lam. 1:12; 1:22; 2:11; 1:2, 16; 2:11, 18; 3:20.
[450] Lam. 1:9, 21; 2:17.
[451] Lam. 1:4-8.

do occur given with as much detail and correspondence to the complaint as was found in the Psalter.

4.6.3.1 Appeal for Deliverance from the Calamity

As we have already noted in the discussion of the addressee, chapter one presents Jerusalem, the desolate city, crying out, "Look Oh LORD, at my affliction . . . Look Oh LORD! For I am distressed." At this point, however, it must be noted that while the comfort and restoration which only her covenant LORD can bring is surely in the background of this poem,[452] it is not part of an explicit appeal for deliverance. God is only asked to pay attention to her plight.

Chapter two contains a call to Zion to appeal to the LORD (vv. 18-19) followed by the appeal again that the LORD would pay heed to her plight. Still, there is no specific request for deliverance.

Chapter three comes closer. The defeated one recites God's acts of terrible judgment and calls for self-examination and repentance. And as she continues to recount the tragedy which has befallen her, she cries out:

3:55	I called Your name, Oh LORD,	קראתי שמך יהוה
	From out of the lowest pit.	מבור תחתיות
3:56	My voice You have heard,	קולי שמעת
	Do not cover Your ears	אל־תעלם אזנך
	to relieve me—to save me!	לרוחתי לשועתי

Chapter four contains no appeal, and chapter five begins right off:

5:1	Remember, Oh LORD, what has happened to us;	זכר יהוה מה היה לנו
	Give heed, see our reproach.	הביט וראה את־חרפתנו

and goes on to express its complaint for most of the next twenty lines and then, the poignant appeal is made:

5:21	Bring us back to Yourself, Oh LORD,	השיבנו יהוה אליך ונשוב
	And we will return.	
	Renew our days like the old times.	חדש ימינו כקדם

4.6.3.2 Appeal for Cursing of the Cause of the Calamity

As we shall note later, even this category of appeal is affected by the treatment of the calamity and its cause given in Lamentations. Much of that attention is directed selfward. They do not want to curse themselves. Most of the treatment deals with the LORD's hand in the calamity. They cannot curse the LORD. There is, however, some attention paid to the

---

452 Contrast Lam. 1:9c, 11c, 20a with 16b vs. 2b and 7b, c.

external factors which have contributed to the misery and affliction experienced by exiled Judah. Friends and loved ones have dealt treacherously with her.[453] Bystanders did not lift a hand to help but rather to mock and clap in derision.[454] They have been dispossessed[455] and abused.[456] Added to all this is the apparent anomaly of the prosperity of the enemy.[457] Against this background, then, we find the appeals for cursing of the enemy. In the face of the enemy's delight over Jerusalem's calamity, she cries:

1:22	Let all their wickedness come before You	תבא כל־רעתם לפניך
	And deal severely with them,	ועולל למו
	Just as You dealt with me	כאשר עוללת לי
	For all my rebellion;	על כל־פשעי
	For many are my groanings,	כי־רבות אנחתי
	And my heart is faint.	ולבי דוי

Again, the LORD is entreated to act upon all the malevolent scheming of the human antagonist and:

3:63	Look, from their sitting to their rising,	שבתם וקימתם הביטה
	I am their mocking song.	אני מנגינתם
3:64	You will return their compensation, Oh LORD,	תשיב להם גמול יהוה
	According to the work of their hands.	כמעשה ידיהם
3:65	You will give them hardness of heart;	תתן להם מגנת־לב
	Your curse is on them.	תאלתך להם
3:66	You will pursue them angrily and destroy them	תרדף באף ותשמידם
	From under the heavens of the LORD!	מתחת שמי יהוה

In chapter four, there appears a statement which may not positively be an imprecation, but the tone of it would cause it to suit being mentioned here. Judah's consanguineous but treacherous neighbor, Edom, is warned to enjoy it while she may, for:

4:21	The cup will come around to you also,	גם־עליך תעבר־כוס
	You will get drunk and make yourself naked.	תשכרי ותתערי
4:22	He punishes your iniquity, Oh daughter of Edom;	פקד עונך בת־אדום
	He exposes your sins.	גלה על־חטאתיך

Hillers treats this as a curse, understanding the perfect verbs as desiderative or precative: "May he punish your iniquity, O Edom! May he lay bare your sins!"[458]

---

453 Lam. 1:2, 19.
454 Lam. 1:7; 2:15, 16; 3:14, 61-63.
455 Lam. 1:7, 10, 11; 5:2.
456 Lam. 1:2, 3, 19; 5:11-13.
457 Lam. 1:5.
458 D. R. Hillers, *Lamentations*, AB-7A (Garden City, N.Y.: Doubleday, 1972), p. 77.

4.6.3.3 Motivation

There are only two main elements brought forward in these laments as reasons why the LORD ought to act as requested. Overwhelmingly, the abject misery and the tragic reversal of the glory of Zion is the main motivational argument which is woven throughout.[459] The second is Jerusalem's repentance. The admission of guilt and acceptance of responsibility for the calamity appears quite frequently. All this has happened:

1:5	For the LORD caused her to suffer	כי יהוה הוגה
	Because of her many rebellions.	על רב פשעתה
1:8	Jerusalem has sinned profusely	חטא חטאה ירושלם
	Therefore she has become as an impure thing.[460]	על־כן לנידה היתה

To a much lesser degree, the wickedness and treachery of the enemy is something Jerusalem wants to be sure the LORD has noticed,[461] and this is the reason given for the curses pronounced.

At at least one point there appears to be a claim of innocence made. The afflicted man of chapter three asserts:

3:52	They hunted me down like a bird,	צוד צדוני כצפור
	My enemies, without cause.	איבי חנם

4.6.4 Expression of Confidence and Hope

Lamentations does not present much expression of confidence and hope, and in this it differs from the general tone of the Psalm laments as well. But the LORD is faithful to His Word,[462] and it is this, His faithfulness, which gives rise to a new hope:

3:21	This I will keep in my mind,	זאת אשיב אל־לבי
	Therefore I wait expectantly.	על־כן אוחיל
3:22	It is the LORD's covenant loyalty that we are not consumed,	חסדי יהוה כי לא־תמנו
	For his compassions never end.	כי לא־כלו רחמיו
3:23	They are new every morning.	חדשים לבקרים
	Great is Your faithfulness!	רבה אמונתך
3:24	The LORD is my portion, I tell myself,	חלקי יהוה אמרה נפשי
	Therefore I wait expectantly for Him.	על־כן אוחיל לו

---

459 Cf. e.g., Lam. 2:18-20; 5:1-18.
460 Cf. Lam. 1:18-20; 3:39-66.
461 Lam. 1:9c, 11c, etc.
462 Lam. 2:17.

But the picture remains dark until we get to the difficult verses at the end of chapter four. There, חם "is over" is used to refer to Zion's punishment. It is past—at least the worst of it. Or, as Hillers argues,

> One might also take the perfect as precative. Though this line, even if read as a declarative sentence and not as a wish, is not yet a clear announcement of salvation for Zion (cf. e.g. Isa. 40:2 "Her iniquity is pardoned"), yet it comes closer to being an expression of hope than almost anything else in the book. It is recognized that with the fall of the city and the beginning of the exile the flood of Yahweh's wrath had passed.[463]

4.6.5 Thanksgiving and Praise

Again, given the subject and the theological underpinnings of the treatment here, it should perhaps come as no surprise that there is little adulation. Reverence even seems to be stretched a bit thin at times. Especially does this seem to be so in the almost accusatory recitation of His calamitous judgment. But He is declared righteous in His judgment.[464] The only paean in the book appears at the end:

| 5:19 | You, Oh LORD, rule forever! | אתה יהוה לעולם תשב |
| | Your throne is from generation to generation. | כסאך לדר ודור |

although it is tempered somewhat by the למה " why" of the next line.

4.6.6 Summary

That the God of Jerusalem as portrayed in the book of Lamentations is the God Who had entered into covenant with Judah and that the problems Judah faced were related to her behavior or misbehavior under the terms of that covenant seems to be the point, at least in part, of the recital of these laments. The close connection with Deuteronomy and the frequency with which Zion's mishandling of her heritage is dealt with in Lamentations seems to verify this. In the main, this body of communal lamentation differs from the Psalter in that the subject is the city of Jerusalem personified. It is a dirge over the city. The preponderant element is that of the lament proper—the complaint with the recital of all its details. The other elements can hardly be called incidental but it seems clear that 1) the appeal for deliverance and/or 2) the appeal for the cursing of the enemy with the motivation, 3) the expression of confidence and hope and 4) the expression of thanksgiving and praise are secondary.

---

463 *Lamentations*, p. 93.
464 Lam. 1:18.

Each of the poems offers a different treatment. The acrostic devise undoubtedly influenced the poetic expression somewhat.[465] There lacks a bold expression of overt optimism. It is there, however, and its basis is God's faithfulness and His covenant love. At this point in Israel's history, the lament apparently takes on an additional function to that mentioned in the treatment of the Psalms: that of reminding the covenant people that they cannot sin with impunity; that a covenant relationship entailed both blessings and curses, theirs was the choice and the responsibility.

4.7 Analysis of the Thematic Elements in the Hebrew Laments

In analyzing the communal laments found in the Hebrew Psalter and the book of Lamentations it becomes apparent that there are both significant similarities and significant dissimilarities between and among the two collections of laments. There are strong affinities among the laments and the themes treated, yet there are some distinct variations on the themes apropos to the occasion and purpose of the composition and use of the given lament.

4.7.1 Speaking Voice

The matter of the speaking voice has already been mentioned in connection with the book of Lamentations.[466] The use of personae may be demonstrated in other Hebrew literature as well. Clear distinctions are sometimes difficult to make because at times it may be difficult to discern the role of the cultural phenomenon known as corporate personality, a feature common in the ancient Near East.[467] Indeed, in a number of the Psalm laments both "we" and "I" are used as the poet swings from the congregation as a whole to the representative of the congregation. In light of this feature, Mowinckel argues cogently that the occurrence of "I" or "we" in the Psalms cannot necessarily be taken at face value. Thus, the "I"-speaking voice may indeed be the congregation speaking through its national and cultic representative.[468] Indeed, in a number of the Psalm laments, both "we" and "I" are used as the poet swings from the congre-

---

465 See P. Munch, "Die alphabetische Akrostichie in der jüdischen Psalmendichtung," ZDMG 90 (1936):703-710.

466 See above sect. 4.6.1.

467 Cf. A. R. Johnson, The Vitality of the Individual in the Thought of Ancient Israel (Cardiff, Wales: University of Wales, 1949); H. W. Robinson, "The Hebrew Conception of Corporate Personality," in Werden und Wesen des Alten Testaments, ed. P. Volz, BZAW 66 (1936):49-62. Cf. Idem., Corporate Personality in Ancient Israel (Philadelphia: Fortress, 1964).

468 Mowinckel, Psalms, vol. I, pp. 38-39, 42-80, 193-246.

gation as a whole to the representative of the congregation.[469] Thus, from the Psalm laments, may be seen the following personae: the reporter or poet himself, the king in the so-called royal Psalms of lament, the congregation, and occasionally, God Himself. These same personae are represented in the book of Lamentations with these variations: other than the briefest quotation, God is not represented as speaking; the poet or reporter speak, as do the people; and, in Lamentations, the city of Jerusalem itself is personified and speaks.[470]

4.7.2 Direct Address

In the analysis of the feature of direct address, it was seen that every one of the Psalms treated evidenced both the use of the vocative and the second person singular in directing the complaint and appeal to the LORD God.[471] The book of Lamentations varies only slightly. While direct address is prevalent, there are two extended passages in which God is referred to in the third person and is not invoked directly. These are the first nineteen verses of chapter two and the whole of chapter four. The significance of this feature is hard to discern since the Psalm laments use the third person in speaking of God as well. If the book of Lamentations is to be regarded as a unit, the extended disuse of the second person in these two chapters could be explained simply in terms of the relative length of the book as compared with the Psalms. The fact remains, however, that the acrostic device clearly marks out five distinct poems. And the arrangement of those five poems seems not to provide any real progression. At the least, the lack of direct address in a Hebrew lament is very unusual.

4.7.3 Complaint or Lament Proper

The actual complaint in the Psalm laments and Lamentations is treated next. As indicated above there is no standard formulaic introduction to the complaint unit. The claim that איכה is the normative introduction and ending of the dirge does not seem to apply to the Psalm laments.[472] The forms איך and איכה occur only four times in the entire Psalter.[473] Of these, only one is considered a communal lament.[474] איכה is

---

[469] Cf. Pss. 44, 74, 83, 89, 123.
[470] Cf. W. F. Lanahan, "The Speaking Voice in the Book of Lamentations," JBL 93 (1974):41-49.
[471] See above fig. 3, p. 93.
[472] Cf. II Sam. 1:19,25,27 איך נפלו נברים.
[473] Pss. 11:1; 73:11,19; 137:4.
[474] See fig. 1, p. 16. Psalm 11 is a psalm of confidence and 73 is a wisdom psalm.

used more frequently in Lamentations and comes close to fitting the supposed formula.[475] However, even here, it is missing from the beginning of chapters three and five and does not recur at or near the end of the lament compositions as suggested.[476]

In the book of Lamentations, the various chapters bring their treatment of the complaint into fairly fine focus centering on Zion. Whereas in the Psalter, we found laments dealing with a relatively broad range of calamitous events in the life of the nation, here we find the many incidents treated are all related, either on the cause or the effect side of one climactic tragedy: the fall, destruction and exile of Jerusalem.

4.7.3.1 Enemy

For the most part, the biblical laments seem purposely to avoid the naming of specific enemies. As we have seen, the 83rd Psalm is an exception.[477] The prefatory material to Psalm 60 also cites specific enemies: Aram-naharaim, Aram-zobah, and Edom. Even when the destruction of Jerusalem is the subject of lament, the enemy is generalized as the גוים "nations."[478] One possible reason might be that such a treatment, while referring to a specific event which gave rise to the composition of the given lament, enables subsequent users both to commemorate a past calamity and to contemporize, mentally identifying with some current trouble.

The enemy motif, of course, is widely represented in the Hebrew canon as witnessed by the range of usage of terms such as אויב "enemy," צר "foe," צורר "oppressor," קים "adversary," שורר "(insidious) watcher," שנא "enemy."

4.7.3.2 Calamity

The treatment of calamity in both the Psalm laments and the book of Lamentations contains both an objective and a subjective aspect. It is not only physical havoc wreaked upon the city or nation, but also the estrangement of the people from their God that is lamented.

Both the Psalm laments and Lamentations complain of the physical destruction experienced as a result of a catastrophe. But it seems that this destruction is not always an ultimate kind. Lamentations does mourn the

---

475 Lam. 1:1; 2:1; 4:1; 4:2.
476 See above sect. 4.6.2.
477 See above p. 110.
478 See Pss. 44:3,12,15; 59:6,9; 79:1,6,10; 80:9; 94:10; 102:16; Lam. 1:1,3,10; 2:9; 4:15,20.

ultimate destruction of Jerusalem as do, e.g., Psalms 74, 79, 89, and 137.[479]
Yet other Psalms seem to refer to other occasions when Jerusalem was
under fire from her enemies in which the calamity was just as real but
not final, e.g., Psalm 60's reference to David's struggle with Aram-
naharaim and Aram-zobah, and Joab's victory over Edom in verse two.

Physical impairment, as indicated above[480] is one of the elements
complained of in the laments. The nature and degree of the impairment
depends on the overall theme of the lament. That is, those which lament
the ultimate destruction of the city also tend to mourn the death of its
inhabitants.[481] But whether dealing with the ultimate destruction of the
city or a lesser catastrophe, the laments are primarily vehicles of expression for the survivors. And survivors do not always escape a catastrophe
unscathed. It is this circumstance that seems best to explain the themes
which speak of physical injury or impairment from battle or from
drought and famine and the emotional distress often accompanied by
psychosomatic symptoms which have come to be identified with acute
stress and grief[482] The book of Lamentations is not as graphic in its
description of the physical effects of the calamity, though they are mentioned. The מכאב "pain" is said to be unparalleled and there is severe
mental and emotional anguish accompanied by protracted weeping.[483]

4.7.3.3 Abandonment/Isolation

The theme of abandonment is represented elsewhere in the Hebrew
canon. As seen in the Psalms, so also in other literature, God's silence or
distance is spoken of as a possible indication of His abandonment. But
there are two aspects of God's silence: estrangement and longsuffering.
In Isa. 42:14, the same term used negatively in Ps. 35:22 "O LORD, do not
keep silent," is used positively, "I [God] have kept silent for a long while,
I have kept quiet and controlled myself." The tension is to be seen
between God's speaking a word of grace and deliverance and His
speaking a word of judgment.[484] Also God's distance is spoken of in Pss.
22:12,20, 35:22, 38:22, and 71:12. The writer of Lamentations bemoans
God's distance in these terms:

---

479 Pss. 42/43 and 69 lament the fall of the city obliquely as the psalmist reminisces of the
days when festivals used to be observed at God's House (42:5) and looks forward to the day
when he can return to the holy hill (43:3), when God will save Zion and build Judah's cities
(69:36).
480 See pp. 115ff. and 121.
481 Cf. Ps. 79:2-3,10; Lam. 1:20; 2:21; 3:43.
482 E.g., Pss. 31:10-11; 42:4; 56:9; 69:4; 77:4-5; 80:6; 89:46; 102:5-8,24. See above, p. 186.
483 Lam. 1:12,22; 2:11; 1:2,16; 2:18; 3:20.
484 *Lamentations*, p. 93.

1:16	My eyes flow down with water	עיני ירדה מים
	Because far from me is a comforter,	כי־רחק ממני מנחם
	One who restores my soul.	משיב נפשי

In Isa. 49:14, Zion complains: "The LORD has forsaken me, and the Lord has forgotten me."[485] In Lamentations, even stronger terms, נאץ "contemn," and זנך "reject" are used of the kingship and priesthood, and the altar respectively, but mitigated by the statement that it is not forever.[486]

4.7.4 Expression of Confidence/Hope

The confidence theme in these laments is broader than the well known "confidence of hearing" (*Gewissheit der Erhörung*) motif. That is, expression is given not only to a confidence that God will hear,[487] but that it is His purpose[488] and that He is able to do something about the predicament being complained of.[489] This expression of confidence and trust or hope seem to be used in two slightly different ways in the laments. In four instances in the Psalter, it is expressed prior to the complaint and appeal.[490] Here it seems to serve as a basis for the complaint and to set up the appeal. It is related to the practice of appealing to God's honor. In the majority of the Psalm laments, the expression of confidence and hope occurs at or near the end of the composition, often close or connected to an expression of thanksgiving or vow of praise.[491] In a few of the lament Psalms, both are used.[492] In the Psalm laments which refer directly to the fall of Jerusalem, the theme is almost unnoticeable, perhaps because of the nature of the subject matter. The same is almost true of Lamentations. Of the five poems, only Lam. 3:21-29, the "great is Your faithfulness" passage, gives an overt expression of hope.

4.7.5 Thanksgiving and Praise

Closely related to the theme of confidence and hope is that of thanksgiving and praise. The latter is based upon the former. But so interrelated are they that several of the Psalms contain one or the other but not both expressions.[493]

---

485 Cf. Isa. 54:7; Ezek. 8:12, 9:9; 2 Chron. 24:20; Pss. 22:2, 71:11; Jer. 23:39; Pss. 10:11, 13:2.
486 Lam 2:6,7; 3:17,31. Cf. Ps. 44:10.
487 See Pss. 31:23; 69:34; 102:21; Lam. 3:56. See p. 140.
488 See Pss. 56:11-14; 60:8-10
489 See Pss. 94:17,22-23; 102:26-29.
490 See Pss. 42:6,12; 43:5; 44:5-9; 56:4-5.
491 See Pss. 31:24-25; 42:12; 43:5; 56:11-12; 59:10-11; 60:8-10,14; 94:22-23; 102:26-29.
492 See Pss. 31; 42; 43; 56.
493 Pss. 31, 35, 60, 69, 79, 89, 94, 102, 109.

Psalms 80, 83, 137, 142, and Lamentations chapters 1, 2, 4, and 5 do not contain a clear development of either theme. The reason for this is not clear and should be the subject of further research.

4.7.6 Summary

The distinctives as well as the similarities seen between the various examples of communal lament composition seem best to be explained on literary grounds. There is no consistent pattern or formula for the use of the device of various personae. While God is addressed overwhelmingly by use of the vocative and the second person singular pronoun, there are exceptions, especially in the book of Lamentations, which, it appears, occur at the discretion of the composer.

Though there is commonly a certain specificity which characterizes the complaints and appeal, there is also a significant degree of generalization in the compositions in order, it seems, to facilitate their usage by subsequent generations.

The themes treated in the communal laments are much the same as those treated in the individual laments. The difference lies in the scope of interest and usage--whether of an individual or of the community at large. While illness or physical impairment might, at first thought, seem to be more appropriate to the laments of the individual, there is due cause for the theme to occur in the communal laments as well. Given the theological viewpoint of the Hebrew prophets, it should come as no surprise that some cause and effect relationship be indicated, at least occasionally in the laments, and that concomitantly, some expression of guilt and penitence might be made. However, the overall tone of the communal laments is not one of penitence.

The very nature of the subject matter of the lament compositions naturally lends itself to the making of an appeal. Indeed, the communal lament is in part a kind of petition. The distinctive of the laments is that the petition is concerned with relief and deliverance from the calamity which plagues the community and from those factors which had contributed to it.

5

Comparisons and Contrasts Between the Sumero-Akkadian and the Hebrew Communal Laments

5.1 *Introduction*

As used in this study, the term "genre" refers to a class of literary texts which share a similar subject area or theme and a similar purpose or function. In this case, the theme is that of complaint and mourning over some sort of public calamity accompanied by an appeal for relief. The purpose or function of the lament is to allow the community, either collectively or through representatives, to give expression to that complaint and thus, serve as a cathartic. There are indeed differences in both content and use between the Sumero-Akkadian and the Hebrew laments as well as among each of the two groups. As "genre" is being used in this study, uniformity among the constituents is not required. Rather, what is looked for is a marked similarity of thought and thought forms as well as of mood.

Since the Hebrew laments are the focus of this study, we begin with a summary of the theoretical origins of the communal lament.

5.2 *Theoretical Origins of the Communal Laments*

There are no known "rough drafts" of a communal lament. It is not possible to document the evolution of a particular lament composition from extant texts. Yet, from a theoretical perspective, I would argue that the communal laments did not just happen. But in speaking of the origins of the lament, I am not just referring to the historical events which triggered them. I am referring also to those cultural phenomena surrounding funeral observances, religious rites of penance, and personal tragedy, mentioned in Chapter Three, which are logically prior to the phenomenon of community laments.

5.2.1 Individual lament.

This, however, is a logical connection rather than a historically demonstrable connection. The fact is that among the extant early Sumero-Akkadian literature the individual laments are not represented. In the Hebrew canon, they are about evenly represented from the earlier to the later sections. The earlier form-critical studies tended to emphasize an "oral original" which had evolved more or less out of the folklore of the community.[494] The point needs to be made, however, that in general, literature is not produced by a community. The "community" may have something to do with its development and even serve to give impetus to its origination. But it is the individual who begins the process of self-expression. This would seem to be true of either oral or written expression. This expression may strike such a chord with the community as to be adopted and/or adapted by it. But there is a logical priority to individual expression. This is not to say that any given communal lament is necessarily an adaptation of an individual lament. Clearly, some of the communal laments dealt with here can be shown to have been composed for some specific situation or specific purpose. But an affinity of style and language between individual and community laments can also be seen. The same factors which give basis to the lament in general are apparent to some degree in both.[495] Some of the same issues and quite similar turns of expression are to be seen in both.[496]

---

[494] See Gunkel, "Die israelitische Literatur," pp. 55-56.
[495] The subject of the lament, the "enemy," and the god to whom the complaint is being made. Cf. Westermann, "Struktur und Geschichte."
[496] Cf. LIIBE; Widengren, *Psalms of Lamentation.*

5.2.2 **Funeral dirges.**

Another aspect of lament-type expression which is logically prior to the community lament per se is the funeral dirge. In Chapter Three, the role of the professional mourner and the nature of the performance of the elegy was discussed. In considering the theoretical origins of the communal lament, it should be noted that to some degree the funeral observance in both form and substance may be assumed to have had a role in the development of public lamentation customs in these cultures.[497]

In light of the common practice of personifying the city-state and referring to it as the "mother" of its "sons and daughters," it comes as no surprise to find some adaptation of a funeral dirge applied to "death" of the city-state.

But it must be seen as a development, an adaptation, and not just a straight application of the dirge genre. In the Sumero-Akkadian canon, the dirge is most clearly adapted to those members of the pantheon whose roles seemed to involve a seasonal cycle of dying and reviving. The Tammuz laments are undoubtedly the classic examples and are quite representative.[498] These belong to a distinct sub-genre of public lament[499] which is unparalleled in Hebrew literature and hence, outside the scope of this work.

In the case of the Hebrew canon, there are bits and pieces of actual funeral observances including the dirge—though none are preserved in full. In the light of these fragments, however, it is fairly common to assert that chapters one, two, and four of Lamentations are "actually funeral dirges, as their characteristic opening איכה "Ah! How!" reveals, and they are in fact funeral dirges given political application."[500] This may be so, but only in a very limited degree. The book as a whole has been cited as an example of a so-called "mixed-type." Indeed even its constituent poems are said so to be.[501] Regarding the assignment of the type "funeral dirge," we have already referred to the results of Jahnow's detailed study

---

497 Cf. Jahnow, *Leichenlied.*

498 T. Jacobsen, *Toward the Image of Tammuz*, ed. W. L. Moran, HSS 21 (Cambridge, Mass.: Harvard, 1970), p. 324, nn. 7, 8, 9.

499 S. N. Kramer, "Sumerian Literature: Survey" in *The Bible and the Ancient Near East*, ed. G. Wright (Garden City, N. Y.: Doubleday, 1961), p. 338; and "Sumerian Literature and the Bible," *Analecta Biblica* 12 (1959): 187-188.

500 Eissfeldt, *Introduction*, pp. 95, 501, Cf. Gunkel-Begrich, *Einleitung*, p. 136.

501 Eissfeldt, *Introduction*, p. 502, analyzes chapter three as partly individual lament (vv. 1-39) and partly national lament (vv. 40-47) with introductory interlude (v. 48) leading to an individual lament again (vv. 49-66). Similarly "mixed-type" analyses are offered for chapters one, two, and four (pp. 501-503), and only the last poem is allowed as a "pure national song of lamentation."

of the funeral dirge in the Hebrew Bible and related sources which indicates a rather marked departure on the part of these chapters of Lamentations from the stylistic features of the old funeral dirge.[502] At any rate, for the sake of this aspect of the discussion, it may be said that with regard to the communal lament, the funeral dirge has demonstrably exerted some "influence"—though perhaps not so much as has commonly been assumed—and hence, should be considered to be logically prior.

5.2.3   Community crises.

The third and fourth factors influencing the origin and development of the communal lament are also sociological. But while the factors just discussed concerned a more limited entity—the individual, family and friends—these last factors concern the larger community.

As social units developed and were confronted with crises which threatened their existence, there was introduced another factor which would give impetus to the origin and development of a means of catharsis. Some way of dealing with the calamity without giving in to it was required: some instrument that would allow the community to re-group and face the future in light of the present. "Each culture must provide an explanation for the major events and crises of life, and particularly for death, which seems to challenge all the meaning of life."[503]

As applied to the community, these practices have been labelled "rites of intensification" by anthropologist W. Haviland. He outlines the range of possible occasions for such rites: from drought and crop failure to the sudden appearance of a hostile enemy. The primary function of the rites of intensification is seen to be to

> unite the people in a common effort in such a way that fear and confusion yield to collective action and a degree of optimism. The balance in the relations of all concerned, which has been upset, is restored to normal.[504]

Haviland also notes that such observance is not limited to "times of overt crisis," but is often practiced apotropaically.[505] This theory is supported by the use of the Sumero-Akkadian laments in *namburbi* rites, for example.

---

[502] *Leichenlied*, pp. 168-190.
[503] P. Hiebert, *Cultural Anthropology* (Phila.: Lippincott, 1976), p. 170.
[504] W. Haviland, *Cultural Anthropology* (N.Y.: Holt, Rinehart, and Winston, 1981), p. 358.
[505] Ibid., p. 359.

5.2.4 Fall of the city-state.

The role of the community as a focal point of personal and national identity in the ancient Near East is most significant. In this regard, the temple also must be considered. In fact, in all probability it has an even greater impact because it represented that which brought some degree of coherence to the life of man and the world around him. Hence, without a doubt, the greatest calamity that might befall a society was the fall of its capital and temple accompanied by their destruction and the displacement of its people. For when these were gone, there commonly followed a sense of utter collapse and a feeling, at least potentially, that their god had abandoned them. Any sense of security the community may have enjoyed seems to have disappeared.[506] It was only natural then to deal with this sense of loss by adapting to these community losses the means surely already in use for dealing with grief. And given the theological implications which such crises had for each of the societies in question, it should be no surprise that these vents of emotion should take on cultic significance. The crisis, be it natural disaster, threat of outside force, or the destruction of their citadel and temple, touched upon the god of the given group and their relationship to that god.

5.3 Types of Hebrew Communal Laments

There are a couple of relatively brief examples of a prototypical community lament preserved in the Hebrew Bible in Josh. 7:7-9 and Jdg. 21:3. These are prayer forms, not of praise nor of supplication per se, but of lamentation.[507] These have been called mediated laments by Westermann; that is, a lament on behalf of the people by a leader or deliverer. It deals with a public distress but "the one who laments is a single individual who has received an office of ministry from God." Characteristic to these very short laments is the fact of their calling out directly to God in the form of a question "Why?" which lays the responsibility of the distress with God. They address a single situation and are concerned with the issue of shame and humiliation—both theirs and God's.[508]

Two stages of the later development need to be identified. The trauma of the Babylonian deportations and destruction of Jerusalem mark the dividing line. In the main, the Psalm laments represent the pre-

---

506 Jacobsen, *Image of Tammuz*, p. 13.

507 Cf. A. Wendel, *Das freie Laiengebet im vorexilischen Israel*, (Leipzig: Pfeiffer, 1931), pp. 123-138; cf. Jdg. 6:22; 15:18; Hos. 8:2?.

508 C. Westermann, "Struktur und Geschichte," pp. 67-69.

exilic state of lament literature. These laments are of two types. On the one hand, there is a development of the mediated lament-type seen above in the early examples. Here, a spokesman or leader of the people, presumably in the person of the king, but possibly some other representative, speaks in the first person singular.[509] On the other hand, there are the "we"-laments in which the psalmist seems unquestionably to be representing the speaking community. As shown above and summarized below, these Psalm laments cover a range of community distresses.

The post-exilic lament par excellence is to be seen in the five poems which make up the Book of Lamentations. Taken together, their 266 lines would be somewhat comparable to the extended city/temple lament of the Sumero-Akkadian canon. As indicated above, the Book of Lamentations utilized a mixture of lament types including a modified funeral dirge.[510]

5.4 Types of Communal Lament

From the standpoint of the topical content of the various laments, there seem to be two main types of community lament represented in the extant Hebrew and Sumero-Akkadian laments. One is the demise of the city-state, the other deals with some other kinds of community crisis. Of this later type are found laments which speak to prospective crises, current crises, and past crises. And as already mentioned, the crises may be natural or political in nature or both.

5.4.1 Demise of City-States

As we have seen, the largest lament texts represented in the Sumero-Akkadian corpus are those dealing with the destruction of a city, or series of cities and invariably they include the destruction of the temple. The loss of the temple is obvious, but it is clearly not the only part of the city destroyed. Rather, it is singled out because of its importance in the life of the community. "Light in darkness is overwhelmed," and the gods have abandoned their houses. In fact, the Sumero-Akkadian city laments seem to focus on two main aspects of the devastating calamity. On the one hand, they describe at length the downfall, deterioration and desolation of the city or group of cities. And on the other hand, they describe

---

509 Mowinckel, *Psalms*, vol. I, pp. 225-246. Cf. H. Birkeland, *Die Feinde des Individuums in der israelitischen Psalmenliteratur* (Oslo: Orondahl and Sons, 1933). See above, p. 160, on personae. Westermann registers some skepticism as to whether or not the mediator in these Psalm laments is in fact the king. "Struktur und Geschichte," p. 67.

510 See above, sect 4.3, p. 98ff.

the appropriate god(s) at length in terms of the destructive power of his word and in terms of his absence.[511]

In the Hebrew canon, Lamentations is the largest collection of laments for Zion, the city of Jerusalem—266 lines in all. To this, we must add Psalms 74, 79, 89, and 137. The focus of these is on the city[512] and the throne/crown, the symbols of authority but also of national identity.[513] Or else, the focus is on the temple itself, as well as other assembly places, as the symbol of God's presence in Israel.[514]

5.4.2 Other Community Crises

As the community addressed itself to other traumata with which it was confronted, three specific chronological perspectives are seen.

5.4.2.1 Lament for a prospective crisis.

A few laments border on being protective prayers as they look forward to certain ominous signs in light of which they address their deity. The clearest examples of this perspective are preserved in the Hebrew canon. They are not, however, merely protective prayers.[515] They ask not for general blessing. They address a specific kind of threat but in somewhat general terms. Psalm 83, for example, implores God not to be at rest but to be active, and not silent in view of the calamity. The enemies (of God) are conspiring against His people. And the portent of great calamity is underscored as the Psalm lists the co-conspirators: Edom and the Ishmaelites, Moab and the Hagrites, Gebal, Ammon, Amalek, Philistia, Tyre and Assyria. Calamity has not yet fallen. It is only threatened. But the threat is real to the people, and they voice their lament to their God with all the classic elements of the communal lament.[516] These particular laments seem to focus more on threats of a political rather than natural origin or nature.[517] This may be due to the fact that on the whole, natural disaster may be less predictable.

---

[511] SKly, pp. 47-48.

[512] Ps. 137; Lam. 1:4, 5.

[513] Ps. 89:5, 19-22, 29-30, 36-37, 39-41; Lam. 2:2, 5, 8-10.

[514] Pss. 74:2-4, 7-8; 79:1-2; Lam. 2:6-7.

[515] Eissfeldt, Introduction, p. 114, calls these "collective songs of trust" of which he gives Ps. 125 as an example. Cf. Birkeland, Feinde des Individuums, pp. 104-105.

[516] See also Pss. 20, 77.

[517] Psalm 2, while not a lament per se, expresses something of a complaint over the "tumultuous thronging" of the nations in a belligerent posture. The tone of the composition gives the sense that the threat is present. But it is still a just a threat; the actual calamity has not yet befallen the nation or its king.

5.4.2.2 Lament for present crisis.

The majority of the extant crisis-laments seem to fall within these next two categories: present crisis or past crisis. The chronological demarcation between a present crisis and a past crisis is often difficult to make. When the crisis has not only affected the stability of the social institutions of the community but also has caused the deportation or other dislocation of a people, then an event which is chronologically past continues to cause current repercussions, both of which may be the legitimate subject of lament.

One indication of a lament over a present crisis in the community is the use of the question, "How long?" For example, CT 15:2, a lament to Enlil in the event of famine:

> Oh lord who hast sent hunger everywhere,
>   how long until he be pacified?
> The wrath of thy heart,
>   can anyone appease it?
> The utterance of thy mouth brings destruction.[518]

The example cited uses another expression common at least to the later Sumero-Akkadian laments, viz., the relating of the "how long?" question to the appeasement of the deity's heart. Eventually, the *eršemma* laments commonly contained the request that the deity may soothe his heart vis-à-vis his people.[519]

Similarly, the Hebrew literature also witnesses the present crisis lament. E.g.,

> How long, Oh God,   עד־מתי אלהים יחרף צר
>   will the adversary revile?[520]
> Be gracious unto me, Oh LORD,   חנני יהוה כי צר־לי
>   because of my distress.[521]

As indicated above, many of both the Sumero-Akkadian and the Hebrew laments of this sort treat something that has happened already but which has continuing consequences for the people. For example, to Istar, the lament CT 15:7-9 wails:

> How long, my queen, shall thy courts be demolished,
>   thy statue kept in captivity?[522]

---

[518] BP, pp. 198-201.
[519] SKly, p. 24. Cf. p. 30. This request is not present in the Old Babylonian *eršemma* songs. Cf. p. 31, n. 67.
[520] Ps. 74:10.
[521] Ps. 31:10.
[522] BP, pp. 14-15.

In SBH no. 49, Bau is said to wail:

> In rage for her city which is plundered,
> In rage for her temple which is plundered,
> Saying, "How long, oh my city,
>   How long, oh my temple!"
> Saying, "How long, oh my husband,
>   How long, oh my son!"
> In the house of wailing,
>   In the night she cries aloud.[523]

In the Hebrew canon, Psalm 42/43 illustrates the dual tense lament. From an apparently exilic point of view, one aspect of crisis is past and mournfully remembered. But the crisis continues, and the psalmist feels God has even forgotten His people who "go on mourning because of the enemy's oppression."[524] The crisis is not over yet.

5.4.2.3 Lament for crisis in retrospect.

Given the nature of the texts that have been preserved, it is to be expected that the only communal laments which appear by their content to be only retrospective are the neo-Sumerian city-state laments which have already been discussed. Other crises, such as natural disasters or enemy attacks, do not seem to have been memorialized in the cult laments.

5.5 *Structure*

The Sumero-Akkadian laments may be viewed structurally from two different perspectives: that of function or other external factors, and of content. Functionally, as the tablets were collected, edited, and transmitted from generation to generation, specific portions became identified with specific aspects of the lament ritual. This was touched upon in Chapter Three under the discussion of musical accompaniment.

The point is that the functional identification of what was usually the first main section of the major laments with the instrument called the *balag*, caused those sections eventually to be called a *balag*.[525] These are structurally distinct units of an extended lament. In the rites of lament, this section is called the *taqribtu=ÉR* [526] and is terminated with the line: 'this prayer . . . in/of *TN* . . .'.[527] Also, if the *balag* section of the tablet is

---

523 Ibid., pp. 170-173, 11. 14-23.
524 Pss. 42:10; 43:2.
525 Jacobsen, "Review of LU," p. 222.
526 SKly, pp. 19-21, n. 9.
527 Ibid. Cf. n. 22 on the difficulty of deciphering the meaning of *ki-gi₄-gi₄*.

marked with a *Stichzeile* "catch line," it points to the following tablet—
usually an *eršemma*.[528]

The *eršemma* is the other functionally distinct structural unit of the
Sumero-Akkadian lament. Again, these are marked so that they are
identifiably distinct.[529] And it has been noted that in some of the collections there may be more than one *eršemma* composition.[530] This particular feature does not appear to have a parallel in the Hebrew canon.

From another perspective, the longer laments are structurally divided into *kirugus* of unequal lengths and other units called *gisgigal*.[531]

The Hebrew texts lack such specific designation. Structurally poetic
strophes are apparent. But the most obvious structural feature is the
acrostic device used in the first four poems of Lamentations, which possibly influenced the fifth as well. The acrostics clearly mark out the five
distinct poems. Functionally, of course, certain of the laments were
included in the main collection of Hebrew hymnody, the Psalter. The
collection of five known as Lamentations was eventually placed among
the Megilloth to be used at specified cultic observances.

As regards the structure of the content of the laments, there seems to
be a greater affinity between the two collections under study. In the case
of the Sumero-Akkadian laments, there seem to be three basic elements
represented to one degree or another. They would be the elements of
praise, descriptive narrative, and entreaty.[532]

Similarly, the Hebrew laments demonstrate certain structural elements. Most space seems to be given to the narrative of complaint itself.
But there is also the entreaty or appeal, whether for deliverance or for
cursing the enemy or both, and thirdly, the expression of confi-
dence/hope, and the expression of thanksgiving/praise.[533] Taken as a

---

[528] Ibid., p. 23.

[529] Krecher points out, two-thirds of the *eršemma* compositions from the Old Babylonian
period that have the closing signature (damage to just less than half of the extant texts has
left them without such signatures) have the designation *eršemma-GN* (two tablets have only
eršemma), SKly, p. 29.

[530] Ibid., p. 23.

[531] Ibid., p. 32.

[532] See above, chapter 2. Cf. BC, p. 7; SKly, p. 46, for examples of each element.

[533] See Mowinckel, *Psalms*, vol. I, pp. 229-230. He outlines the structure of the lament
Psalms as 1) invocation, 2) complaint, 3) prayers for help with motivation, 4) promise of sacrifice and expression of thanksgiving and the assurance that the prayer will be heard. Cf.
Westermann, "Struktur and Geschichte," p. 48, where he offers for the Psalm laments the
structural sequence: 1) introduction (and introductory request), 2) lament, 3) turning to God
(confession of confidence/hope), 4) request, 5) solemn promise of praise. Cf. also Westermann, "Role of Lament in the Theology of the Old Testament," Int 28 (1974):20-22, where he
suggests a structural sequence: 1) prehistory, 2) distress, 3) call for help, 4) hearkening, 5) a
leading out, 6) a leading into, 7) response.

whole, the book of Lamentations demonstrated these structural elements as well but not chapter by chapter. Even in any given chapter, one or another element is often missing.[534] Clearly, in the book of Lamentations the complaint per se is predominant.

This leads to the conclusion that regardless of how one isolates and identifies what appear to be the structural components of the lament— either Sumero-Akkadian or Hebrew—the structural grid cannot be forced upon the individual laments. It will not fit. These structural observations are helpful as heuristic devices. But it must be noted that the elements do not appear to get an equal amount of attention. They do not always occur in the same order, whether it be the more or less normal *balag* + *eršemma* order for which variants such as (*balag*) + (*eršemma*) + (*eršemma*) or (*balag*) alone or (*eršemma*) alone are attested. Or, from a different perspective, there are laments which omit the entreaty and just emphasize the complaint. Yet, others end with praise rather than begin with it. And still others express the entire lament in terms of praise of the mighty destructive working of the deity.[535]

Speaking of yet another way of viewing structural elements,[536] Westermann states that "there are no fixed sequences recognizable. It is also possible that one of the subjects [I would add, or of the other components mentioned above] in the lament is repeated in the Psalm more than one time. It is therefore no fixed form."[537] To miss this flexibility is to invite misunderstanding of the texts.

5.6 *Persona*

In literary criticism, the term "persona" denotes that characterization which an author uses as the medium by which he expresses himself. An author may use more than one persona in his composition. The use of this device is most prevalent in the lament literature. Its importance lies mainly in the fact that it enables the writer to deal with his subject from a much broader perspective than possible with only one character. In the Sumero-Akkadian laments, the poet often assumes the persona of a reporter who narrates the scenario.[538] Then, in order to introduce a somewhat different perspective to the treatment, the poet shifts to the point of view of one of the gods. Then he might shift back to the persona

---

534 See fig. 3, above p. 93.
535 Cf. SKly, p. 46.
536 The three subjects of the lament: subject 1 = God, subject 2 = lamenter, subject 3 = enemies as essential components.
537 "Struktur und Geschichte," p. 50.
538 "LU," *kirugus* one and two.

of the people only to shift once again, this time to the wife of the deity in question.[539] For the people as a community, the poet may assume yet another speaking voice, probably through the representative *kalû* and company. A similar use of personae is demonstrated in the Hebrew literature.[540]

5.7 *The Question of Influence Between the Collections of Lamentations*

Perhaps more than any other aspect of lament study, the question of influence yields only cautious answers. Granted, sweeping conclusions sometimes have been offered. However, they may not be quite so broad as they may have appeared on the surface.

The main problem faced at this point stems from the sociological and historical complexities of the situations being described, the origins and transmission of the texts which describe these situations, and the varying uses to which the poems seem to have been put.

But since the societies in question had demonstrable connections, the question of relationship and influence between the cultural phenomena of public or communal lament as it existed in ancient Mesopotamia and Israel is a valid one.

5.7.1 The Question of Influence Among the Sumero-Akkadian Laments

The earliest extant communal laments have undoubtedly had some influence on the continued development and use in Mesopotamia. The consensus seems to be that the neo-Sumerian laments, the earliest extant laments, were written to deal with a specific historical occasion and once used, probably at the ceremonies held for the restoration of the city(s) and temple(s) in question, they generally came to be treated as *belles lettres*. These early laments were composed predominantly in the main Sumerian dialect *emegir*. The *a-ab-ba hu-luh-ha* is an example of one written in the *emesal* dialect.[541] These laments were preserved in the Old Babylonian period even though the dominant ethnic culture had changed from Sumerian to a Semitic culture in South Mesopotamia. The *eduba* "house of tablets"—the Sumerian Academy—which had become firmly established by the end of the third millennium, was continued by

---

539 See e.g., *kirugus* three, four, and the long soliloquy of Ningal in the Lament over Ur in *kirugu* seven, lines 257-298.
540 See above, ch. 4.7.
541 OAS, p. 32 ff.

Akkadian speaking teachers and men of letters.[542] The Sumerian literary culture at least had exerted such a profound effect on that part of the world that to a substantial degree it would be continued, albeit in adapted form, for centuries all the way into the Seleucid period.[543]

This, then, was the setting in which, at the very end of the neo-Sumerian or beginning of the Old Babylonian period, the great laments over the demise of Ur III and its cities and temples were written. It appears that these lamentations became part of the curriculum of the *eduba*.

The close demonstration of the evolution of the public lament in post-Sumerian times is made impossible by the fact that there is until now a hiatus in the "line" of lament collections after the Old Babylonian period. During the earlier laments, there began to be used a special dialect of Sumerian called *emesal*. The *emesal* dialect was primarily used as the speaking voice of females in the Sumerian literary texts. But the line of extant *emesal* texts breaks off for roughly 600 years when it reappears in neo-Assyrian texts and continues to be found for almost the next millennium. Thus, there may well be assumed a continuity of lament tradition.[544]

The later Sumero-Akkadian laments, however, show marked distinctions from the earlier ones. Stylistically, they seem to have become quite mechanical with stereotyped terms for destruction and mourning and at times gross repetition of cliches. Their descriptions of the calamity or crisis they are supposed to commemorate is quite general, devoid of reference to specific persons or events as found in the neo-Sumerian laments.[545]

Kutscher has now shown with the *a-ab-ba hu-luh-ha*, whose origins can be traced to the Old Babylonian period, that the distinction just mentioned is not so much due to evolution over a long period of time. Rather, it is due to change in usage. The main city laments were indeed composed to commemorate a very specific event and in all probability was used in the cult in connection with the rebuilding of the city/temple(s) mentioned.[546] They demonstrate a "freshness of style and sincere creative effort," and when refrains are used, they are used primarily for emphasis. However, from the early period we have also a lament which has all those marks of the later laments mentioned above. The difference lies in

---

542 Cf. A. Sjoberg, "Old Babylonian Eduba," AS 20 (1976):159-179.
543 SKly, pp. 18-28.
544 Ibid., pp. 18-42.
545 OAS, pp. 4-5.
546 See sect. 2.3.3 above, pp. 47ff.

the usage apparently intended. The more general, less creative, more stereotyped laments were precisely those which were composed to be adapted to cultic observances which were recurrent.[547]

In summary, the neo-Sumerian and Old Babylonian city-laments demonstrate a truly creative effort which bears marks of generic relationship. It seems apparent that they grew out of similar times and circumstances.

The influence seems fairly clear until we are faced with the fact that the a-ab-ba hu-luh-ha seems to break all the conventions including language—it is in the *emesal* dialect. That the majority of the later laments are in this mold seems, on the one hand, to argue for continuity of influence, but on the other hand, to demonstrate that the religious/social usage appears to exert the greater influence.

5.7.2 The Question of Influence Among the Hebrew Laments

As has been argued, the occasion and/or purpose of a lament exerts a significant influence on what is to be said or written in a given lament. But the conventions of a culture do as well. Thus, I have tried to show the connection between the earlier individual laments, the funeral dirge and the communal lament.

The matters of structure, style and terminology are largely the matter of convention, i.e., the customary means of expression for a given subject in a given culture. Influence is inevitable. The measure of flexibility apparent among the communal laments, however, would indicate that the influence is not irresistible.

The ejaculatory expressions common to the culture and appropriate to the subject are amply but not universally used. The vocabulary and the idioms of lament which become cliché are also widely attested but apparently not required by the genre. In my judgment, it is again the culture more than the antecedent stages of a developing genre which bears the greater influence. The Hebrews, like their Semitic cousins and their Sumerian predecessors, demonstrate what to the Western mind is a remarkable proclivity to complain to their deity and consider it in some sense a part of worship. From the early examples of a Moses or an Elijah to Isaiah and Jeremiah, the Israelite, as individual and as community, seemed uninhibited when it came to addressing his God in the face of a crisis.[548]

---

547 OAS, p. 6. Cf. SKly, pp. 26, 27.

548 See W. W. Hallo's treatment of neo-Sumerian letter-prayers in "Individual Prayer in Sumerian: the Continuity of a Tradition," JAOS 88 (1968): 75-80. The letter-prayers are said

From the literary perspective, some influence was doubtless exerted upon the communal lament by the other related forms. But such influence is virtually impossible to define clearly or to describe adequately exclusive of other factors. In speaking of the history of Hebrew laments, Westermann rightly describes this history as a "process in life," (*Lebensvorgang/Daseinsvorgang*).[549] It is most difficult to take one "stop-action" picture of the lament that adequately describes the whole. The point is that there is insufficient evidence of standardized or formalized terminology or syntax or other device, such as meter, to be able to show conclusively that there is a direct evolutionary link or even to determine exclusively the parameters of the genre. Yet, as I have already shown, there are expressions and gestures which come from the common experience of a given culture, such as death and other forms of personal calamity, and are put to use in compositions dealing with death and calamity on a broader social scale.

5.7.3 The Question of Influence Between the Sumero-Akkadian and the Hebrew Laments

As difficult as it may be to specify the literary influence which must exist among laments of a given culture, it is at least as difficult to do so between cultures.[550] Between the cultures in question there is a relationship—historically, socially, linguistically. The question must be, then, how direct or indirect is this relationship? As the record goes, it appears that although there clearly was some direct contact between the Sumero-Akkadian cultural tradition and the Hebrew, that contact was limited.

As mentioned above, Kramer has long been a champion for Sumerian "primacy" and hence, influence. Gadd takes much the same position.[551] From a basically similar perspective, Kraus sees an "astonishing parallel" to the Hebrew Lamentations in the formal begin-

---

characteristically to begin with a salutation followed by a message usually expressing 1) complaint, 2) protests, 3)prayers, 4)formal reinforcements of the appeal. The message is followed by a conclusion which "may occasionally consist of a vow to repay the kindness besought in the body of the text. More often it consists of a brief stereotyped formula either borrowed from the language of secular letters or peculiar to the genre itself."

549 "Struktur und Geschichte," p. 46.

550 Mowinckel declares the question is "often impossible to decide in any particular case." *Psalms*, vol. II, p. 178.

551 He states categorically that the book of Lamentations at least is "manifestly under the influence of these (Sumerian laments)." He takes Gottwald (*Studies in the Book of Lamentations*) to task for virtually ignoring what "has been observed by several writers, and is so naturally to be looked for in a work which is by its subject exilic." "The Second Lamentation for Ur" in *Hebrew and Semitic Studies Presented to Godfrey Rolles Driver*, eds., D. W. Thomas and W. D. McHardy (Oxford: Clarendon, 1963), p. 61, cf. n. 2.

ning and the various motifs of the "Lament over Ur."[552] On the other hand, Eissfeldt, for example, allows no "historical connection" between the book of Lamentations and the Sumerian laments.[553] Driver, Rudolph and Weiser find the parallels lack any indication of direct influence or borrowing.[554]

Two and a half decades ago, T. McDaniel, in a concise and cogent paper, argued that Kramer's theory of the primacy of Sumerian influence particularly on the book of Lamentations was untenable.[555] Recently, W. Gwaltney has taken issue with McDaniel and attempts, unsuccessfully to our mind, to prove that "McDaniel's conclusions can no longer be maintained and that Kramer's views are more defensible now than when he made them in 1959 and 1969."[556]

Gwaltney set up a typology for comparing the Mesopotamian and Hebrew laments under four major headings: ritual occasions, form/structure, poetic techniques, and theology.[557]

The first category yields the least similarity in Gwaltney's comparative analysis. He states that "on this question we are without documentation to inform us," with regard to the cultic setting of the Hebrew laments. He postulates, however, the restoration of the temple as the "most likely candidate for the biblical" laments. He concludes: "we may assume from the statement in Jer. 41:5 that some form of religious practice continued on the site of the largely demolished Temple."[558]

As I have already indicated, there is evidence, albeit meager, which seems to point to both a regular usage in relation to the temple, and an occasional usage in relation to specific calamities, past or impending.[559] However, Gwaltney is arguing for a close formal, "genetic" relationship on this basis. By his own admission, he does not succeed at this point. Indeed, any similarity seems only coincidental at best. Such similarity in

552 Kraus, Klagelieder, pp. 9-10.
553 Introduction, p. 504.
554 G. R. Driver, "The Psalms in the Light of Babylonian Research" in The Psalmists, ed. D. C. Simpson (London: Oxford, 1926), p. 172. W. Rudolph, Die Klagelieder, p. 9; A. Weiser, Klagelieder, Das Alte Testament Deutsch, Vol. 16 (Göttingen: Vandenhoeck und Ruprecht, 1962), pp. 297-370.
555 T. McDaniel, "The Alleged Sumerian Influence upon Lamentations," VT 18 (1968): 198-209.
556 W. Gwaltney, "The Biblical Book of Lamentations in the Context of Near Eastern Lament Literature," in Scripture in Context II, ed. W. Hallo, et al. (Winona Lake, Ind.: Eisenbrauns, 1983), p. 192. Cf. S. N. Kramer, "Sumerian Literature and the Bible," Analecta Biblica 12 (1959):185-204, see also Kramer, "Lament over Nippur."
557 Gwaltney, "Lamentations," p. 205.
558 Ibid., p. 209-210. Gwaltney cites Jer. 41:5, Zech.7:3-5; 8:19.
559 See above, ch. 3.4, ch. 4.4.

cultic setting is best explained by the similarity in themes developed by the two corpora of public laments and by the fact that they are indeed public, rather than private laments. This is hardly a sound basis for the conclusion that there exists some "genetic" relationship between Gwaltney's second category of form and structure. At this point in his typology, he discovers "a decided lack of similarity."[560] Indeed, we concur. In fact, we have argued that form and structure are not very reliable criteria by which to determine a genre.

The third aspect of Gwaltney's typology deals with poetic techniques. These he itemizes:

1. interchange of speaker (third, second, first person) involving description (third person), direct address (second person), monologue (first person), dialogue (first, second, and third persons)
2. use of woe-cries and various interjections
3. use of Emesal dialect apparently to simulate high-pitched cries of distress and pleading
4. heavy use of couplets, repeating lines with one word changed from line to line, and other devices of parallelism
5. antiphonal responses
6. tendency to list or catalog (gods, cities, temples, epithets, victims, etc.)
7. use of theme word or phrase which serves as a cord to tie lines together, or whole stanzas.[561]

He concludes that of all these characteristics, "only the Mesopotamian predilection for cataloging is lacking in the biblical Lamentations.[562]

A careful analysis, however, shows this not to be the case. First, there is absolutely no basis for arguing that a special dialect is used in the Hebrew laments. Although he does not directly state that he thinks a dialect is used in the Hebrew laments, this is one of his key characteristics listed above. In his discussion of those characteristics, Gwaltney seems to imply in his concluding statement just quoted that some special dialect is used without offering any evidence.

Furthermore, Gwaltney's limitation of his comparison to the book of Lamentations has the effect of skewing his results. In fact, these five compositions are not the only Hebrew communal laments. When the wider collection is analyzed, it is clear that there are other significant distinctions, for example, the profusion of refrains and repetends in the

---

560 Gwaltney, "Lamentations," pp. 209-210.
561 Ibid., p. 208.
562 Ibid. p. 209.

Mesopotamian compositions.[563] Neither is the use of woe-cries as pronounced in the Hebrew laments.[564] The other so-called characteristics
Gwaltney identifies can hardly be distinctive of laments.

Again, with reference to the usage of these poetic techniques by the
composers of both groups of laments, it seems the better explanation lies
in those aspects of ancient Near Eastern culture and experience which
the two have in common. Both societies faced both the normal calamities
of life such as death by natural causes, and the extraordinary crises of
plagues, famine and war. Although not identical, there were similarities
between their respective views on kingship and nation. The king was
seen to have held that office by divine right; the city-state was viewed as
the "mother" of her citizens.[565] Hence, political problems took on
"theological" significance. For both, the community played a significant
role in responding to the vicissitudes of life. Thus, the community
became involved in expressing its collective woe to its deity accompanied
by a request for deliverance and restoration because both saw a
significant if not causal role being played by their respective deity or
deities.[566]

The fourth of Gwaltney's typological categories is theology which he
subdivides into divinity, humanity, and causality. He acknowledges both
similarities and differences. However, he is not successful, in my judgment, in making his case. Of the theological underpinnings of the

---

[563] See discussion of repetends and refrains in chapter 2 in the treatment of the *balag*.
Compare the scarcity and brevity of refrains in the Hebrew laments: Pss. 42-43, 80 stand in
stark contrast to their meager use in the Hebrew laments.

[564] See chapter 4 above. The other so-called characteristics Gwaltney identifies can
hardly be distinctive of laments. Again, it seems the better explanation of the usage of these
poetic techniques by the composers of both groups of laments lies in those aspects of ancient
Near Eastern culture and experience which the two have in common. Both societies faced
both the normal calamities of life such as death by natural causes, and the extraordinary
crises of plagues, famine, and war. Although not identical, there were similarities between
their respective views on kingship and nation. The king was seen to have held that office by
divine right; the city-state was viewed as the "mother" of her citizens.

[565] Cf. the use of an expression such as "daughter of PN (city)." It is used frequently in
the second poem of Lamentations and more sparingly in chapters 1, 3, and 4. It does not
occur in the fifth chapter and is used only once in the Psalm laments. בת ירושלם :Lam.
2:13,15. בת ציון :Lam. 1:6; 2:4,8,10,11,13,18; 4:22 (cf. 2:11; 3:48; 4:3,6,10: בת עמי; בנות עירי;
Lam. 3:51). בת יהודה :Lam. 1:15; 2:2,5. בת בבל :Ps. 137:8. בת ארום :Lam. 4:21,22. The expression has been found thus far among the city-laments only in an Akkadian lament (Published
in PSBA 1901, translated by Langdon SBP XXV, pp. 263-266.) dated to the Seleucid period by
Pinches. In lines 3,4, and 12 of this composition are found "daughter of Erech," "daughter of
Agade," "daughter of Larak," and "daughter of Nippur." Cf. LU 283-284 where Ningal
laments "My daughters and my sons verily...have been carried off...etc."—the closest to the
use of the expression I
could find.

[566] See chapter 2, pp. 53ff.

Mesopotamian laments, Gwaltney observes concerning their view of deity:

1. The god of wrathful destruction, usually Enlil, abandons the city, a signal for devastation, often called a "storm," to begin.

2. This chief god may bring the havoc himself or may order another deity to attack the city or the sanctuary.

3. In any case, Enlil's will is irresistible; he has the backing of the council of gods.

4. Enlil is described and addressed in anthropomorphic terms:
   - a warrior
   - the shepherd of the people
   - his word destroys
   - his "heart" and "liver" must be soothed
   - he must be roused from sleep
   - he must inspect the ruins to see what has occurred
   - he must be cajoled to change his mind

5. Yet there is an unknowable quality to Enlil; he is unsearchable.

6. Lesser deities must intercede with the chief god to bring an end to the ruin.[567]

Gwaltney goes on to show parallels in the Hebrew material noting the lack of a goddess wandering about and bemoaning the destruction of the city but postulating that the city of Jerusalem substitutes for this feature in Lam. 1:12-17. The other distinctions he notices are the lack of lesser gods who intercede, the absence of God's needing to be aroused from sleep, and the absence of any call to soothe God's "heart and liver."[568]

There can be no doubt that indeed the God of Israel is depicted as majestic and mighty, a fortress of strength, the LORD of hosts;[569] that He is seen at work in the calamity being lamented;[570] that He is seen to have withdrawn from the city and is pleaded with to return and restore.[571] However, by simply citing these similarities and differences, Gwaltney does not prove that they establish a "genetic" connection between the Mesopotamian and Hebrew laments. Rather, it can be argued that the similarities are adequately explained on the basis of the similarity of subject matter. The themes of God's greatness and His wrath are not unique to the lament genre but are represented not only in other genres

---

567 Gwaltney, "Lamentations," pp. 206-207.
568 Ibid. p. 208.
569 Pss. 31:4; 42:11; 80:5,8; 102:13; Lam. 5:19.
570 Pss. 60:3,4; 80:5-7; Lam. 1:5, 12-15, 17; 2:1-8, 17; 3:1-16, 32-38, 43-45; 4:11, 16; 5:22.
571 Pss. 42:4,11; 74; 77:8,10; Lam. 2:1,6-8; 5:22, etc.

within the Psalter but also in other genres throughout the Hebrew Bible. It is to be expected that if one is dealing with a lament over some calamity, and that lament is composed in a theistic milieu of any kind, the deity or deities of that culture are going to be involved. In most cases, at least some level of responsibility will be attributed to deity by definition. Again, this does not demonstrate a "genetic" relationship.

The motif of rousing deity from sleep to attend to the calamity which is found in the Mesopotamian laments is not unique to them. This motif is found in Egyptian texts from the third millennium B.C. to the Roman period.[572] It is exhibited in Elijah's confrontation with the prophets of the Canaanite deity Baal when Elijah taunts them to "call with a loud voice" to get the attention of an otherwise distracted deity or "perhaps he is asleep and he must be awakened."[573] Although Gwaltney states that this is one theme which "is totally lacking in the biblical Lamentations,"[574] it is to be found in the larger collection of communal laments. The psalmist cries in the forty-fourth Psalm: "Arouse Yourself! Why do You sleep, Oh Lord? Awake!" The motif arises out of a common experience: tragedy in the face of the apparent lack of intervention of deity, either to have prevented it or to redress it. It does not prove a "genetic" literary relationship. In fact, each of the similarities identified by Gwaltney is adequately explained on much the same basis. The differences he points out are sufficiently explained against the distinctives of the respective cultures, e.g., Israelite monotheism over against the Mesopotamian polytheism, etc.

Each of the four pillars which Gwaltney offers in support of his typological arguments is inadequate. Even taken together, they do not support his thesis.

The other main aspect of Gwaltney's approach is to show that the "significant spatial and temporal gap between the Mesopotamian congregational lament form and the biblical book" of Lamentations does not exist. He sets this gap notion up as the keystone of McDaniel's thesis: "the most crippling to Kramer's, Gadd's, and Kraus's position."[575] This is not the case, however. On the one hand, Gwaltney identifies the cornerstone of his thesis as the "advances in the realm of Sumerian and Akkadian literary analysis during the 1970s."[576] He declares, "on the

---

572 A. Erman, *Die Literatur der Aegypter*, (Leipzig: J.C. Hinrichs, 1923), p. 37. Porphyry, *De Abstinentia*, trans. S. Hibberd (1857), iv. 9.

573 I Kgs 18:27.

574 Gwaltney, "Lamentation," p. 208.

575 Gwaltney, "Lamentations," p. 194.

576 Ibid., p. 192.

basis of the discoveries of the 1970s we can now fill the gap in time between the city-laments and biblical Lamentations with the lineal liturgical descendants of the city-laments, the *balag-eršemmas*."[577] The Seleucid *balag-eršemma* material he adduces to close the spatial and temporal "gap" is not a new discovery of the 1970's as he suggests. A significant sampling had been available long before Kramer addressed the question in 1959.[578] But more importantly, the weight of McDaniel's thesis is based on literary, not spatial or temporal factors.[579]

As some have pointed out, there are indeed some very close similarities in style and substance between these two lament traditions. The conclusions are mixed. But when the specific details are studied, it seems that indeed the parallels are best explained as coincidental and the result of a common experience addressed by a similar, if not common, culture.

One reason already cited in support of this conclusion is that most of the coincidental features demonstrate significantly distinctive characteristics, or else have been shown to be so widely used among the various societies in the ancient Near East as to make a direct connection impossible.[580]

On the other hand, there are features which are preponderant in the Sumerian laments—so much so as to be almost a hallmark—but which are noticeably absent from the Hebrew laments. A prime example is the "evil storm" motif so prevalent in the Ur Laments which one "would expect to find . . . somewhere in the biblical lamentation if there were any real literary dependency."[581] Other dominant Sumero-Akkadian motifs not present in the Hebrew laments would be: the abandoned sheepfold, the divine flood, the destructive divine word, the appeasing of the divine heart.

Still, a third factor is that while there is clear evidence of some significant level of social intercourse between the two cultures in question in,

---

577 Ibid., p. 210.

578 E.g., Langdon's treatments in SBP in 1909.

579 This is true of the McDaniel study to which Gwaltney is responding and is bolstered by the fact that this McDaniel's article is a sequel to a forty-nine page philological analysis of Lamentations which McDaniel published in that same year. See "Philological Studies in Lamentations" pts. I and II, Bib 49 (1968): 27-54, 199-220.

580 See the comparison done by T. McDaniel, "The Alleged Sumerian Influence." McDaniel takes the parallels cited by Rudolph as well as some others which might suggest Sumerian influence, and one by one suggests quite plausibly that direct influence of Sumerian cannot thus be proven, and that the given feature is better explained by elements of Canaanite literary tradition or merely by the nature of the subject matter. Hillers seems to concur in denying any "*direct* influence" and that the "genuine, and occasionally close, parallels in wording . . . are to be explained in a wider context." *Lamentations*, p. XXXIX.

581 McDaniel, "Sumerian Influence," p. 207.

e.g., the fragment of a copy of the Gilgamesh Epic found at Megiddo dating to the 14th century[582] and the Amarna material, there remains to be found any example of any type of Sumero-Akkadian lament, individual or communal, in the West. While this is clearly an argument from silence, the fact remains that there is no clear evidence of a line of influence between the Sumero-Akkadian lament tradition and that of the Hebrews. As Jacobsen put it:

> In all questions of cultural influence it is not the abstract and the simple but the particular and the complex which furnish reliable evidence.
>
> This must be kept clearly in mind when one evaluates the implications of even such attractive suggestions as that the Sumerian lamentations are forerunners of the "Book of Lamentations." (Forerunners in the sense of compositions in an earlier age treating of similar subjects? Yes, certainly. Forerunners in the sense that the "Book of Lamentations" stands in a Sumerian literary tradition from which it derives literary patterns and phraseology? Surely not until it has been shown that the extant similarities go beyond what similar subject matter and similar situations will naturally suggest to any good poet.)[583]

5.8 Conclusion

There can be no doubt that there was a historical-cultural continuum which produced both collections of lament and did indeed affect the respective literary traditions as well as religious and social traditions. Though direct evidence seems to be lacking in this particular area, it would seem reasonable to assume that indeed Israel did learn from her neighbors as she did in other areas.

But the tradition is both a long one and widespread. A close look at the data available just does not seem to support the theory that lament was something learned directly from the Babylonians during the exile.[584] The Hebrew communal laments are sufficiently distinct and demonstrate an almost unique flexibility of form and style[585] so as to warrant the conclusion of literary dependence within the ancient Near Eastern milieu. The data does support a cultural dependence upon what

---

[582] See A. Goetze and S. Levy, "Fragment of Gilgamesh Epic from Megiddo," *Atiqot* 2 (1959): 121-128.

[583] Jacobsen, *Tammuz*, p. 364.

[584] Cf. Gadd, "Second Lament," p. 61.

[585] Cf. Castellino, though dealing with individual laments, addresses the question of dependence and concludes in the negative. LIIBE, pp. 252-256.

Mowinckel calls "the common oriental culture" and hence, "participation in a common literary culture.[586]

---

[586] "Psalms, vol. II, p. 178.

Bibliography

Albrektson, B. *Studies in the Text and Theology of Lamentations*. Lund: G. W. K. Gleerup, 1963.

Albright, W. F. *Archaeology and the Religion of Israel*. Baltimore: Johns Hopkins, 1956.

————. "The Old Testament and Canaanite Language and Literature." *CBQ* 7 (1945):5-31.

Alexiou, M. *Ritual Lament in Greek Tradition*. London: Cambridge University Press, 1974.

Amirtham, S. "To be Near and Far Away from Yahweh: The Witness of the Individual Psalm of Lament to the Concept of the Presence of God." *Bangalore Theological Forum* 2 (1968):31-55.

Anderson, A. A. *The Book of Psalms*. 2 vols. New Century Bible, eds. R. E. Clements and M. Black. London: Oliphants, 1972.

Archibald, H. et al. "Bereavement in Childhood and Adult Psychiatric Disturbance." *Psychosomatic Medicine* 24 (1962):343-351.

Baird, J. A. "Genre Analysis as a Method of Historical Criticism." *Society of Biblical Literature Proceedings* 108, 2 (1972):385-411.

Ball, C. J. "The Metrical Structure of Quinoth, the Book of Lamentations Arranged According to the Original Measures." *Society of Biblical Literature Proceedings* (1887):131-53.

Baltzer, C. *The Covenant Formulary*. Philadelphia: Fortress,1971.

Barr, J. *The Bible in the Modern World*. New York: Harper, 1973.

Baumgartner, W. *Die Klagegedichte des Jeremia*. BZAW 32 (1917). Giessen: A. Töpelmann, 1917.

Begrich, J. "Die Vertrauensäusserungen im israelischen Klageliede des Einzelen und in seinem babylonischen Gegenstück." *ZAW* 46 (1928):221-260.

Birkeland, H. *Die Feinde des Individuums in der israelitischen Psalmenliteratur*. Oslo: Orondahl, 1933.

Blayney, B. *Jeremiah and Lamentations*. Edinburgh: Oliphant and Balfour, 1810.

Blenkinsopp, J. "The Search for the Prickly Plant: Structure and Function Found in the Gilgamesh Epic." *Structuralism*. Edited by S. Wittig. Pittsburg: Pickwick Press, 1975.

Böhmer, J. "Ein alphabetisch-akrostiches Rätsel und ein Versuch, es zu lösen." *ZAW* 28 (1908):53-57.

Bonnet, H. "Dichotomy of Artistic Genres." In *Yearbook of Comparative Criticism*. Vol. 8: *Theories of Literary Genre*, pp. 3-16. Edited by J. P. Strelka. University Park: Pennsylvania State University, 1978.

Bottero, J. et al. eds. *Delacorte World History*. New York: Delacorte, 1967. Translated by R. Tannenbaum. Vol. 2: *The Near East: Early Civilizations*.

Briggs, C. A. and E G. Briggs. *The Book of Psalms*. 2 vols. ICC. Edinburgh: T. and T. Clark, 1909.

Broadribb, D. A. "A Historical Review of Studies of Hebrew Poetry." *AbrN* 13 (1972-3):66-87.

Brueggemann, W. "From Hurt to Joy. From Death to Life." *Int* 28, 1 (1974):3-19.

Brunet, G. *Les lamentations contre Jérémie: Réinterprétation des quatre premieres lamentations*. Paris: Presses Universitaires de France, 1968.

Budde, K. "Die Klagelieder," in *Die fünf Megilloth. Kurzer Hand-Commentar zum Alten Testament* 17. Leipzig, 1898.

———. "Das hebräische Klagelied." *ZAW* 2 (1882):1-52.

Burke, K. "Poetic Categories." *Attitudes toward History*. Vol. 1, pp. 41-119. New York: New Republic, 1937. 2 vols.

Buss, M. J. "The Idea of Sitz im Leben—History and Critique." *ZAW* 90 (1978):157-170.

———. *The Prophetic Word of Hosea: A Morphological Study*. BZAW 111. Berlin: Töpelmann, 1969.

Buttenwieser, M. *The Psalms: Chronologically treated with new Translation*. Chicago: University of Chicago Press, 1938.

Cannon, W. W. "Authorship of Lamentations." *BSac* 81 (1924):42-58.

Caplice, R. *The Akkadian Namburbi Texts: An Introduction*. Sources from the Ancient Near East. Vol. 1, fasc. 1. Los Angeles: Undena, 1974.

———. "Namburbi Texts in the British Museum." Part 1: *Or* NS 34 (1965): 105-131; Part 2: *Or* NS 36 (1967): 1-38; Part 3: Or NS 36 (1967): 273-298; Part 4: *Or* NS 39 (1970): 111-151; Part 5: *Or* NS 40 (1971): 133-183.

Castellino, G. R. Le *Lamentazione Individuali e gli Inni in Babylonia e in Israele*. Torino: Societa Editrice Internationale, 1940.

Cheyne, T. K. *The Book of Psalms*. London: Kegan Paul, Trench and Co., 1848.

Childs, B. *Biblical Theology in Crisis*. Philadelphia: Westminster, 1970.

Clements, R. E. *A Century of Old Testament Study*. London: Lutterworth, 1976.

Cohen, M. E. "Analysis of the *balag*-Composition to the God Enlil Copied During the Seleucid Period." Ph.D. dissertation, University of Pennsylvania, 1979.

———. *Balag-compositions: Sumerian Lamentation Liturgies of the Second and First Millennium B. C.* Sources from the Ancient Near East. Vol. 1, fasc. 2. Malibu, Calif.: Undena, 1974.

———. *Sumerian Hymnology: the Eršemma*. Hebrew Union College Annual Supplements, no. 2. Cincinnati: Hebrew Union College, 1981.

Colie, R. L. *The Resources of Kind*. Edited by B. K. Lewalski. Berkeley: University of California Press, 1973.

Collins, T. "Line-Forms in Hebrew Poetry." *JSS* 23, (Fall, 1978):228-244.

Condamin, A. "Symmetrical Repetitions in Lamentations I and II." *JTS* 7 (1906):137-140.

Contenau, G. *Everyday Life in Babylon and Assyria*. Translated by K. R. and A. R. Maxwell-Hyslop. London: Arnold, 1954.

Cooper, J. *The Curse of Agade*. Johns Hopkins Near Eastern Studies. Baltimore: Johns Hopkins University, 1983.

———. "Sumerian and Akkadian in Sumer and Akkad." *Or* NS 42 (1973):239-246.

Craig, J. A. *Assyrian and Babylonian Religious Texts*. Leipzig: J. C. Hinrichs, 1895-1897.

Craigie, P. C. "A Note on Fixed Pairs in Ugaritic and Early Hebrew Poetry." *JTS* 22 (1971):141-43.

———. "The Poetry of Ugarit and Israel." *TynBul* 22 22(1971):3-31.

Crane, R. S. *Critical and Historical Principles of Literary History*. Chicago: University of Chicago, 1971.

Cross, F. M., Jr. and D. N. Freedman. "*Studies in Ancient Yahwistic Poetry*." Ph.D. dissertation, Johns Hopkins University, Baltimore, 1950.

Culley, R. C. *Oral Formulaic Language in the Biblical Psalms*. Toronto: Toronto University, 1967.

Dalglish, E. R. "Hebrew Penitential Psalms with Special Reference to Psalm 51." Ph.D. dissertation, Columbia University, 1951.

———. *Psalm Fifty-One in the Light of Ancient Near Eastern Patternism*. Leiden: Brill, 1962.

Dahood, M. *The Psalms*. 3 vols. Anchor Bible, 16017. New York: Doubleday, 1966-1970.

Diakonoff, I. M. "Ancient Writing and Ancient Written Language: Pitfalls and Peculiarities in the Study of Sumerian." In *Sumerological Studies in Honor of Thorkild Jacobsen*, pp. 99-122. *AS*, 20. Edited by S. J. Lieberman. Chicago: University of Chicago, 1976.

Donohue, J. J. *The Theory of Literary Kinds*. Vol. I: *Ancient Classifications of Literature*. Vol. II: *Ancient Classes of Poetry*. Dubuque, Ia.: Loras College, 1943-1949.

Dossin, G. "Un rituel du Culte d'Istar." *RA* 35 (1938):1-13.

180   THE GENRE OF COMMUNAL LAMENT

Doty, W. G. "The Concept of Genre in Literary Analysis." *Society of Biblical Literature Proceedings* 108, 2 (1972):413-448.

Driver, G. R. The Books of Joel and Amos with Introduction and Notes. Cambridge: University Press, 1897.

———. "Hebrew Notes on 'Song of Songs' and 'Lamentations'." *Festschrift Alfred Bertholet zum 80 Geburtstag.* pp. 134-146. Edited by W. Baumgartner, et al. Tübingen: J. C. B. Mohr, 1950.

———. "Notes on the Text of 'Lamentations.'" *ZAW* 52 (1934):308ff.

———. "The Psalms in the Light of Babylonian Research." *The Psalmists.* Edited by D. C. Simpson. London: Oxford, 1926.

Ebeling, E. *Die akkadische Gebetsserie "Handerhebung."* Berlin: Akademie, 1953.

Edzard, D. *Die "zweite Zwischenzeit" Babyloniens.* Weisbaden: Harrassowitz, 1975.

Ehrenpreis, I. *The "Types Approach" to Literature.* New York: King's Crown Press, 1945.

Eissfeldt, O. "Etymologische und archaeologische Erklärung alttestamentlicher Worter." *Oriens Antiquus* 5:167-171.

———. "Kultvereine in Ugarit." In *Ugaritica.* Vol. VI, pp. 187-195. Edited by C. Schaeffer. Paris: Paul Geuthner, 1969.

———. *The Old Testament: An Introduction.* Translated by P. Ackroyd. New York: Harper and Row, 1965.

Ellis, M., ed. *Essays on the Ancient Near East in the Memory of Jacob Joel Finkelstein.* Memoirs of Conn. Grad. Arts Science. Vol. 19. Hamden, Conn.: Ardion Books, 1977.

Emerton, J. A. "Meaning of אבני־קדש in Lamentations 4:1." *ZAW* 79 (1967):2:232-6.

Falkenstein, A. "Die Ibbisin-Klage." *Die Welt des Orients* I (1950):377-384.

———. "*Fluch über Agade.*" *ZA* 57 (1965):43 ff.

———. "Hymn to Sulpae." *ZA* 55 (1960):11 ff.

———. "Review of Lamentation over the Destruction of Ur, by Samuel Noah Kramer." *ZA* 49 (1949):320-24.

———. "Sumerische religiöse Texte: 1. Drei 'Hymnen' auf Urninurta von Isin." *ZA* 49 (1949): 80-150.

———. "Zur Chronologie der sumerischen Literatur: Die nachaltbabylonische Stufe." *Mitteilungen der Orientgesellschaft in Berlin* 85 (1953): 1-13.

———. and Wolfram von Soden. *Sumerische und akkadische Hymnen und Gebete.* Die Bibliothek der alten Welt. Zurich: Artemis-Verlag, 1953.

Fisher, L. R. *Ras Shamra Parallels.* 2 vols. AnOr 49, 50. Rome: Pontificium Institutum Biblicum, 1972.

Fowler, A. "The Life and Death of Literary Forms." *New Literary History* 2 (1971): 199-216.

Freedman, D. N. "Archaic Forms in Early Hebrew Poetry." *ZAW* 72: (1960):101-107.

———. "The Structure of Psalm 137." *Near Eastern Studies in Honor of W. F. Albright.* Edited by H. Goedicke. Baltimore: John Hopkins, 1971.

Freehof, S. B. "Note on Lamentations 1:14." *JQR* 38 (1947/8):343 ff.

Frye, Northrup. *Anatomy of Criticism: Four Essays*. Princeton: Princeton University, 1957.

Gadamer, H. G. *Truth and Method*. New York: Seabury, 1975.

Gadd, C. J. "Babylonia 2120-1800." In *Cambridge Ancient* History. 3d ed., vol. 1, pt. 2. *Early History of the Middle East*, pp. 595-643. Edited by I. E. S. Edwards, C. J. Gadd, et al. Cambridge: University Press, 1971.

————. "Second Lamentation for Ur." *Hebrew and Semitic Studies Presented to G. R. Driver*. Edited by D. W. Thomas and W. D. McHardy. Oxford: Clarendon Press, 1963.

————. and S. N. Kramer. *Ur Excavation Texts 6*, pt. 2, *Literary and Religious Texts*. Publications of Joint Expedition of the British Museum and the University Museum, University of Pennsylvania, to Mesopotamia. Philadelphia: University of Pennsylvania, 1966.

Galpin, F. W. *The Music of the Sumerians and Their Immediate Successors, the Babylonians and Assyrians*. Cambridge: University Press, 1937.

Galling, K. *Biblisches Reallexicon*. Vol. 1: *Handbuch zum Alten Testament*. Tübingen: J. C. B. Mohr, 1937.

Gaster, T. H. "An Ancient Eulogy on Israel, Deuteronomy 33:3-5, 26-29." *JBL* 66 (1947):53-62.

————. *Myth, Legend and Custom in the Old Testament*. New York: Harper and Row, 1969.

————. *Thespis*. New York: Harper and Row, 1950.

Gerstenberger, E. "Der klagende Mensch. Anmerkungen zu den Klagegattunger in Israel." *Festschrift G. Von Rad: Probleme biblischer Theologie*. pp. 64-72. Edited by H. W. Wolff. Munich: Kaiser, 1971.

Gevirtz, S. *Patterns in the Early Poetry of Israel*. Studies in Ancient Oriental Civilization, 32. Chicago: University of Chicago, 1963.

Ginsberg, H. L. "The Rebellion and Death of Ba'lu." *Or* 5 (1936):161-198.

Goetze, A. and Levy, S. "Fragment of Gilgamesh Epic from Megiddo." *Atiqot* 2 (1959): 121-128.

Gordis, R. "Commentary on Text of Lamentations II." *JQR* 58 (July 1967):14-33.

————. "Conclusion of the Book of Lamentatons." *JBL* 93 (June 1974):289-93.

————. "A Note on Lamentations 2:13." *JTS* 34 (1983):162ff.

Gordon, C. H. *Ugaritic Textbook*. AnOr, 38. Rome: Pontifical Biblical Institute, 1965.

Gorer, G. *Death, Grief and Mourning*. Garden City, New York: Anchor Books, 1967.

Gottlieb, H. "*Ligklagen over Krt, II K I-II*." Dansk Teologisk Tidsskrift 32 (1969):88-105.

Gottwald, N. K. "Lamentations." *Int* 9 (July 1955):320-38.

————. *Studies in the Book of Lamentations*. London: SCM., 1954.

Gray, G. B. *Forms of Hebrew Poetry*. London, 1915. Rev. ed. Prolegomenon by D. N. Freedman. New York: KTAV, 1972.

Green, M. W. "The Eridu Lament." *JCS* 30/3 (1978):127-167.

———. "Eridu in Sumerian Literature." Ph.D. dissertation, University of Chicago, 1975.

Gressmann, H. *Altorientalisch Texte und Bilder zum alten Testament*. 2d ed. Tübingen: Mohr, 1926-7.

Gunkel, H. *Ausgewählte Psalmen*. 4th rev. ed. Göttingen: Vandenhoeck und Ruprecht, 1917.

———. "The Israelite Prophecy from the Time of Amos." In *Twentieth Century Theology in the Making*. Edited by J. Pelikan, translated by R. W. Wilson. New York: Harper and Row, 1969.

———. "Die israelitische Literatur." *Die Kultur der Gegenwart*. Div. I/vol. 7. Edited by P. Hinneberg. Berlin: B. G. Teubner, 1906.

———. "Jesaia: eine prophetische Liturgie." *ZAW* 42 (1924):177-208.

———. *Die Propheten*. Göttingen: Vandenhoeck und Ruprecht, 1917.

———. *Die Psalmen übersetzt und erklärt*. 4th ed. Göttingen: Vandenhoeck und Ruprecht, 1926.

———. *The Psalms*. Biblical Series 19. Philadelphia: Facet Books, 1967.

———. *Reden und Aufsätze*. Göttingen: Vandenhoeck und Ruprecht, 1913.

———. *Die Sagen der Genesis*. Göttingen: Vandenhoeck und Ruprecht, 1901.

———. *What Remains of the Old Testament*. Translated by A. K. Dallas. New York: Macmillan, 1928.

———. and J. Begrich. *Einleitung in die Psalmen. Die Gattungen der religiösen Lyrik Israels*. Göttingen: Vandenhoeck und Ruprecht, 1928, 1933. 2d ed. 1966.

———. and O. Scheel, eds. *Die Relgion in Geschichte und Gegenwart*. 5 vols. Tübingen: Mohr, 1909.

Guthrie, H. *Israel's Sacred Songs*. New York: Seabury, 1966.

Gwaltney, Jr., W. C. "The Biblical Book of Lamentations in the Context of Near Eastern Lament Literature." *Scripture in Context II*. Edited by W. W. Hallo, J. C. Meyer, and L. G. Perdue. Winona Lake, Ind.: Eisenbrauns, 1983.

Hallo, W. W. "The Cultic Setting of Sumerian Poetry." *RAI XVIIe* (Ham-sur-Henre: University Library de Bruxelles, 1970):116-34.

———. "On the Antiquity of Sumerian Literature. *JAOS* 83 (1963):167.

———. "Review of Literary and Religious Texts, First Part, by C. J. Gadd and S. N. Kramer." *JCS* 20, 2 (1966):89-93.

———. "Toward a History of Sumerian Literature." In *Sumerological Studies in Honor of Thorkild Jacobsen*, pp. 181-203. AS, 20. Edited by S. J. Lieberman. Chicago: University of Chicago, 1976.

———. and J. J. A. van Dijk. *The Exaltation of Inanna*. New Haven: Yale, 1968.

Harner, P. B. "The Salvation Oracle in Second Isaiah." *JBL* 88 (1969):418-434.

Harris, Z. S. *Development of the Canaanite Dialects*. American Oriental Series no. 8. New Haven: American Oriental Society, 1939.

Hartmann, H. "Die Musik der sumerischen Kultur." Inaugural dissertation, Universität Frankfurt am Main, 1960.

Hayes, J. *An Introduction to Old Testament Study.* Nashville: Abingdon, 1979.

————, ed. *Old Testament Form Criticism.* San Antonio: Trinity University, 1974.

Held, M. "Studies in Ugaritic Lexicography and Poetic Style." Ph.D. dissertation, Johns Hopkins University, Baltimore, 1957.

Herdner, A. *Corpus des tablettes en cuneiformes Alphabetiques (decouvertes a Ras Shamra—Ugarit de 1929 a 1939) I (texts) II (plates).* Paris: P. Geuthner, 1963.

Herzog, E. *Psyche and Death: Archaic Myths and Modern Dreams in Analytical Psychology.* London: Hodder and Stoughton, 1966.

Hibbard, F. G. *The Psalms Chronologically Arranged with Historical Introduction.* New York: Carlton and Lanahan, 1856.

Hillers, D. R. *Lamentations.* Anchor Bible, 7A. New York: Doubleday, 1972.

————. "Roads to Zion Mourn (Lamentations 1:4)." *Perspective* 12, no. 1-2 (1971):121-34.

————. *Treaty-Curses and the Old Testament Prophets.* Rome: Pontifical Biblical Institute, 1964.

Hirsch, E. D. *Validity in Interpretation.* New Haven: Yale University Press, 1967.

Holladay, W. "Form and Word Play in David's Lament over Saul and Jonathan." *VT* 20 (1970):153-89.

Hulst, A. R. et al. *Old Testament Translation Problems.* Leiden: Brill, 1960.

Hurvitz, A. "The Date of the Prose-tale of Job Linguistically Reconsidered." *HTR* 67 (1974):17-34.

Jacobsen, T. "Review of Lamentation over the Destruction of Ur, by S. N. Kramer." *AJSL* 58 (1941):219-224.

————. *Toward the Image of Tammuz.* Edited by W. L. Moran. Harvard Semitic Series, vol. 21. Cambridge, Mass.: Harvard, 1970.

Jahnow, H. *Das hebräische Leichenlied im Rahmen der Völkerdichtung.* BZAW 36 (Giessen: A. Töpelmann, 1923).

Janzen, W. *Mourning Cry and Woe Oracle.* BZAW 125. Berlin: de Gruyter, 1972.

Johnson, A. R. *The Cultic Prophet in Ancient Israel.* 2d ed. Cardiff, Wales: University of Wales, 1962.

————. The *One and the Many in the Israelite Conception of God.* Cardiff, Wales: University of Wales, 1961.

————. *The Vitality of the Individual in the Thought of Ancient Israel.* Cardiff, Wales: University of Wales, 1949.

Jakobson, R. "Poetry of Grammar and Grammar of Poetry." *Lingua* 21 (1968):597-609.

Jolles, A. *Einfache Formen.* 2d ed. Tübingen: Max Niemeyer 1958.

Kaiser, O. *Introduction to the Old Testament.* Minneapolis: Augsburg, 1975.

Keil, C. F. *The Lamentations of Jeremiah.* Translated by Jas. Kennedy. Edinburgh: T. S. and T. Clark, 1874.

Kirkpatrick, A. F. *The Psalms: Cambridge Bible*. Cambridge: Cambridge University Press, 1902.

Kissane, E. J. *The Book of Psalms*. Mystic, Conn.: Lawrence Verry, Inc., 1964.

Kitchen, K. *The Ancient Orient and the Old Testament*. Chicago: Inter-Varsity, 1966.

Klein, J. "Šulgi D: a neo-Sumerian Royal Hymn." Ph.D. dissertation, University of Pennsylvania, 1968.

Kline, M. *The Treaty of the Great King*. Grand Rapids: Eerdmans, 1963.

Knierim, R. "Old Testament Form Criticism Reconsidered." *Int* 27 (Oct. 1973):435-468.

Knight, D. A. *Rediscovering the Traditions of Israel*. SBLDS 9 Missoula, MT. Scholars Press (1975).

Kramer, S. N. "Keš and its Fate: Laments, Blessings, Omens." In *Gratz College Anniversary Volume*, p. 172. Edited by I. D. Passow and S. T. Lachs. Philadelphia: Gratz College, 1971.

———. "Lamentation Over the Destruction of Nippur: A Preliminary Report." *Eretz-Israel*, vol. 9. W. F. Albright Volume, pp. 89-93. Jerusalem: Israel Exploration Society, 1969.

———. "Lamentation Over the Destruction of Sumer and Ur." In *ANET*, pp. 611-619. Edited by J. Pritchard.

———. "Lamentation Over the Destruction of Ur." In *ANET*, pp. 455-463. Edited by J. Pritchard.

———. *Lamentation Over the Destruction of Ur*. AS 12 (1940). Chicago: University of Chicago.

———. "Literary Texts from Ur. VI, pt. II, Lamentation Ur." *Iraq* 25 (1963):171-176.

———. *Sumerian Literary Texts from Nippur in the Museum of the Ancient Orient at Istanbul*. AASOR 23 (1944).

———. "Sumerian Literature: A General Survey." *The Bible and the Ancient Near East*. Edited by G. E. Wright. Garden City, New York: Doubleday, 1961.

———. "Sumerian Literature and the Bible." *Analecta Biblica* 12 (1959):185-204.

———. *The Sumerians*. Chicago: University of Chicago Press, 1963.

———. "Two British Museum ir emma 'Catalogues.'" *StOr* 46 (1975):141-166.

Kraus, H. J. "hôj als prophetische Leichenklage über das eigene Volk im 8. Jahrhundert." *ZAW* 85 (1973):15-46.

———. *Psalmen*. BKAT 15. Edited by M. Noth. Neukircher: Neukirchener Verlag, 1960.

———. *Worship in Israel*. Translated by G. Buswell. Richmond: John Knox Press, 1966.

Krecher, J. *Sumerische Kultlyrik*. Wiesbaden: Harrassowitz, 1966.

Krupp, G. "The Bereavement Reaction: A Special Case of Separation Anxiety—Socio-Cultural Considerations," *Psychoanalytic Study of Society* 2 (1962):42-74.

Kubler-Ross, E. *On Death and Dying*. New York: Macmillan, 1969.

Kunstmann, W. G. *Die babylonische Gebetsbeschwörung*. Leipziger semitistischen Studien, n.f. Bd. 2. Leipzig: n.p., 1932.

Kurylowicz, J. *Studies in Semitic Grammar and Metrics*. London: Curzon Press, 1973.

Kutscher, R. *Oh Angry Sea*. YNER 9. New Haven: Yale University Press, 1975.

———. *Words and Their History*. Jerusalem: Kiryat-Sefer, 1965.

Lachs, S. T. "Date of Lamentations V (168-165 BC)." *JQR* 57 (July 1966):46-56.

Lambert, M. "La littèrature sumerienne à propos d'ouvrages recents." *RA* 55 (1961):177-1966; 56 (1962):81-90, 214.

Lambert, W. G. *Babylonian Wisdom Literature*. Oxford: Oxford University Press, 1960.

Lanaham, W. F. "Speaking Voice in the Book of Lamentations." *JBL* 93 (1974):41-9.

Lane, E. W. *An Account of the Manners and Customs of Modern Egyptians*. 5th ed. London: J. Murray, 1871.

Langdon, S. *Babylonian Liturgies*. Paris: Geuthner, 1913.

———. *Babylonian Penitential Psalms*. OECT 6. Paris: Geuthner, 1927.

———. "Calendars of Liturgies and Prayers: I. The Assur Calendar." *AJSL* 4 2 (1926):110-127.

———. *Historical and Religious Texts from the Temple Library of Nippur*. Babylonian Expedition, vol. 31. Munich: n.p., 1914.

———. "Lamentation to the Goddess of Sirpurla." *AJSL* 24 (1907-08):282-285.

———. *Sumerian and Babylonian Psalms*. Paris: Paul Geuthner, 1909.

———. *Sumerian Liturgical Texts*. Publication of Babylonian Section, vol. 10., no. 2. Philadelphia: University of Pennsylvania museum, 1917.

Leedy, P. "Genres Criticism and the Significance of Wharton's Essay on Pope." *Journal of English and Germanic Philology* 45 (1946):142.

Leslie, E. A. *The Psalms: Translated and Interpreted in the Light of Hebrew Life and Worship*. New York: Abingdon Cokesbury, 1949.

Leslau, W. "Observation on Semitic Cognates in Ugaritic." *Or* 37 (1968):347-366.

Lindemann, E. "Symptomatology and Management of Acute Grief," *American Journal of Psychiatry* 101 (1944):141-148.

Lohfink, N. "Enthielten die im Alten Testament bezeugten Klageriten eine Phase des Schweigens?" *VT* 12 (1962):260-77.

Lohr, M. "Alphabetische und alphabetisierende Lieder im Alten Testament." *ZAW* 25 (1905):173-198.

———. *Die Klagelieder des Jeremias*. Göttingen: Vandenhoeck und Ruprecht, 1906.

———. "Der Sprachgebrauch des Buches der Klagelieder." *ZAW* 14 (1894):31-50.

———. "Threni III und die jeremianische Autorschaft des Buches der Klagelieder." *ZAW* 24 (1904):1-6.

Long, B. O. "This Divine Funeral Lament." *JBL* 85 (1966):85-86.

Lowth, R. *Lectures on the Sacred Poetry of the Hebrews*. Translated by G. Gregory. Edited by C. E. Stowe. New York: J. Leavitt, 1829.

Lundbom, J. *Jeremiah: A Study in Ancient Hebrew Rhetoric.* SBLDS 18. Missoula, MT: Scholars Press (1975).

Lutz, H. F., ed. *Selected Sumerian and Babylonian Texts.* Publications of the Babylonian Section, Vol. I, no. 2. Philadelphia: University Museum, 1919.

McDaniel, T. F. "Alleged Sumerian Influence on Lamentations." *VT* 18 (1968):198-209.

———. "Philological Studies in Lamentations I, II." *Bib* 49 (1968):27-53, 199-220.

Marino, A. "Toward a Definition of Literary Genres," in *Yearbook of Comparative Criticism*, vol. 8: *Theories of Literary Genre.* Edited by J. P. Strelka. University Park: The Pennsylvania State University, 1978.

Martinengo-Cesaresco, E. *Essays in the Study of Folk-Songs.* London: Dent, 1914.

Mayer, W. *Untersuchungen zur Formensprache der babylonischen "Gebetsbeschwörungen."* Studia Pohl, Series Maior 5. Rome: Pontifical Biblical Institute, 1976.

Meek, T. J. *Cuneiform Bilingual Hymns, Prayers and Penitential Psalms.* Baltimore: Johns Hopkins, 1913.

———, and W. P. Merrill. "Book of Lamentations." *IB* 6 (1956).

———. "The Structure of Hebrew Poetry." *JR* 10 (1929):523-50.

Meissner, B. *Die Babylonisch-Assyrische Literatur.* Wildpark-Potsdam: Akademische Verlagsgesellschaft. Athenaion, 1928.

———. *Kulturgeschichtliche Bibliothek: Babylonien und Assyrien II.* Heidelberg: Carl Winter, 1925.

Moore, G. F. *Judaism.* 3 vols. Cambridge: Harvard, 1948.

Moran, W. L. "The Hebrew Language in its Northwest Semitic Background." *The Bible and the Ancient Near East: Essays in Honor of Wm. Foxwell Albright*, pp. 59-84. Edited by G. E. Wright. New York: Anchor/Doubleday, 1965.

Morgenstern, J. *Rites of Birth, Marriage, Death and Kindred Occasions among the Semites.* Cincinnati: Hebrew Union College, 1966.

Moscati, S. *The Face of the Ancient Orient.* Garden City N.Y.: Doubleday, 1962.

Mowinckel, S. *The Psalms in Israel's Worship.* Translated by D. R. Ap-Thomas. 2 vols. Oxford: Oxford University Press, 1962.

———. *Psalmstudien.* 6 vols. Skriftur utgitt av Det Norske Videnskaps-Akademi i Oslo. Kristiana: J. Dybwad, 1921-24.

———. "Zum Problem der hebräischen Metrik." In *Festschrift für Alfred Bertholet zum 80 Geburtstag*, pp. 379-394. Edited by W. Baumgartner, et al. Tübingen: J. C. B. Mohr, 1950.

Munch, P. "Die alphabetische Akrostichie in der jüdischen Psalmendichtung." *ZDMG* 90 (1936):703-710.

Myers, J. *I Chronicles.* Anchor Bible, 12. Garden City: Doubleday, 1965.

Myhrman, D. W., ed. *Babylonian Hymns and Prayers* Publications of the Babylonian Section, Vol. I, no. 1. Philadelphia: University Museum, 1911.

Nagelsbach, E. *The Lamentations of Jeremiah.* Translated by W. H. Hornblower. Edinburgh: T. and T. Clark, 1871.

O'Callaghan, R. T. "Echoes of Canaanite Literature in the Psalms." *VT* 4 (1954):164-76.

Oesterly, W. O. E. *The Psalms.* London: S.P.C.K., 1939.

Ogden, G. S. "Joel 4 and Prophetic Responses to National Laments." *JSOT* 26 (1983): 97-106.

————. "Prophetic Oracles Against Foreign Nations and Psalms of Communal Lament: The Relationship of Psalm 137 to Jeremiah 49:7-22." *JSOT* 24 (1982): 89-97.

————, and T. H. Robinson. *Introduction to the Books of the Old Testament.* London: S.P.C.K., 1934.

Peake, A. S. *Jeremiah and Lamentations.* London: T. C. and E. C. Jack, 1912.

Perowne, J. J. S. *The Book of Psalms.* 7th ed. London: George Bell and Sons, 1890.

Pettinato, G. *Testi Lessicali Bilingui della Biblioteca L. 2769.* Seminario di Studi Asiatici, Series maior, IV: *Materiali Epigraphici di Ebla.* Naples: Istituto Universitario Orientale di Napoli, 1982.

Peters, J. P. *The Psalms as Liturgies.* New York: Macmillan, 1922.

Plöger, O. *Die fünf Megilloth.* Tübingen: J. C. B. Mohr, 1969.

Pope, M. H. *Job.* Anchor Bible, 15. Garden City: Doubleday, 1965.

————. *Song of Songs.* Anchor Bible, 7A. Garden City: Doubleday, 1977.

Porten, B. "The Marzeah Association." In *The Archives from Elephantine,* pp. 177-186. Berkeley: University of California, 1968.

Pritchard, J. B., ed. *Ancient Near Eastern Texts.* 3d ed. Princeton: Princeton University, 1969.

Rabinowitz, H. R. "Terms for Eulogies in Bible." *Beth Mikra* l7 (1972):235-255.

Rad, G. von, *Old Testament Theology.* Translated by D. Stalker, 2 vols. New York: Harper, 1962

Reallexikon der Assyriologie und vorderasiatischen Archaeologie. S.v. "Klagelied," by D. Edzard.

Reichert, J. F. "'Organizing Principles' and Genre Theory." *Genre* 1 (1968):1-12.

Ricoeur, P. "The Hermeneutical Function of Distanciation," *Philosophy Today.* 1 7 (1973):129-141

Robinson, H. W. *Corporate Personality in Ancient Israel.* Philadelphia: Fortress, 1967.

————. "The Hebrew Conception of Corporate Personality," *BZAW* 66 (1936): 49-62.

Robinson, T. H. "Notes on the Text of Lamentations." *ZAW* 51 (1933):255ff.

————. *The Poetry of the Old Testament.* London: Duckworth, 1947.

Rowley, H. H. *Rediscovery of the Old Testament.* Philadelphia: Westminster, 1946.

————. *Worship in Ancient Israel.* Philadelphia: Fortress Press, 1967.

Rudolph, W. *Das Buch Ruth, Das Hohe Leid, Die Klagelieder.* KAT, 17. Gütersloh: G. Mohn, 1962.

Sachs, A. "Ritual for the Repair of a Temple." In *ANET*, pp. 339-342. Edited by J. Pritchard.

———. "Ritual to be Followed by the Kalu-Priest when Covering the Temple Kettle-Drum." In *ANET*, pp. 334-338. Edited by J. Pritchard.

Sakenfeld, K. D. *The Meaning of ḥesed in the Hebrew Bible.* Harvard Semitic Monographs, 17. Missoula, MT.: Scholars Press, 1978.

Schmidt, H. *Die Psalmen.* HAT 15. Tübingen: J. C. B. Mohr, 1934.

Schrank, W. *Babylonische Sühnriten.* Leipziger semitische Studien 3. Leipzig: n.p., 1908.

Sellin, E. *Introduction to the Old Testament.* Translated by W. Montgomery. London: Hodder and Stoughton, 1923.

Seux, M.-J. *Hymnes et Prières aux Dieux de Babylonie et d'Assyrie.* Paris: Editions de Cerf, 1976.

Shea, W. H. "David's Lament." *BASOR* 221 (1976):141-144.

———. "The qinah Structure of the Book of Lamentations." *Bib* 60:1 (1979):103-107.

Sjöberg, A. W. "The Old Babylonian Eduba." In *Sumerological Studies in Honor of Thorkild Jacobsen*, pp. 159-179. *AS*, 20. Edited by S. J. Lieberman. Chicago: University of Chicago, 1976.

———, and E. Bergmann. "Sumerian Hymns to Temples." *Texts from Cuneiform Sources.* Vol. 3. Locust Valley, N.Y.: J. J. Augustin, 1969.

Streane, A. W. *The Book of the Prophet Jeremiah Together with Lamentations.* Cambridge: University Press, 1913.

Strelka, J. P., ed. *Theories of Literary Genre.* Yearbook of Comparative Criticism. Vol. 8. University Park, Pa.: Pennsylvania State University, 1978.

Stummer, F. *Sumerisch-akkadisch Parallelen zum Aufbau alttestamentlicher Psalmen.* Paderborn: Ferdinand Schöningh, 1922.

Thureau-Dangin, F. *Rituels accadiens.* Paris: Geuthner, 1921.

———. *Die Sumerischen und Akkadischen Königsinschriften.* Leipzig: J. C. Hinrichs, 1907.

Todorov, T. *The Fantastic: A Structural Approach to the Literary Genre.* Cleveland: Case Western Reserve University, 1973.

Tromp, N. *Primitive Conceptions of Death and the Nether World in the Old Testament.* Biblica et Orientalia, 21. Rome: Pontifical Biblical Institute, 1969.

Ungnad, A. and H. Gressmann. *Altorientalische Texte und Bilder zum alten Testament.* Tübingen: Mohr, 1909.

Vanderburgh, F. A. *Sumerian Hymns from Cuneiform Texts in the British Museum.* New York: Columbia University Press, 1908.

Virolleaud, C. *Palais royal d'Ugarit II, V.* Paris: Imprimerie Nationale, 1957.

Wahl, T. P. "Strophic Structure of Individual Laments in Psalms Books I and II." Th.D. dissertation, Union Theological Seminary, New York, 1976.

Wanke, G. " אוי und הוי." *ZAW* 78 (1966):215-218.

Watters, W. R. *Formula Criticism and the Poetry of the Old Testament.* Berlin: de Gruyter, 1976.

Weiser, A. *Klagelieder.* ATD, 16. Göttingen: Vandenhoeck und Ruprecht, 1962.

―――. *The Psalms.* Translated by H. Hartwell. OTL. Philadelphia: Westminster Press, 1962.

Welch, A. C. *The Psalter in Life, Worship and History.* Oxford: Clarendon, 1926.

Wendel, A. *Das freie Laiengebet im vorexilischen Israel.* Leipzig: Pfeiffer, 1931.

Wellek, R. and A. Warren. *Theory of Literature.* 3d ed. New York: Harcourt, Brace and World, 1956.

Westermann, C. *Basic Forms of Prophetic Speech.* Translated by H. C. White. Philadelphia: Westminster, 1967.

―――. *The Praise of God in the Psalms.* Translated by K. Crim. Richmond, Va.: John Knox, 1965.

―――. *The Psalms:* Structure, Content and Message. Translated by R. Gehrke. Minneapolis: Augsburg, 1980.

―――. *The Structure of the Book of Job.* Translated by C. Muenchow. Philadelphia: Fortress, 1981.

―――. "Role of Lament in the Theology of the Old Testament." *Int* 28:1 (1974):20-38.

―――. "Struktur und Geschichte der Klage im Alten Testament." *ZAW* 66 (1954):44-80.

Wevers, J. W. "A Study in the Form Criticism of Individual Complaint Psalms." *VT* 6 (1956):80-96.

Widengren, G. *Accadian and Hebrew Psalms of Lamentations as Religious Documents.* Stockholm: Bokforlags Aktiebolaget Thule, 1937.

Wieder, A. A. "Ugaritic-Hebrew Lexicography." *JBL* 84 (1965):160-164.

Wilcke, C. "Der aktuelle Bezug der Sammlung der sumerischen Tempelhymnen und ein Fragment eines Klageliedes." *ZA* 62 (1972):35-61.

Willessen, F. "The Cultic Situation of Psalm LXXIV." *VT* 2 (1952):289-306.

―――. "Formale Geschichtspunkte in der sumerischen Literatur." In *Sumerological Studies in Honor of Thorkild Jacobsen*, pp. 205-316. AS, 20. Edited by S. J. Lieberman. Chicago: University of Chicago, 1976.

Witzel, M. "Die Klage über Ur." *Or* NS 14 (1945):185-234; 15 (1946):46-63.

Yaron, K. "The Dirge Over the King of Tyre." *Annual of the Swedish Theological Institute* 3 (1964): 28-57.

Young, G. D. "Semitic Metrics and the Ugaritic Evidence." *The Bible Today* (Feb. 19 '49):150-55.

Yoder, P. B. "Fixed Word Pairs and the Composition of Hebrew Poetry." Ph.D. dissertation, University of Pennsylvania, 1970.

Young, M., et al. "The Mortality of Widowers," *Lancet* 2 (1963): 454-456.

Zimmern, H. *Babylonische Hymnen und Gebete in Auswähle.* Leipzig: Hinrichs, 1905.

―――. *Babylonische Hymnen und Gebete, Zweite Auswähle.* Leipzig: Hinrichs, 1911.

————. *Sumerische Kultlieder aus altbabylonischer Zeit 1, 2*. Vorderasiatische Schriftdenkmäler der königlichen Museen zu Berlin. Leipzig: Hinrichs, 1912, 1913.